NEW PENGUIN SHAKESPEARE
SAMUEL JOHNSON

Samuel Johnson was born in Lichfield in 1709, the son of a bookseller, and was educated at Lichfield Grammar School and, for a short time, at Pembroke College, Oxford. He taught for a while, after which he worked for a Birmingham printer, for whom he translated Lobo's *A Voyage to Abyssinia*. In 1735 he married Elizabeth Jervis Porter and with her money opened a boarding academy. The school was a failure and in 1737 Johnson left for London. There, he became a regular contributor to the *Gentleman's Magazine* and struggled to earn a living from writing. His *London: A Poem In Imitation of the Third Satire of Juvenal* was published anonymously in 1738 and attracted some attention. *The Vanity of Human Wishes: The Tenth Satire of Juvenal Imitated* appeared under his own name in 1749. From 1750 to 1752 he issued the *Rambler*, a periodical written almost entirely by himself, and consolidated his position as a notable moral essayist with some twenty-five essays in the *Adventurer*. The *Idler* essays, lighter in tone, appeared weekly between 1758 and 1760. When his *Dictionary of the English Language* was published in 1755, Johnson took on the proportions of a literary monarch in the London of his day. In need of money to visit his sick mother, he wrote *Rasselas* (1759) reportedly in the evenings of one week, finishing a couple of days after his mother's death. In 1763 Boswell became his faithful follower and it is mainly to his *Life* that we owe our intimate knowledge of Johnson. Founded in 1764, 'The Club' (of literary men) was the perfect forum for the exercise of Johnson's great conversational art. His edition of Shakespeare's plays appeared in 1765. From August to November 1773 he and Boswell toured Scotland and in 1775 his *Journey to the Western Islands of Scotland* appeared. His last major work was *Lives of the Poets*. He died in December 1784.

H. R. Woudhuysen was educated at St Paul's School, Pembroke College, Oxford, and was a Junior Research Fellow at Lincoln College, Oxford. Since 1982 he has been a Lecturer in the Department of English at University College London.

SAMUEL JOHNSON
ON
SHAKESPEARE

EDITED WITH AN INTRODUCTION AND NOTES BY
H. R. WOUDHUYSEN

PENGUIN BOOKS

PENGUIN BOOKS

Published by the Penguin Group
27 Wrights Lane, London W8 5TZ, England
Viking Penguin Inc., 40 West 23rd Street, New York, New York 10010, USA
Penguin Books Australia Ltd, Ringwood, Victoria, Australia
Penguin Books Canada Ltd, 2801 John Street, Markham, Ontario, Canada L3R 1B4
Penguin Books (NZ) Ltd, 182–190 Wairau Road, Auckland 10, New Zealand

Penguin Books Ltd, Registered Offices: Harmondsworth, Middlesex, England

First published 1989
1 3 5 7 9 10 8 6 4 2

Introduction and notes
copyright © H. R. Woudhuysen, 1989
All rights reserved

Made and printed in Great Britain by
Cox and Wyman Ltd, Reading, Berks.
Filmset in Bembo Linotron 202 by
Rowland Phototypesetting Ltd, Bury St Edmunds, Suffolk

Except in the United States of America,
this book is sold subject to the condition
that it shall not, by way of trade or otherwise,
be lent, re-sold, hired out, or otherwise circulated
without the publisher's prior consent in any form of
binding or cover other than that in which it is
published and without a similar condition
including this condition being imposed
on the subsequent purchaser

CONTENTS

Preface	vii
Introduction	1
Notes to the Introduction	36
Further Reading	39
A Note on the Text	42

MISCELLANEOUS OBSERVATIONS ON THE TRAGEDY OF MACBETH (1745)	43
PROPOSALS FOR PRINTING SHAKESPEARE'S PLAYS (1745)	84
DRURY LANE PROLOGUE (1747)	85
TWO ESSAYS FROM *THE RAMBLER* (1751)	87
DEDICATION TO MRS CHARLOTTE LENNOX'S *SHAKESPEARE ILLUSTRATED* (1753)	95
SELECTIONS FROM THE *DICTIONARY* (1755)	98
PROPOSALS FOR PRINTING BY SUBSCRIPTION SHAKESPEARE'S PLAYS (1756)	113
PREFACE TO THE EDITION OF SHAKESPEARE'S PLAYS (1765)	120
SELECTIONS FROM THE NOTES TO THE EDITION OF SHAKESPEARE'S PLAYS (1765)	166
The Tempest	166
A Midsummer Night's Dream	169
The Two Gentlemen of Verona	172
Measure for Measure	173

The Merchant of Venice	177
As You Like It	179
Love's Labour's Lost	180
The Winter's Tale	183
Twelfth Night	184
The Merry Wives of Windsor	186
The Taming of the Shrew	188
Much Ado About Nothing	188
All's Well That Ends Well	188
King John	191
Richard II	195
1 Henry IV	198
2 Henry IV	201
Henry V	206
1 Henry VI	211
2 Henry VI	211
3 Henry VI	212
Richard III	215
Henry VIII	216
[Epilogue to the Histories]	218
King Lear	219
Timon of Athens	223
Titus Andronicus	225
Macbeth	226
Coriolanus	229
Julius Caesar	230
Antony and Cleopatra	230
Cymbeline	232
Troilus and Cressida	235
Romeo and Juliet	236
Hamlet	238
Othello	244
Miscellaneous Remarks, Conversations and Anecdotes	249
Notes	255

PREFACE

❧

Samuel Johnson's writings on Shakespeare have been collected several times during the past eighty or so years, most familiarly and enduringly by Walter Raleigh in 1908. W. K. Wimsatt edited a new and wider selection of Johnson on Shakespeare, which appeared in 1960 and again as a Penguin in 1969. Since the first appearance of Wimsatt's anthology Arthur Sherbo's two invaluable volumes in the Yale Edition of the Works of Samuel Johnson have been published (1968). As well as the Preface, the *Miscellaneous Observations on the Tragedy of Macbeth*, the two sets of *Proposals* and the dedication to Mrs Lennox's *Shakespeare Illustrated*, these collected almost all of Johnson's notes to the plays and record their textual history. Anyone interested in Johnson and Shakespeare must acknowledge a profound debt to Arthur Sherbo's great scholarship. A selection from Sherbo's edition appeared in one volume in 1986, edited by Bertrand H. Bronson and Jean M. O'Meara.

The aim of this new selection of Johnson on Shakespeare is to make Johnson's most interesting critical ideas about Shakespeare more widely available. It offers newly edited and modernized texts of all Johnson's major pieces of Shakespearian criticism, including a large number of his critical and explanatory notes. On the whole, his discussions of proposed emendations have been omitted. For the first time it collects new, critical and illustrative material from the *Dictionary* and prints some of Johnson's stray comments on Shakespeare from a wide variety of sources, most notably, of course, from Boswell's *Life* of him.

For their help, advice and encouragement in preparing this selection I should like to thank Miss K. Duncan-Jones, Dr J. D. Fleeman, Dr F. P. Horne, Miss D. J. Loudon, Dr J. Pitcher and Dr K. Walker.

INTRODUCTION

❦

I

Samuel Johnson's life was bounded by his imaginative engagement with Shakespeare. In her *Anecdotes* of 1786 his old friend Mrs Piozzi records this childhood story:

I have heard him relate another odd thing of himself too, but it is one which everybody has heard as well as I: how, when he was about nine years old, having got the play of Hamlet in his hand, and reading it quietly in his father's kitchen, he kept on steadily enough, till coming to the Ghost scene, he suddenly hurried upstairs to the street door that he might see people about him: such an incident, as he was not unwilling to relate it, is probably in everyone's possession now; he told it as a testimony to the merits of Shakespeare. (*JM*, i.158–9)

Boswell repeats the elements of this story when he reports (*Life*, i.70)[1] 'that he read Shakespeare at a period so early, that the speech of the Ghost in *Hamlet* terrified him when he was alone'. Of Johnson's last days, Boswell also has the following account:

About eight or ten days before his death, when Dr Brocklesby paid him his morning visit, he seemed very low and desponding, and said 'I have been as a dying man all night.' He then emphatically broke out in the words of Shakespeare:

> Canst thou not minister to a mind diseased,
> Pluck from the memory a rooted sorrow,
> Raze out the written troubles of the brain,
> And with some sweet oblivious antidote
> Cleanse the stuffed bosom of that perilous stuff
> Which weighs upon the heart?

To which Dr Brocklesby readily answered from the same great poet:

> Therein the patient
> Must minister to himself.
> (*Macbeth*, V.3.40)

Johnson expressed himself much satisfied with the application (*Life*, iv.400–401).

To the end of his life Johnson's involvement with Shakespeare's works, whether as reader, critic, lexicographer, traveller or editor, was profound: only the Bible meant more to him. Johnson was buried in Westminster Abbey in Poets' Corner, close to the statue of Shakespeare erected there in 1741.

Johnson does not seem to have been at all curious about Shakespeare's life. On his only recorded visit to Stratford-upon-Avon in March 1776 on the way to Lichfield, Boswell and Johnson contented themselves with drinking tea and coffee there; Johnson studiously avoided any discussion of the town's most famous son, and appears to have been quite unconcerned about the dramatist's birthplace. If he knew it, he never referred to the fact that his friend Henry Thrale's Bankside brewery occupied the site of Shakespeare's Globe Theatre. He had little to say about Shakespeare's life, except that he always maintained 'Shakespeare had Latin enough to grammaticize his English' (*Life*, iv.18). What sort of a man Johnson thought Shakespeare was remains unknowable. Even our essential ignorance about how to spell Shakespeare's name correctly was more a source of amusement to Johnson than of regret. In Scotland, Boswell records:

Dr Johnson observed that there had been great disputes about the spelling of Shakespeare's name; at last it was thought it would be settled by looking at the original copy of his will; but upon examining it, he was found to have written it himself no less than three different ways. (*Life*, v.124)

The man for whom it was 'the biographical part of literature, which is what I love most' (*Life*, i.425) appears to have had a striking lack of interest in the life, literary career and also in the personality of the author he most admired.

For Johnson it was the plays that mattered. He almost completely ignored the poems: if he had ever read the Sonnets he said nothing about them, having a low opinion of their literary form. On the same visit to the Highlands in 1773, *Macbeth* was inevitably uppermost in Johnson's mind. It was as though he saw no material difference between the places Shakespeare wrote about in his play and the real places he was visiting – as if there were no distance between the dramatic fiction and the authentic, historical location. There is a marked difference between his behaviour in Scotland and his lack of interest in Stratford. 'We went forwards the same day to Forres,' he wrote in his *A Journey to the Western Islands of Scotland*, 'the town to which Macbeth was travelling when he met the weird sisters in his way. This to an Englishman is classic ground. Our imaginations were heated and our thoughts recalled to their old amusements.'[2] Boswell has Johnson 'solemnly' ask Macbeth's 'How far is't called to Forres? What are these, / So withered and so wild in their attire?' (I.3.38) and adds that he 'repeated a good deal more of *Macbeth*' (*Life*, v.115). For Johnson this was where Macbeth met the witches; for Boswell this was where Macbeth 'according to tradition' met the witches. They went on to visit the old castle of Cawdor, the Thane's seat, and then saw what was generally taken to be Macbeth's castle. From first to last *Macbeth* always held a special place in Johnson's imaginative life. It was with that play, and its study of the guilty mind, he made his earliest contribution to Shakespearian scholarship and criticism, the *Miscellaneous Observations on the Tragedy of Macbeth*.

II

Johnson's initial publication on Shakespeare was an anonymous pamphlet issued during the first half of 1745, just before the second Jacobite rebellion began in Scotland. The pamphlet came in two parts: appended on a single large folded leaf to his

Miscellaneous Observations on the Tragedy of Macbeth (1745) were his set of *Proposals* for a new edition of Shakespeare's plays, with a specimen pair of pages from *Macbeth*. The edition was to be printed in ten octavo volumes at a cost to subscribers of £1 5s. (£1.25), with 10s. 6d (52½p) due at the time of subscribing. Johnson's scholarly attention had no doubt turned to the literature of the sixteenth and seventeenth centuries through his first major literary undertaking. This was his work of examining and cataloguing the thousands of books and pamphlets contained in the Harleian library undertaken during the early 1740s. The primary impetus for publishing his work on *Macbeth* came from Johnson's own desire to edit Shakespeare and to give a specimen of what he could achieve as critic and editor; the chance to respond to Sir Thomas Hanmer's edition, the most recently issued one, seems only to have come after Johnson had written most of his notes. Few of the emendations Johnson proposed are now accepted by Shakespeare scholars and Johnson himself was to reject several of them in his edition of 1765. But they already show his grasp of the problems of emending the text, which might need alteration because of verbal corruption (sometimes due to mistakes in reading handwriting correctly), metrical errors or faulty punctuation. The text had to make sense: if it could not be adequately paraphrased, then as a last resort, not as a good opportunity for the display of supposed editorial brilliance, it had to be changed. Before doing this, however, Johnson established the principle that what appeared incomprehensible to modern readers might have been understood by those of Shakespeare's own time. Therefore, as he announced in the first sentence of the *Miscellaneous Observations*, in order to judge a writer correctly 'it is always necessary to examine the genius of his age and the opinions of his contemporaries'; and the only way to do this is to read the books the author might have read and those which record the ideas and the language which he might have known. In this he was to some extent following the example Lewis Theobald had set in his edition of Shakespeare first published in 1733.

Much of the *Miscellaneous Observations* is taken up with

explaining words and phrases by verbal parallels and with illustrations of ideas about witchcraft with which Shakespeare and his audience would have been familiar. It is in these illustrative notes (in particular I, XVI, XX and XXXV) that Johnson displays some of his wide reading and his powers as a critic. His response is above all one of imaginative sympathy and engagement; he enters into the fearful and guilty world of witches, night and murder wholeheartedly but not uncritically. Already Shakespeare has been identified by his 'knowledge of human nature' (XVI), his ability to create 'a very just and strong picture of a man . . .' (XX); Shakespeare 'exactly . . . conformed to common opinions and traditions' (XXXV); close examination will reveal his extraordinary power as a poet, a producer of striking images (XX). On the other hand Shakespeare's tragedies have too many people in them (XXXIV), he is careless about narrative details (VI), and he lets opportunities to draw a moral point pass by (XVI). Johnson does not read the play as a dramatic poem but as a drama in the mind; what characters say in it must be understood in the light of their mental states and the play's overall dramatic context (XX and XXIII).

When he returned to edit *Macbeth* for the edition of 1765 he reprinted nineteen of his forty-six notes without altering them; seven notes were either omitted, rejected or reprinted with a new comment signalling his repudiation of them. He clearly felt dissatisfied with several of the remainder: in particular he became far more wary of his conjectural emendations.[3]

The *Miscellaneous Observations* and the *Proposals for Printing* Shakespeare's plays issued with it show that Johnson had already thought deeply about working on Shakespeare. The *Proposals* also reveal that by then he had considered the typographical arrangement of an edition of Shakespeare's plays, in which for the first time the notes would be printed in double columns rather than, as they had always been previously arranged, across the page. The lay-out of the page imitated that of contemporary editions of the Greek and Roman authors: Shakespeare had become a classic text. The scale of the edition Johnson envisaged in 1745 can be judged from its proposed size here of ten volumes; when it finally came out twenty years later in 1765 it filled only eight. There is some evidence that *Macbeth* was not the only play on which Johnson had worked at the time of writing the *Miscellaneous Observations*.[4] How far Johnson had progressed in his earliest Shakespearian editorial labours is uncertain. The proposed edition foundered mainly because of problems over copyright, exacerbated by the imminent publication of Warburton's edition in 1747. But the experience of writing the notes to *Macbeth* may have suggested to Johnson that his knowledge of Shakespeare's language and grammatical style was not yet adequate for such an undertaking.

III

The failure of the Shakespeare project left Johnson free to undertake another. By the end of April 1746 he had drafted a short scheme to compile a dictionary of the English language; a month and a half later he signed a contract with the publishers to produce the work. Johnson worked on the *Dictionary* for nine years until it finally appeared in 1755. During this time he wrote two essays for the periodical *The Rambler* which show that he was still brooding on Shakespeare. He also provided a dedication for, and may perhaps have had some hand in the writing of, his friend Charlotte Lennox's *Shakespeare Illustrated*. This work appeared – to a very mixed reception – in three volumes, two being published in 1753 and the third coming out in 1754. Together they comprise the first attempt to collect and analyse Shakespeare's treatment of his sources, covering twenty-two plays. On the whole Mrs Lennox finds that Shakespeare spoiled the stories which he took from his sources, to produce 'absurdities in the plot and unnatural manners in the characters' (*Cymbeline*), 'useless incidents, unnecessary characters and absurd and improbable intrigue' (*Measure for Measure*), 'incidents unnatural and absurd' (*Twelfth Night*), 'miracle upon miracle' (*The Winter's Tale*), 'a succession of incidents, without order, connection or any dependence upon each other' (*Troilus and Cressida*) and 'improbable contrivance' (*Much Ado About Nothing*). She only really approves of the plays which are 'regular'; *Romeo and Juliet* and *Othello*, reserving her highest praise for *Macbeth*. On the other hand she has a number of striking things to say about the other plays. *Measure for Measure*, for example, is a tragedy turned to comedy by the force of its plot, 'a riddle without a solution'; Imogen's rejection of Iachimo's first attempt on her in *Cymbeline* is 'Lucretia-like'; *Hamlet* could almost be called 'the tragedy of Laertes' and Hamlet seems to revenge his own, not his father's, death.

Despite her general lack of sympathy with Shakespeare's failure to write credibly realistic plays, some of her other ideas about Shakespeare are strikingly different from those of other critics of her time. Some, however, are close to Johnson's views of the plays: in *Hamlet*, she objects, the guilty and the innocent are overwhelmed by one fate, and the Prince's death (like those of Lear and Cordelia) violates poetical justice. She admires Falstaff's 'inimitable humour' in *1 Henry IV*, pays a surprising amount of attention to *Henry VIII*, disapproves of the puns and quibbles in *The Two Gentlemen of Verona*, and throughout feels that Shakespeare is too eager to tie up the strands of his plots at the end of his plays. She also reprints two of Johnson's notes in full from the *Miscellaneous Observations* (I and VI) as well as all but the last paragraph of Note XXXV. Johnson's rather self-contradictory dedication is not wholly in sympathy with what Mrs Lennox provided in her book. More surprisingly, despite his promise to examine Shakespeare's sources, Johnson made little use of *Shakespeare Illustrated* in his edition, drawing on it directly or indirectly in his discussion of the sources of only seven plays.

When the *Dictionary* was published in 1755 it contained about 116,000 quotations (many more had been collected), illustrating some 40,000 words; of the poetical quotations, it has been estimated that about a third came from Shakespeare.[5] The quotations were often transcribed slightly inaccurately, usually in a lightly edited form intended to save space without sacrificing intelligibility. At the end of most of these quotations the name of the play they came from was printed, in some cases not always correctly. Johnson looked on the quotations in the *Dictionary* not only as illustrative examples of the words he was defining, but also as a collection of moral and useful *exempla*. When Johnson quotes a passage in the *Dictionary* it can usually be taken that he agrees with, or at least approves of, what is being said: the book is in some respects a vast commonplace book or collection of favourite quotations. On at least one occasion Johnson deliberately changed what Shakespeare had written to make it conform with what he believed. Under the verb 'to learn' Johnson used Caliban's speech from *The Tempest* (I.2.363) to illustrate sense 2, but inserted a 'not' in the phrase 'I know how to curse', so reversing Shakespeare's meaning:

> You taught me language, and my profit on't
> Is, I know not how to curse. The red plague rid you
> For *learning* me your language![6]

As an anthology of quotations the *Dictionary* is quite rich in comments on Shakespeare. The most interesting of these come from Charlotte Lennox's recently published *Shakespeare Illustrated*, but they do not appear to begin until the letter 's'. This is the only modern work of Shakespearian criticism or scholarship on which Johnson drew, apart from earlier editions of Shakespeare. He had undoubtedly read Dryden, Addison and Dennis, as well as Thomas Rymer's works, from all of which he quotes, but rarely with direct reference to Shakespeare. He makes much more use of the only other substantial piece of early Shakespeare criticism with which he seems to have been familiar. Most of Milton's sonnet contributed to the second folio of 1632 appears in the *Dictionary* under 'relic' 2, 'livelong' 2, 'slow' (adv.), and 'sepulchre' (v.a.). Milton's other lines on Shakespeare in *L'Allegro* appear under 'fancy' 1, and 'woodnote'.

Johnson's range of quotation from Shakespeare in the *Dictionary* is extraordinarily wide. He seems to have taken the text for the quotations from Warburton's edition of 1747. It has always been thought that with one exception he only quoted from the plays. Under 'cloth' 3 he ascribes two lines (244–5) to

Shakespeare's *Tarquin and Lucrece*, that is *The Rape of Lucrece*. A second instance of Johnson's knowledge of Shakespeare's non-dramatic works is evident in the entry for 'goddess'. There his second quotation is from *The Passionate Pilgrim* (3.5). Johnson could have read both of these in one of the small number of early eighteenth-century editions of the poems, but he certainly took one and probably borrowed the other from illustrative quotations supplied by other editors.[7]

A full analysis of all the quotations in the *Dictionary* would provide a fascinating picture of Johnson's reading in Shakespeare, of which plays and which parts of plays were most frequently cited. Nobody has yet undertaken such an analysis and without it generalizations are bound to be only partially accurate: Johnson's habits and practices changed while he was engaged in writing the *Dictionary*. Nevertheless, samples of two letters provide some interesting and revealing material. Under 'g', which fills 77 pages in the *Dictionary*, he quotes 670 passages from Shakespeare; under 't', which occupies 110 pages, 976 passages. *Macbeth* is the play quoted from most often (under 'g' 50 times; 69 times under 't'), *King Lear* the play most often cited under 't' (79 times; 45 times under 'g'). As one might expect, *Hamlet* is used heavily for both letters (31 times under 'g' and 39 times under 't'), but *Coriolanus* (26 and 50 times under 'g' and 't') and *Richard III* (31 and 41 times under the same letters) are also used more often than one might expect. *Henry VIII* and *The Merchant of Venice* consistently supplied a high number of quotations. Among the least frequently quoted plays are *The Tempest*, *The Comedy of Errors*, *Titus Andronicus* and *All's Well That Ends Well*. Johnson drew surprisingly heavily on *2 Henry VI* (18 quotations are cited under 'g' and 30 under 't'). Exactly what these figures show remains open to argument, but the predominance of the tragedies (*Othello* is quoted 27 and 28 times under 'g' and 't' respectively) and the affection for *Henry VIII* (vividly recalled in the passages about Wolsey's fall in *The Vanity of Human Wishes*) and *The Merry Wives of Windsor* are interesting reflections of Johnson's general comments on the plays in his edition. It is also clear that some passages from Shakespeare were particularly close to Johnson's heart: he used one descriptive passage of two and a half lines from *Macbeth* (III.4.5) to illustrate eight separate words in the *Dictionary*.[8]

If the quotations show Johnson's astonishingly detailed reading of the plays, the definitions reveal his usually firm grasp of Shakespeare's language and syntax. It had always been Johnson's intention to illustrate unusual or idiosyncratic usages in the *Dictionary*. In the 1747 *Plan*, to demonstrate his determination to define 'the peculiar sense in which a word is found in any great author', he quoted *Macbeth*, I.7.16 to show that '"faculties" in Shakespeare signifies the powers of authority';[9] in the *Dictionary* under 'faculty' (n.) 6 he defined the word as 'Power; authority' and quoted the same passage from *Macbeth*. But another source for Shakespeare's 'hard' words was more immediately at hand. Johnson's use of the glossary Sir Thomas Hanmer printed at the end of the sixth and last volume of his edition of Shakespeare is not entirely straightforward. Hanmer included about 550 words in this glossary, and in the *Dictionary* Johnson drew on Hanmer's definitions for about eighty of these, each time acknowledging the source of his definition: these words only occur between 'chough' and 'pin'. Elsewhere in the *Dictionary* he drew on Hanmer's definitions without acknowledging his debt, but also omitted many words which Hanmer had included. Johnson's reasons for working in this way are unknown. As well as Hanmer's edition he drew on Pope's (see under 'editor' and 'nonsense' 1) and Warburton's (see under 'crash' (v.a.), 'demurely' 2, 'faithfully' 7, 'gourd' 2 and 'mystery' 3). He also acknowledged his debt to his Scottish assistant Alexander Macbean in his definition of 'munch' in *Macbeth* I.3.5, and Edward Phillips's *New World of Words* for 'guilder' in *The Comedy of Errors*, IV.1.4.

Many of Johnson's definitions in the *Dictionary* overlap with the notes he wrote for the edition of Shakespeare's plays, but the earlier work is an unrivalled and largely unexplored source for his detailed comments on Shakespeare's language, which he saw, he says in the Preface, as his chief resource for 'the diction of common life'. He most frequently remarks that Shakespeare uses words or phrases that are obsolete or no longer used. But he also takes pains to point out what he sees as 'low', 'ludicrous', 'cant', 'not proper' or 'harsh' usages. What Johnson meant when he said 'Shakespeare never has six lines together without a fault' becomes clear when his detailed comments on Shakespeare's language in the *Dictionary* are examined. He often admits his own uncertainty as to Shakespeare's meaning and likes to note what he thought of his unique usages. The question of correct pronunciation also received his attention. Under 'sepulchre' (v.a.) he notes: 'It is accented on the second syllable by Shakespeare and Milton; on the first, more properly, by Jonson and Prior', and he condemns Shakespeare for 'falsely' putting the stress on the first syllable of 'horizon'.

The *Dictionary* gave Johnson a firm grounding in the language Shakespeare used. It brought him face to face with the question of what the very words in the plays actually meant. Johnson saw that Shakespeare often used language incorrectly, but also that there were frequent occasions when he could not satisfactorily explain the meaning of the words Shakespeare had chosen to write. This semantic uncertainty was to affect Johnson's critical response to the plays in the edition of 1765: some of the critical open-mindedness of his later work on Shakespeare comes, perhaps, from the realization that the meaning of many of the words and phrases the playwright had used was not determinable. Nevertheless, in the process of compiling the *Dictionary* Johnson had also in effect produced the first, primitive, concordance to Shakespeare's works.

Two further editions of the *Dictionary* reflect Johnson's involvement with Shakespeare. A third edition was issued in 1765 to coincide with the publication of the edition of the plays: this did not contain new material. In 1773, the year in which his revised edition of Shakespeare was published, he also brought out a fourth edition of the *Dictionary*. This incorporated some of the new material which Steevens supplied to the edition of Shakespeare, but also revealed a few of Johnson's own new and second thoughts about Shakespeare's language.[10]

IV

Before looking at the edition of the plays which finally appeared in 1765, two related areas need to be considered. What was Johnson's reaction to Shakespeare's plays in performance and what was the state of Shakespeare scholarship in the first part of the eighteenth century? The key to answering the first question lies in Johnson's relationship with his former pupil, David Garrick.

David Garrick (1717–79) commanded the Shakespearian stage in London between 1741, when he first appeared in his outstanding *Richard III*, and 1772, when his version of *Hamlet* was produced. His share in the Drury Lane Theatre allowed him to produce Shakespeare as he wished, putting on twenty-four of the plays in productions which sometimes, but by no means always, returned to the original texts, abandoning the rewritten and 'improved' versions which had been performed since the Restoration. Garrick's acting, and the productions themselves, emphasized the psychological realism of the plays, replacing the old declamatory style of acting with a rapid and naturalistic performance. Nor was it just in the theatre that Garrick came to be identified with Shakespeare; he put together a fine collection of early quartos of the plays (now in the British Library), commissioned the statue of Shakespeare by Roubiliac for Westminster Abbey and organized the Stratford Jubilee of 1769, which Johnson did not attend. To his contemporaries, including Johnson, it must sometimes have seemed as though Garrick 'owned' Shakespeare: he was the king of the bardolators.

Johnson's relations with Garrick were complicated by their long association and by Johnson's ambivalent attitude towards the stage which his former pupil so dominated. The satirical portrait of Prospero who consistently does down his old friend in *The Rambler* 200 has usually been taken to be Johnson's revenge on Garrick's success and supposed meanness. Johnson rarely missed an opportunity to mock Garrick's pretensions and thirst for fame, yet in the Preface to the edition of the plays Johnson did not mention him by name. He hinted, however, that Garrick would not let him use his collection of old plays in quarto while he was at work on the edition. Boswell, who greatly admired the actor, defended Garrick, suggesting that Johnson expected the books to be lent to him, while Garrick wanted Johnson to collate the plays at his house where he had made them freely available (*Life*, ii. 192).

The omission of Garrick's name from the Preface irked Boswell (see below, p. 253), but Johnson's firm view was that as an actor Garrick had already been paid for his Shakespearian performances and that he knew nothing about Shakespeare. George Steevens records (*Life*, v.244, n.2) Garrick's remark, 'Now I have quitted the theatre I will sit down and read Shakespeare', to which Johnson replied, ''Tis time you should for I much doubt if you ever examined one of his plays from the first scene to the last.'[11] Johnson's dislike of the essential falsehood and hypocrisy of actors and acting in general, of their self-importance ('Punch has no feelings'), and of Garrick's acting in particular, were also influenced by his theoretical dislike of the representation of tragedy on the stage. It was Garrick, however, who produced and acted in Johnson's only play, *Irene*, when it was put on at Drury Lane in 1749.

How often, or even whether, Johnson went to the theatre to see Shakespeare's plays acted remains unknown. As the periodical essays show, Johnson was interested in theatrical criticism. He knew full well that the plays were written for the stage, to be performed, and he must have seen some of them acted in the altered and improved versions that were popular in his time, but in their twenty or so years of friendship, Boswell, for one, records no visits to the theatre with Johnson to see Shakespeare acted: his failing eyesight and hearing no doubt helped to keep him away. Johnson's notes to his edition of Shakespeare often show his awareness of the demands of stagecraft and theatrical production, of the need to get entrances and exits clear, of the close relatedness between reading and watching a play and of the effect the plays have on their audiences: this is, perhaps, what lies behind the uncharacteristic comment that the 'pretended madness of Hamlet causes much mirth'. Yet he seems to have nothing in general to say about how Shakespeare ought to be acted and produced, and little about Shakespeare's skill as a dramatist, as a writer of theatrical scenes which go to make up a dramatic whole. In the notes to the edition he constantly repeats that act and scene divisions in the printed texts are arbitrary and their true division is for the reader to decide. He seems not to have tried to find out about Elizabethan and Jacobean theatrical conditions.

If Johnson's interest in Shakespeare was an imaginative rather than a biographical or purely theatrical one, it was also a scholarly pursuit. Johnson played a leading part in the creation and development of English literary scholarship. He did much to promote the idea that English literature had a history which deserved to be investigated and written. His edition marks the end of the old amateur world of editing Shakespeare and the beginning of its movement into the hands of professional scholars. The main outlines of the story of the treatment of Shakespeare's works by his eighteenth-century editors and of contemporary Shakespeare scholarship and criticism may be told briefly as follows.

Shakespeare's plays have survived in two sorts of texts distinguished by their different formats. During his lifetime many single plays were published in quartos; after his death his friends and fellow actors Heming and Condell collected his plays, including those which had never appeared in quartos, in a folio volume which was published in 1623 and reprinted three more times during the seventeenth century. For plays which survive alone in the folio (*The Tempest*, *Macbeth*, *Twelfth Night*, among others) an editor has only one text to print. Plays which also survive in quartos (*King Lear*, *Hamlet* or *The Merchant of Venice*, for example), present the editor with a choice: either to print the quarto text, or the folio, or to print a mixed or conflated text of the two. In the seventeenth century Shakespeare's plays were on the whole only known from the folio texts and the quartos were ignored. The history of editing from the next century to the present day revolves around the recovery of the quartos and the attempts of editors to sort out the relationship between quarto and folio texts of the plays.

Johnson himself knew of most of the important quartos

which survive; his primary editorial resource was the first folio of 1623. The copy of it which he used for his edition has not been identified, although it appears to have been owned in October 1790 by George Steevens.[12] His own copy of the second folio of 1632, formerly owned and annotated by Theobald, survives in the Folger Shakespeare Library. He possessed a copy of the second impression of the third folio of 1664, in which *Pericles* as well as the Shakespeare apocrypha were first printed.[13] As he explained in the Preface, Johnson soon realized that only the first folio had any textual authority; its later reprintings merely tended to corrupt and silently modernize the text. The quartos Johnson used were listed by George Steevens at the end of the edition of 1765; it is not known how or where Johnson had access to these. In the 1756 *Proposals* he stated that he would print from the early texts all the variant readings he could find, so that the reader would have all the witnesses to judge which was correct: in the event, when the edition came out in 1765, this was one of the editorial tasks which Johnson neglected. The study of the quartos only got under way in the year after the edition came out, when Steevens made them more generally available through his reprinting of some of them in *Twenty of the Plays of Shakespeare*: Johnson owned a set of these, which were sold at his death.[14] Edward Capell (1713–81) continued the investigation of the quartos, collecting a large number of them (now in Trinity College, Cambridge), publishing an edition of Shakespeare which drew heavily on their readings in 1768, a commentary on nine of the plays in 1774 and more *Notes and various Readings* in 1779. With Capell and Edmond Malone (1741–1812) the modern editing of Shakespeare began.

Its intermediate phase had begun with the edition of Shakespeare by the dramatist Nicholas Rowe (1674–1718). This was the first to break from the folio format of the four seventeenth-century collections. It came out in six octavo volumes in 1709, with a second edition of nine volumes in 1714 which included the poems. He followed the folio order for the plays and based his text on the fourth folio, emending it carefully and often correctly, marking act and scene divisions, supplying entrances and exits and lists of characters, where the folio had omitted or muddled them. He also included the first formal life of Shakespeare which, heavily altered by Pope, was generally included in editions of the works until it was superseded by Malone's more scholarly account. The second editor of Shakespeare was Alexander Pope (1688–1744) who published his edition of the plays in six quarto volumes in 1725; a seventh volume edited by George Sewell contained the poems and an essay on the history of the stage. Pope was the first editor to give the text any serious critical attention. He recognized the importance of the quartos, but made generally poor use of them, basing his text mainly on Rowe's edition while including his own emendations and conjectures and further refining on Rowe's scene divisions. He 'improved' and modernized Shakespeare's spelling, punctuation and metre. Pope rearranged the order of the plays, distinguishing between 'Tragedies from History' and 'Tragedies from Fable'. At the foot of the page, in a smaller type, Pope printed passages (some 1,500 lines) whose authenticity he suspected.

In 1726 Lewis Theobald (1688–1744) published *Shakespeare Restored*, an attack on the text of Pope's edition, which earned him the honour of being made the hero of the first, three-book version of the *Dunciad*. He issued his own seven-volume edition of Shakespeare, based on Pope's but incorporating his emendations to the text, many of which are still accepted by editors, in 1733. Theobald's was the first scholarly edition of Shakespeare, drawing on most of the quartos as well as the first folio. He had read widely in Elizabethan literature and began the study of Shakespeare's sources; perhaps more importantly, he saw that difficult or corrupt passages in one play were best understood by looking at parallel passages in other plays. It was with Theobald's edition that the writing of scholarly and critical notes became a significant feature of the editor's duty. A second and cheaper edition of Theobald's Shakespeare appeared in 1740 with a few more conjectural emendations, and it was printed again in 1752, but a new posthumous edition (known as the 'third') with some unattributed emendations came out in 1757.

Sir Thomas Hanmer (1677–1746) was the fourth editor of Shakespeare, his illustrated edition being published at Oxford in six quarto volumes in 1743–4. While sometimes successful in his emendations, Hanmer used no edition of Shakespeare earlier than Pope's. The most valuable part of his edition was an important glossary to the plays. The last editor of Shakespeare before Johnson was Pope's friend and executor, later Bishop of Gloucester, William Warburton (1698–1779). His edition came out in eight volumes in 1747, drawing freely on Theobald's text but introducing Warburton's own notes. Johnson's copy of this edition survives in the library of the University College of Wales, Aberystwyth, and shows that Johnson annotated it for use while he worked on the *Dictionary*. He turned to it again when he was editing Shakespeare. Some time after 1753 he borrowed from Sir Edward Walpole a copy of this same edition which contained manuscript notes and annotations by Styan Thirlby. Johnson drew on these notes, of which he had a low opinion, for his edition (*Life*, iv.161; *JM*, ii.431). He failed to return the sixth volume of the Thirlby set, which is now included among the rest of Johnson's copy of this edition at Aberystwyth.[15]

Warburton's edition came out at a crucial time in the history of Shakespeare scholarship. The year before it appeared, the Spenserian scholar John Upton (1707–60) had published his important *Critical Observations on Shakespeare*. He issued a second edition of this in 1748 in which he responded to Warburton's edition of the previous year. Johnson refers to this work in the Preface and also drew on Upton's book in his annotation of the plays. Warburton's edition provoked another attack in the influential book by Thomas Edwards (1699–1757), *The Canons of Criticism*, which first appeared in 1747 as a Supplement to Warburton but was frequently reprinted, reaching a seventh edition in 1765. Johnson knew Edwards's attack on Warburton but he said, according to Boswell (*Life*, i.263, n.3), 'there is no proportion between the two men; they must not be named together. A fly, Sir, may sting a stately horse and make him wince; but one is but an insect and the other is a horse still.' Yet another opponent of

Warburton's who had already published two books attacking the edition, in particular for the unacknowledged debts to Hanmer, was Zachary Grey (1688–1766). For the first edition of his Shakespeare Johnson borrowed notes and conjectural emendations from his *Critical, Historical and Explanatory Notes on Shakespeare*, issued in two volumes in 1754: Johnson's copy was sold after his death.[16]

From about this time detailed comments on the plays began to appear more frequently. Johnson was able to borrow six notes from John Holt's *Remarks on The Tempest* (1750) for his edition and he knew Joseph Warton's series of articles on *King Lear* contributed to the *Adventurer* in 1753–4, referring to them in his general observations on the play.

Johnson sums up his attitude to these earlier editions of Shakespeare in the Preface to his own edition; unsurprisingly he declares he is not over-impressed by the labours of his predecessors. But there is some evidence that he tried to moderate his critical views of some of the other editors. In his later *Life* of Rowe he comments that he did 'more than he promised and that, without the pomp of notes or boasts of criticism, many passages are happily restored . . . He at least contributed to the popularity of his author' (*Lives*, ii.71).[17] Johnson is equally gentle with Pope's edition in his *Life* of him:

> Pope in his edition undoubtedly did many things wrong, and left many things undone; but let him not be defrauded of his due praise: he was the first that knew, at least the first that told, by what helps the text might be improved. If he inspected the early editions negligently, he taught others to be more accurate. In his Preface he expanded with great skill and elegance the character which had been given of Shakespeare by Dryden; and he drew the public attention upon his works, which though often mentioned had been little read. (*Lives*, iii.139)

Furthermore, Johnson undoubtedly revised and omitted some of his sharper remarks on Warburton in the edition when it was in proof (*Life*, i.544) and his attitude to Sir Thomas Hanmer underwent several changes. Hanmer died in May 1746 and in May 1747 Johnson contributed an affectionate poem about him to the *Gentleman's Magazine*, loosely based on a Latin epitaph written by Robert Freind.[18] In it Johnson referred to the 'lettered ease' to which Hanmer retired during the period when he produced his edition of Shakespeare. Johnson's true valuation of Hanmer appears clearly in the many times he uses definitions from Hanmer's edition of Shakespeare in the *Dictionary*.

After Johnson had finished most of the work on his edition which appeared in 1765 he continued to keep up with new publications about Shakespeare. He owned a copy of Benjamin Heath's anonymously published *A Revisal of Shakespeare's Text*, issued early in 1765.[19] This contained many new notes to the plays and was largely intended as yet another attack on Warburton's edition. It came out just in time for Johnson to respond to some of its emendations in the Appendix to his edition of 1765: he evidently knew the book quite well. For his own 1773 edition he drew on Thomas Tyrwhitt's *Observations and Conjectures upon some Passages of Shakespeare* (1766), which first made use of the list of Shakespeare's plays printed in Francis Meres's *Palladis Tamia: Wit's Treasury* of 1598. Richard Farmer sent him a copy of his *Essay on the Learning of Shakespeare* (1767) through Thomas Percy: Johnson thought very highly of Farmer's book, which, he said, settled the question and showed that Shakespeare's primary debt for his sources was to English translations rather than to the foreign originals (*Life*, iii.38–9 and 477–8).[20] He thought much less well of Mrs Elizabeth Montagu's defence of Shakespeare against Voltaire's criticisms. Her *Essay on Shakespeare* came out anonymously in 1769: on 16 October of that year Boswell records Johnson as saying, 'there is not one sentence of true criticism in her book' (*Life*, ii.88). There is no direct evidence that he took an interest in the publication of Malone's first major contribution to Shakespeare scholarship, the *Attempt to Ascertain the Order in which the Plays of Shakespeare were written* (1778), although by the time it appeared he was well acquainted with its author.

Johnson seems to have had less interest in later textual scholarship. It does not appear that he thought much of Edward Capell's work on the quartos. Boswell records Bennet

Langton's anecdote which reports Johnson as saying: 'If the man would have come to me, I would have endeavoured to "endow his purposes with words"; for, as it is, "he doth gabble monstrously"' (*Life*, iv. 5; cf. *The Tempest*, I.2.356). Instead of acquiring Capell's important researches he owned a twelve-volume edition of the works, which may well have been a 1772 reprint of Theobald's edition.[21] The publisher of the 1788 Supplement to Sir John Hawkins's edition of Johnson's works, John Stockdale, issued a one-volume edition of Shakespeare in 1784, which Johnson also possessed.[22] He dismissively noted the appearance of Charles Jennens's critical edition of *Hamlet* when it came out in 1773; in 1772 Jennens had issued an edition of *King Lear* which had abused Johnson's edition of Shakespeare.[23] Joseph Ritson gave him a copy of his *Remarks Critical and Illustrative on the Text and Notes of the Last Edition of Shakespeare* (1783), which was an attack on his 1778 edition.[24]

V

In 1755 the *Dictionary* on which he had been working for nearly ten years was published. His next literary project was the edition of Shakespeare's plays. He issued a second set of *Proposals*, which were published in London with the date 1 June 1756 on the title-page.[25] The following day Johnson signed an agreement with Jacob Tonson, the chief of the proposed edition's publishers, relinquishing his copyright in the edition in exchange for 250 free sets of the edition in sheets, and half their price – a guinea (£1.05) – for any sets sold above the original number. The terms of the agreement and the title-page of the *Proposals* show that Johnson's undertaking was defined as being to correct and illustrate Shakespeare's plays. The *Proposals* promised that the edition would be delivered to the subscribers by Christmas 1757.

The reasons for the slow progress of Johnson's work on the edition between June 1756 and its publication on 10 October 1765, other than Johnson's characteristic dilatoriness, remain obscure; perhaps he felt that the work he had undertaken on the *Dictionary* and in the mid 1740s on Shakespeare meant that there was little new research to be done. His choice of title for the new periodical he wrote between 1758 and 1760, the *Idler*, may indicate a certain sense of guilt that he was not getting on with the task in hand. The printing history of the edition has never been fully investigated.[26] A change in Johnson's working methods was undoubtedly marked by the appearance of the 1757 edition of Theobald's Shakespeare, which led him to abandon his primary reliance on Warburton. Johnson probably worked on the edition until the last possible moment. Boswell met Johnson on 16 May 1763 but says nothing of Johnson's edition of Shakespeare until he deals with its publication in 1765.[27] The idea of including an appendix of further notes was current at least as early as 14 April 1758, by which time part of the edition was certainly in print – printing may even have begun as early as the summer of 1757 (*Life*, i. 335–6). One of the few certain facts is that the Preface was written at a very late stage, during August and September 1765.

Johnson undertook most of the work on the edition in London. Where he obtained the early texts on which he worked is unknown: the two best collections in London at the time were Garrick's and Capell's. He visited Oxford in 1759 (*Life*, i. 347), the year of his mother's death. In 1762 he first received his valuable pension. In September 1763 he wrote to Thomas Percy saying he hoped to stay with him: 'I purpose to bring Shakespeare with me, and strike a stroke at him with your kind help. Be pleased to get together all observations that you have made upon his works'; the visit did not in fact take place until the next year.[28] Later in 1763 he was reported to be staying at Twickenham in a house belonging to Sir Joshua Reynolds, 'where he is busily employed in putting the finishing hand to that work [the edition of Shakespeare]; resolved not to return to London until he has completed it' (*Life*, iii. 451), and early in 1764 he stayed with the Langton family in Lincolnshire, where he 'had the advantage of a good library' (*Life*, i. 476). From late June to mid August he visited Thomas Percy at Easton Maudit, where he helped with the glossary to the *Reliques of Ancient English Poetry* (*Life*, i. 553–4) and was in Oxford in October (*Life*, iii. 452). About this time he first met and began to stay with the Thrale family at Streatham. He made a brief visit to Cambridge towards the middle of February 1765, when he saw Richard Farmer who told Percy 'he asked my assistance and refused my subscription' (*Life*, i.517–18 and 555); he might well have looked at some of Farmer's fine collection of early English printed books. As well as Percy, Langton, Farmer and others, he was also in touch with Thomas Birch, Charles Burney, Thomas Warton, Joseph Baretti and Garrick about his work, all of whom could have helped him with it. It was on the very eve of the appearance of his edition that he first made the acquaintance of the two rising stars of the next generation of Shakespearian scholars. Between 1763 and 1765 he met George Steevens (1736–1800) who contributed to the Appendix to the edition of 1765, may even have been in the room while Johnson wrote the Preface, and supervised the edition of 1773. In 1764 he first came across the young lawyer and future hero of Shakespeare studies, Edmond Malone.[29]

Johnson evidently worked desultorily and slowly on the edition: what had been promised for Christmas 1757 finally appeared in the autumn of 1765.

His main editorial tool for the Shakespeare was his own *Dictionary* which, as well as supplying hundreds of definitions of words Shakespeare used, also allowed him to examine Shakespeare's parallel uses of the same word in different places. It made him embark on a course of reading through the authors of Shakespeare's time (in particular Sidney, Spenser, Hooker, Raleigh, Bacon, Donne and Jonson and the poems of Chapman), and on a study of the language of the Authorized Version of the Bible. Despite this work Johnson seems to have remained unrepentantly ignorant of Elizabethan and Jacobean drama. Of contemporary dramatists he owned five volumes of Ben Jonson's works, which may have belonged to Peter Whalley's 1756 seven-volume edition, and the 1750 ten-volume edition of the works of Beaumont and Fletcher:[30] he had, apparently, no interest in Marlowe, Kyd, Middleton or any of Shakespeare's fellow dramatists. But Johnson had been considering the problems of editing Shakespeare from at least as early as the *Miscellaneous Observations* of 1745. His friendship with Bishop Percy and Thomas Warton had allowed him to see how sixteenth-century scholars studied and edited texts: he himself had experienced the practice of editing in his edition of Sir Thomas Browne's *Christian Morals* (1756) and in the substantial help he gave to James Bennet in his edition of Roger Ascham's *English Works* (1761). Among the things that this work taught Johnson was that an editor must be pragmatic rather than dogmatic in his procedures and views.

The exact way in which Johnson worked on his edition of Shakespeare still awaits full investigation. The precise textual basis of his edition is similarly unexplored. The *Proposals* showed that Johnson saw how to edit the text of Shakespeare's plays by collating the early quartos and the folio, but he had not the patience nor the materials to do so. Instead, Johnson partly based his text on Warburton's edition of 1747 and partly on the 1757 edition of Theobald: both of these essentially derive from Theobald's 1740 edition. But his use of these texts was unsystematic and the reasons behind his apparent switching in some plays in mid-scene from Theobald to Warburton have not been satisfactorily explained.[31] The fullest general account of what he did to the texts he used shows that Johnson radically altered, simplified and clarified not only the punctuation of the plays, but that he also took advantage of the liberty which he had described in the Preface to change 'particles or other words of slight effect' to 'correct' and 'improve' Shakespeare's grammar.[32] Johnson's thousands of changes included the addition of more explicit stage directions and adjustments to the punctuation (over 10,000 variations from Warburton's punctuation) to make the text more theatrically immediate, accessible and vivid for the reader.

A more detailed study of his treatment of the text of *King Lear*, to which he seems to have paid particular attention, suggests that he worked from the posthumous (1757) revision of Theobald's edition, but freely consulted and used the first quarto and the first folio to produce the most conservative and carefully considered of early eighteenth-century editions of the play.[33] A similar method of proceeding, working from

Theobald's 1757 edition but also drawing on Warburton's text, has been discovered in an examination of the textual history of *1 Henry VI*.[34]

Above all Johnson respected the integrity of the first folio, believing that what was in it was Shakespeare's and that only the first of the folio editions was of any textual use. He knew that some quartos preserved good texts and others poor texts. He saw that for two plays, *Richard II* and *A Midsummer Night's Dream*, the folio text was based on that of earlier quartos. If the folio had passages not in the early quartos he consulted, then it appeared to him that this was because Shakespeare had revised the plays. In this view, despite Shakespeare's reputation as a hasty and often careless writer, he anticipated some of the most recent scholarly research which has found evidence of minute and detailed revision in several plays, in particular in *King Lear*.

The willingness to emend which Johnson had earlier shown in his *Miscellaneous Observations* was gradually tempered by his experience of editing until he eventually became fundamentally unwilling to emend the text unless he had to. This came partly from his recognition that Shakespeare was capable, if not of writing nonsense, at least of making mistakes which, he believed, should be left as they stood: 'Had Shakespeare had a dictionary,' he wrote in *The Plan of a Dictionary of the English Language* (1747) alluding to *A Midsummer Night's Dream*, IV.1.41, 'he had not made the "woodbine" entwine the "honeysuckle".' The chief cause of corruption in the text, he seemed to think, was inaccuracy in its copying or printing: not, as others had before him believed, playhouse contamination. He was extremely cautious about suggesting that speeches or whole scenes had been interpolated by actors or other writers. Johnson was perhaps the first editor to consider the use to which a knowledge of Elizabethan handwriting could be put in the emendation of Shakespeare's text. But above all else he established the important principle that the best text of Shakespeare was the one which reproduced most fully and accurately what Shakespeare had written, not the one which reflected the good taste and inspired critical judgement of the editor.

Johnson's edition met with a general sense of disappointment from other critics and scholars when it finally appeared. So much had been promised, but only part of it had been fully carried out. There were too many evident signs of haste, unsystematic and inconsistent work, changes of mind and editorial intention, and of material added or removed at will. However much Johnson achieved in the edition, he had not fulfilled the promises either of the *Proposals* of 1756 or of the rationale of editorial method and duty put forward in the Preface. He had not read all the other commentators on Shakespeare with all their emendations; he had not read widely enough in the literature of Shakespeare's day, especially in his sources and in the works of contemporary dramatists, and he had not collated sufficient of the old quartos, let alone reprinted all their variant readings. In the end he had simply not done enough work.

For his editorial labours Johnson may only have received £375 for the first edition of the works and £100 for the second edition issued later in 1765.[35] The annotation for this second edition and for the third edition of 1768 remained unchanged: while some errors in the text were corrected, more were newly introduced. A separate printing of the Preface was issued in 1765 from the same setting of type used for the second edition. The fourth edition of 1773, edited by George Steevens, included revisions by Johnson both to the Preface and more substantially (in just under 500 places) to his annotation. He was not afraid to change his mind: many of the harsher criticisms of Warburton were cut. In the preparation of this edition Johnson wrote to Richard Farmer and the brothers Thomas and Joseph Warton requesting help (*Life*, ii. 114–15). Another important new influence on Johnson's work was the labour of revising the *Dictionary* for its fourth edition, which was published in the same year as the Shakespeare.

This fourth edition of Shakespeare's plays is sometimes known as the first variorum edition. The second variorum edition of 1778 contains a new sentence in the Preface and some other changes and further revisions to about fifty of Johnson's notes. The text of the plays printed in 1773 and 1778 gradually departs from Johnson's and begins to incorporate the fruits of Edward Capell's researches published in his edition of 1768 and his commentary of 1774. To the 1780 Supplement to Steevens's edition produced by Edmond Malone, Johnson is supposed to have introduced two corrections to the text of the Preface and one to his note on the Epilogue to *Henry VIII*. The third variorum edition of 1785 appeared after Johnson's death and contains no new material from his pen. Johnson probably started to lose interest in undertaking serious new work on Shakespeare when he began work on the *Lives of the Poets*; by March 1777 the London booksellers had asked him to undertake this new project. Nevertheless, it seems almost certain that he was aware of the publication of Malone's Supplement in 1780, which began the systematic, scholarly study of Shakespeare's life and works.

VI

Despite Johnson's failure to carry out what he had proposed, the purchaser of his eight volumes of Shakespeare still got the best and fullest edition of the plays so far published in the eighteenth century. As well as his own Preface, Johnson reprinted the earlier Prefaces of Pope, Theobald, Hanmer and Warburton; these were followed by Rowe's life of Shakespeare in Pope's revised version, a copy of the grant of arms to John Shakespeare, a transcript of Shakespeare's will, the story that when Shakespeare first arrived in London he held horses outside the theatre during performances, and Ben Jonson's verses to Shakespeare from the first folio.[36]

After all this preliminary matter the plays then follow, with five plays in each of the first four volumes and the sixth, four in volumes five and seven and three in volume eight, which contained the Appendix of supplementary notes and George Steevens's list of the quartos. Johnson departed from the order in which Warburton had printed the plays but retained the folio classifications of comedies, histories (printed in the order of their historical narratives) and tragedies, which included *Cymbeline* and the Roman plays. Within these categories the organizing principle behind Johnson's arrangement of the plays, which begin with *The Tempest* and end with *Othello*, is not clear. Before each play Johnson included a list of the characters in it, which again usually departed from those given by Warburton. He tended to simplify these lists of *dramatis personae* and shorten the descriptions of the characters. In *Measure for Measure*, for example, he noted that 'Varrius might be omitted for he is only once spoken to and says nothing'; for *The Tempest* he expanded Warburton's direction taken from the folio, 'Scene, an uninhabited island' to 'Scene, the sea with a ship, afterwards an uninhabited island'.

The Preface to the edition is probably Johnson's most famous piece of critical writing, perhaps the most famous essay on Shakespeare ever to have been written. In it, one great imagination and intellect records its response to another. Yet there are problems in the Preface which continue to puzzle the reader and which have prevented Johnson's views from ever becoming, in the strict sense of the word, definitive. Coleridge described it as 'strangely overrated, contradictory, and most illogical'.[37] While its structure is clear, some of its arguments – that love is generally unimportant on the stage and yet that Shakespeare's comedies are his best works, for example – do appear paradoxical. Johnson implicitly sets himself almost on the same level with Shakespeare: as a critic he is entitled and qualified to judge the work he has edited. His criticism will be large and general, refusing to descend to actual details. It puts itself forward as the converse of 'the petty cavils of petty minds'. Nevertheless, while he avoids being too specific the Preface shows how far Johnson's literary criticism had developed from the more purely abstract and theoretical periodical essays of the 1750s. In addition to this, the Preface also acted as a defence of Johnson's editorial work: if he had not done what he should have done as well and as quickly as he said he would, he had, all the same, done a great deal.

It was the longest Preface to an edition of Shakespeare's plays which had so far appeared and yet it is still a short work which covers a great deal of ground. The structure of the

Preface is clear and straightforward. Johnson begins by describing Shakespeare's strengths as a writer; he then briefly admits that there are faults in his works and goes on to defend him in the three areas where he appears at his most vulnerable: in respect of his treatment of the unities, of the time and culture in which he lived, and of his learning. Finally he turns to the work of Shakespeare's previous editors before describing the principles behind his own edition.

As with much of Johnson's writing, the Preface contains a striking mixture of his own personal views and more objective critical theories. Its tone moves between cool irony, weighty satire and detached, critical observation. Johnson is never prescriptive except when he seeks to undermine prescriptive criticism: 'there is always', he says, 'an appeal open from criticism to nature'. And while Shakespeare is the poet of nature, who 'caught his ideas from the living world', he was not a god to be worshipped and admired uncritically. 'Of all modern and perhaps ancient poets', in Dryden's words, he 'had the largest and most comprehensive soul', but also he was human and could err. His faults – his willingness to sacrifice morality to dramatic expedience, his hurrying to finish off the plays, his lack of natural talent for writing tragedy, the weaknesses of his plots and so on – make him a suitable candidate for criticism. Yet his powers as a writer – his skill in comedy, his well-discriminated, realistic characters, his truthful 'mingled drama' and his supreme knowledge of human nature – make him superior to all other authors.

Johnson is not specifically concerned with Shakespeare's theatrical skills. He realizes that the plays would fail if they were put on in their original forms: that is why they have to be performed in improved and adapted versions. Yet to the reader they are the supreme imaginative dramas. Even so, what Shakespeare wrote is often not immediately intelligible to the reader, and the editor has a duty to explain it and to point out in closer detail Shakespeare's beauties and faults.

There are about 5,600 notes in Johnson's edition; about half of these are Johnson's original explanations and critical comments; a further 800 represent his reaction to previous annotations. The notes Johnson wrote to the plays occupy some 900 pages in the Yale edition of his works. They range from the explanatory to the critical, from elaborate paraphrases to illustrative quotations from other Renaissance writers. They gather up and respond to much of what had already been written about the plays. Johnson reprinted most of Warburton's notes and, as the Preface makes clear, felt he had a duty to comment favourably or unfavourably on them as he judged best. Yet he did not work systematically, sometimes failing to acknowledge the sources of his material, sometimes adding new notes which interrupted the system of numbering for those he had already written. Most of the notes are brief and reasonable in their tone; they get to the heart of the matter as quickly as possible, for Johnson did not seek to score points off the errors and ignorance of previous editors.

A full edition of Johnson's notes would reprint not only his short glosses to single words and phrases in the plays, but also the notes by other editors which he reprinted without comment and with whose opinions he presumably agreed. These reveal, for example, that with Pope he thought *Troilus and Cressida* one of Shakespeare's last plays and that Posthumus's vision in *Cymbeline* (V.4) was added by another author to the play after Shakespeare had written it; with Theobald that Oberon and Puck, although 'invisible', are on stage throughout *A Midsummer Night's Dream*; with Warburton that Gonzalo's speech in *The Tempest* (II.1.150) belongs to the tradition of Utopian discourses. Most striking to modern eyes, perhaps, is Johnson's willingness to believe that the plays contain numerous contemporary allusions which can be identified: he follows Warburton who proposed that Oberon's speech about 'a fair vestal thronèd by the west' (*A Midsummer Night's Dream*, II.1.155) refers to Queen Elizabeth and Mary Queen of Scots; he reprints without comment Theobald's note that Sir Toby Belch's 'Taunt him with the licence of ink' (*Twelfth Night*, III.2.42) reveals that 'our author intended to show his respect for Sir Walter Raleigh'; and that King John's speeches beginning 'It is the curse of kings' (IV.2.208) refer to William Davison's troubles with the case of Mary Queen of

Scots in 1586–9 and so must have been interpolated 'long after' the play was first written.

The notes make consistently interesting and diverting reading; many of Johnson's explanations and paraphrases of difficult words, phrases and passages are still quoted by modern editors: some of his emendations are still accepted. Johnson was not afraid to confess his inability to understand what Shakespeare wrote or to leave the text alone. Nor, as the example of his work on *Macbeth* showed, did he feel embarrassed in changing his mind about what he had once said or thought. Indeed his whole approach to annotating Shakespeare in 1765 was quite different, more restrained, sparer, less antiquarian, than it had been in 1745. Shakespeare, he believed, was quite capable of making gross mistakes, historical and geographical errors, flagrant anachronisms and simple blunders. But he also reserves a large number of his more critical comments for Shakespeare's linguistic and grammatical practices.

The reason for the usefulness and success of the notes has been variously explained. Johnson's interest in Lockean mental psychology, it has been argued, made him aware that an important part of Shakespeare's manner was that 'the equality of words to things is very often neglected', that he 'attends more to his ideas than to this words', that his 'mind was more intent upon notions than words'. Johnson was able to follow Shakespeare's fullness and quickness of mind and to explain how the ideas related to the words which Shakespeare used to express them. Furthermore, he was able to move in his notes from the immediate dramatic context which he was annotating to illustrating the more general or common experience which was being described. The notes slow down Shakespeare's darting imagination, show what is being said in relation to how it is being said and go on, where appropriate, to illustrate the wider application of the immediate theatrical experience.[38]

To the end of each play (apart from *Much Ado About Nothing*) Johnson attached a short 'stricture'. These have become known as his 'general observation' on the play, although he never called them by that term. Many of these comments were revised in 1773 (most of the general observation on *The Tempest*, for example, first appeared then). They reveal Johnson at his most critically informal and some are the only extant records of what he thought of individual plays. They presage the sort of direct, practical criticism of individual works of which Johnson was to show himself a master in the *Lives of the Poets*.

VII

For Johnson in the Preface Shakespeare is first and foremost the poet of nature, the greatest English creator of character and plot: his critical vocabulary reflects this unerringly, but sometimes imprecisely. In the notes his chief critical terms are on the one side 'elegant',[39] and on the other 'harsh'. He takes pains to point out what is 'sublime' and 'pathetic' in Shakespeare, but is also aware of 'mean', 'coarse' and 'gross' passages in his plays. Above all he praises what is 'proper' (defined in the *Dictionary* as: 4 'Natural; original' and 6 'Exact; accurate; just'), and to a lesser extent 'just' (defined as: 3 'Exact; proper; accurate') and 'natural'.

The critic's duty is to point out what is beautiful in Shakespeare, but he cannot leave what is wrong unnoticed: many of Johnson's comments on Shakespeare (the general observation on *Cymbeline*, for example) appear at first wrongheaded, but often contain elements of what he feels are complex truths about the plays. But for Johnson there were more obvious faults in Shakespeare than just his wilfulness. As well as the puns of which he so disapproved there was the sacrifice of moral justice for dramatic effect: whatever he might have said in the Preface about Shakespeare's genius for comedy, it is the tragedies which seem to haunt and distress Johnson. Beyond the immediate moral question posed by tragedy, he often finds something crude and distasteful in Shakespeare: 'It were to be wished that the poor merriment of this dialogue [in *Henry V*, III.2.20] had not been purchased with so much profaneness.' Shakespeare's willingness to let his characters swear, blaspheme, perjure and tell lies shocks Johnson deeply.

For Johnson this is a personal, moral failing on Shakespeare's part, which in the end affects his critical judgement of the plays. Johnson is, perhaps, finally caught by a suspicion that Shakespeare, the poet who had 'the largest and most comprehensive soul' of all times, may not have been a morally good man, that he may have been more interested in his art than his duty as a Christian to his faith. Two features of Johnson's work on Shakespeare may reflect this uneasiness on his part. The *Dictionary* shows over and over again that Johnson thought Shakespeare a careless and corrupt user of the English language; he used 'bad', 'improper' and 'barbarous' words in 'forced' and 'harsh' constructions. No doubt Shakespeare did abuse the language and no doubt Johnson was one of the few writers to be in a position of authority and confidence to point this failure out. But Johnson returns with disturbing regularity, both in the *Dictionary* and in the notes to the edition of Shakespeare, to his linguistic depravities. It is almost as though, unwilling entirely to condemn the plays, Johnson shows his disapproval of them by his minute criticism of their fabric.

Secondly and more importantly, Johnson's determined lack of interest in Shakespeare himself must strike modern readers as odd. He takes almost no interest in the question of the development of Shakespeare's art, apart from arguing that he probably got better as he grew older: his apparent ignorance of the poems, however great his general contempt for the sonnet might have been, appears almost wilful. Despite his retailing of some rather dubious anecdotal stories about Shakespeare, Johnson, who was so much concerned with Shakespeare's art, has next to nothing to report or to surmise about his life or, more curiously, about his personality. Johnson is quite unwilling to tell the reader what sort of a man Shakespeare was. He goes so far as to say he was a 'genius', he was 'favoured by nature' and he had 'the largest and most comprehensive soul', but there is apparently nothing more to say, and nothing more that needs to be said, about it.

This silence and lack of curiosity may indicate an unease about his favourite writer, a fear that a too close examination of

Shakespeare might reveal personal and moral defects upon which Johnson would prefer not to dwell. Johnson, whose imaginative response to the plays was often so overwhelmingly open ('I cannot reconcile my heart to Bertram', 'But Falstaff unimitated, unimitable Falstaff, how shall I describe thee?'), closed his mind to the man who wrote them, preferring to look at 'soul' and to talk about 'the poet of nature'. Johnson saw that Shakespeare was a genius, but also a man; he admires the genius but is more cautious about the man. There is something of this divided view of him in Johnson's comment in the Preface, that 'We fix our eyes upon his graces and turn them from his deformities and endure in him what we should in another loathe or despise.' Similarly at the end of the Preface there is a clear sense that Johnson thought Shakespeare was aware of the discrepancy between what he did and what he morally ought to have done: he had, Johnson says, 'that superiority of mind which despised its own performances when it compared them with its powers'.

The possible motives behind this attitude towards Shakespeare's personality deserve some consideration. A decade or so later Johnson was willing to attend to such matters when he was writing the lives of Milton, Pope and Gray, but for Shakespeare he avoids the issue. While Johnson may have lacked documentary facts, there was enough material elsewhere with which he might have recreated a version of Shakespeare's life. Apart from the plays themselves, there was the question of their chronology and order; there were the places Shakespeare had lived, the testimony and example of his friends and fellow playwrights (in particular Jonson) and the anecdotes which accumulated around him, however spurious they may have appeared to be. Johnson will have none of this: in the end he will not openly reveal what sort of a man he thought Shakespeare was – whether he was good or bad.

There is one passage in the Preface, however, which comes near to a sympathetic portrait of Shakespeare. 'He came to London,' Johnson wrote, 'a needy adventurer and lived for a time by very mean employments . . . The genius of

Shakespeare was not to be depressed by the weight of poverty, nor limited by the narrow conversation to which men in want are inevitably condemned.' As so often with Johnson (especially in the *Life of Savage*), it is tempting here to draw a parallel between the biographer and his subject: this may be what Johnson, who had written for *The Adventurer*, himself was doing. He began composing his only play, *Irene*, at Edial, while he was a schoolmaster, in 1736: the next year he set off for the capital. In his late twenties he arrived in London with one potentially profitable literary property, a play, and began to learn what it was to live in poverty as a hack writer. His description of Shakespeare's arrival in the town inevitably reflects his own. But their subsequent careers and lives were quite different. The playwright enjoyed apparently effortless success; Johnson's life was one in which periods of extremely hard work were succeeded by bouts of idleness compounded by a strong sense of guilt and personal uncertainty: he had serious and recurrent doubts about his moral being.

In Johnson's view Shakespeare triumphed in his chosen profession of dramatist. Writing appeared to cost him little effort – Jonson's verses on Shakespeare which were reprinted in the 1765 edition reported that. His carelessness was, in part, a product of this very facility. The contrast between Shakespeare's literary ease and Johnson's own dilatoriness, his unwillingness to commit himself to paper until the last possible moment, must have been painful. Johnson was aware of his own powers as a writer, but was equally aware of his own personal weaknesses, which in the end he regarded as moral ones. To investigate Shakespeare's life was bound to make him examine his own and to express the similarities and profound differences between the two. From the plays, Johnson understood what Shakespeare had achieved in his writing and how easily he had done it: from his own life he knew what a price had to be paid personally and so morally for what he had achieved. However disturbing an experience it was for Johnson to read the plays, the consideration of the personality which had produced them was bound to be equally, perhaps even more, painful. Finally, Johnson may have thought that investigating Shakespeare's infirm moral being would prove too personally damaging an enterprise.

Yet this turning away, this not wishing to look at what evidently offends, is necessarily part of Johnson's essentially imaginative response to Shakespeare. His weakness in Johnson's eyes was his mortality; his strength, that he was a force of nature.

NOTES TO THE INTRODUCTION

1. *Johnsonian Miscellanies*, ed. George Birkbeck Hill, 2 vols, Oxford 1897; abbreviated as *JM*. *Boswell's Life of Johnson*, ed. George Birkbeck Hill, rev. L. F. Powell, 6 vols, Oxford 1934–64; abbreviated as *Life*.
2. Samuel Johnson, *A Journey to the Western Islands of Scotland*, ed. J. D. Fleeman, Oxford 1985, p. 18.
3. The changes between Johnson's notes have been studied by Arthur Sherbo in 'Dr Johnson on *Macbeth*: 1745 and 1765', *Review of English Studies* new series 2 (1951), 40–47.
4. Arthur Sherbo, 'Sanguine Expectations: Dr Johnson's *Shakespeare*', *Shakespeare Quarterly* 9 (1958), 426–8.
5. James L. Clifford, *Dictionary Johnson: Samuel Johnson's Middle Years*, 1979, pp. 143–7.
6. Robert DeMaria, *Johnson's Dictionary and the Language of Learning*, Chapel Hill and London 1986, p. 17; the quotation is unchanged in the fourth edition. Warburton's 1747 edition from which Johnson took the illustrative quotations for the *Dictionary* has the correct reading.
7. W. B. C. Watkins, *Johnson and English Poetry Before 1660*, Princeton Studies in English 13 (1936), reprinted New York 1965, pp. 70 and 103–4. Theobald quotes the passage from *The Rape of Lucrece* to illustrate *As You Like It*, III.2.266: in Warburton's edition of Shakespeare the note is reprinted at ii.341.
8. C. S. Lim, 'Dr Johnson's Quotation from *Macbeth*', *Notes and Queries* 231 (1986), 518. See also note 10 to *Rambler* 168 below.
9. *The Plan of a Dictionary of the English Language*, 1747, p. 24.
10. Some of the connections between the revised *Dictionary* and the revised Shakespeare are explored by Arthur Sherbo in '1773: The Year of Revision', *Eighteenth-Century Studies* 7 (1973–4), 18–39.
11. See also *Life*, v.244–5 and 541–2.
12. J. D. Fleeman, *A Preliminary Handlist of Copies of Books Associated with Dr Samuel Johnson*, Oxford Bibliographical Society Occasional Publication 17, 1984, no. 245; abbreviated as *Books Associated with Johnson*.
13. *The Sale Catalogue of Samuel Johnson's Library: A Facsimile Edition*, ed. J. D. Fleeman, English Literary Studies Monograph 2, 1975, lot 353; abbreviated as *Sale Catalogue*.
14. *Sale Catalogue*, lot 179.

15. This copy has been described by A. Cuming in 'A Copy of Shakespeare's Works which Formerly Belonged to Dr Johnson', *Review of English Studies* 3 (1927), 208–12.
16. *Sale Catalogue*, lot 45.
17. Samuel Johnson, *Lives of the English Poets*, ed. George Birkbeck Hill, 3 vols, Oxford 1905; abbreviated as *Lives*.
18. Samuel Johnson, *The Complete English Poems*, ed. J. D. Fleeman, Harmondsworth 1971, p. 76.
19. *Books Associated with Johnson* no. 80; this is now in the Folger Shakespeare Library, Washington DC.
20. *Books Associated with Johnson* no. 67; this is now in the Victoria & Albert Museum.
21. *Sale Catalogue*, lot 516.
22. *Sale Catalogue*, lot 493.
23. *The Letters of Samuel Johnson*, ed. R. W. Chapman, 3 vols, Oxford 1952, no. 304; abbreviated as *Letters*.
24. *Books Associated with Johnson* no. 236; this is now in the Folger Shakespeare Library, Washington DC.
25. The printer charged the publisher for 3,000 copies; see Donald D. Eddy, 'Samuel Johnson's Editions of Shakespeare (1765)', *Papers of the Bibliographical Society of America* 56 (1962), 428–44. Arthur Sherbo records what is known of the edition's printing history in *Samuel Johnson, Editor of Shakespeare with an essay on 'The Adventurer'*, Illinois Studies in Language and Literature 42, Urbana 1956, pp. 8–13.
26. Donald D. Eddy (op. cit., p. 429) distinguishes between the two editions of 1765 and finds that considerable sections in four volumes of the second edition were themselves printed from a new setting of type. There are some valuable comments on the printing history of the edition of 1765 and the relationships of the later reprints and editions in letters to *The Times Literary Supplement* from Tom Davies on 19 April and J. D. Fleeman on 17 May 1974.
27. Arthur M. Eastman attempts to reconstruct Johnson's work on the edition during its year of publication in 'Johnson's Shakespearean Labors in 1765', *Modern Language Notes* 63 (1948), 512–15.
28. See Mary Hyde, '"Not in Chapman"', in *Johnson, Boswell and their Circle: Essays Presented to Lawrence Fitzroy Powell*, Oxford 1965, p. 306.
29. See John H. Middendorf, 'Steevens and Johnson', in *Johnson and his Age*, ed. James Engell, Harvard English Studies 12, Cambridge, Mass. and London 1984, pp. 125–35; and James M. Osborn, 'Edmond Malone and Dr Johnson', in *Johnson, Boswell and their Circle*, pp. 1–20.
30. *Sale Catalogue*, lots 123 and 612. See also W. B. C. Watkins, *Johnson and English Poetry Before 1660*, pp. 63–6 and 101–3.
31. Arthur M. Eastman, 'The Texts from which Johnson Printed his Shakespeare', *Journal of English and Germanic Philology* 49 (1950), 182–91.
32. Arthur M. Eastman, 'Johnson's Shakespeare and the Laity: A Textual Study', *Publications of the Modern Language Association of America* 65 (1950), 1112–21.
33. Shirley White Johnston, 'Samuel Johnson's Text of *King Lear*: "Dull Duty" Reassessed', *Yearbook of English Studies* 6 (1976), 80–91.

34. G. Blakemore Evans, 'The Text of Johnson's *Shakespeare* (1765)', *Philological Quarterly* 28 (1949), 425–8 and *Shakespeare Research Opportunities* 2 (1966).
35. See J. D. Fleeman, 'The Revenue of a Writer: Samuel Johnson's Literary Earnings', in *Studies in the Book Trade in Honour of Graham Pollard*, Oxford Bibliographical Society Publications new series 18, 1975, 211–30, and *JM*, i.422, n. 8.
36. The copy of the grant of arms was first printed by Pope from a College of Arms manuscript transmitted to him by John Anstis; the transcript of Shakespeare's will was reprinted from the inaccurate version included in volume six of *Biographia Britannica*, 1763 (see Samuel Schoenbaum, *Shakespeare's Lives*, Oxford 1970, pp. 137–9). Johnson reports the story about holding the horses as told to Pope by Rowe, although neither used it in their editions; Johnson may have borrowed it from Theophilus Cibber's *Lives of the Poets* (1753).
37. Letter to Daniel Stuart, 13 May 1816, in *Collected Letters of Samuel Taylor Coleridge*, ed. Earl Leslie Griggs, 6 vols, Oxford 1956–71, iv (1959), p. 642.
38. See John H. Middendorf's 'Ideas vs. Words: Johnson, Locke, and the Edition of Shakespeare', in *English Writers of the Eighteenth Century*, ed. John H. Middendorf, New York and London 1971, pp. 249–72.
39. On Johnson's use of this term, see Patricia Ingham, 'Dr Johnson's "Elegance"', *Review of English Studies* new series 19 (1968), 271–8.

FURTHER READING

The literature on both Shakespeare and Johnson is of course enormous. The following suggestions for further reading, which generally exclude books and articles referred to in the Introduction, can only suggest a few items which may be of interest.

Walter Raleigh's *Johnson on Shakespeare*, Oxford 1908, presents an old-spelling text with a characteristically engaging Introduction. W. K. Wimsatt's modernized *Dr Johnson on Shakespeare*, 1960, Harmondsworth 1969, is still valuable. Despite some weaknesses (principally in B. H. Bronson's Introduction), Arthur Sherbo's *Johnson on Shakespeare*, The Yale Edition of the Works of Samuel Johnson, Vols VII and VIII, New Haven and London 1968, is invaluable; it contains an index of words and phrases glossed. A selection from the two-volume edition with a slightly revised Introduction, *Selections from Johnson on Shakespeare*, ed. Bertrand H. Bronson and Jean M. O'Meara, New Haven and London 1986, contains the 1756 *Proposal*, the Preface and many of the notes to the plays; in it particular attention has been paid to the notes of previous editors to which Johnson responded. The Preface has been reproduced in facsimile from the fourth edition of 1778 and exhaustively annotated by P. J. Smallwood, *Johnson's Preface to Shakespeare*, Bristol 1985.

The background to Johnson's work on Shakespeare is best studied in the six volumes of Brian Vickers's *Shakespeare: The Critical Heritage*, London and Boston 1974–81. This reprints and comments on a vast quantity of the Shakespeare adaptations, scholarship and criticism produced between 1623 and 1801, allowing Johnson's work to be seen in the context of contemporary views of Shakespeare. The fifth volume (1979), covering 1765–74, contains the Preface, reviews of the edition and a valuable discussion of Johnson's achievements and failures. The introductory essays refer to most of the important secondary material. A more concise account of the contemporary context of Johnson's work is available in *Eighteenth Century Essays on Shakespeare*, ed. D. Nichol Smith, 2nd edn, Oxford 1963. The story of the developing interest in Shakespeare's biography and the history of bardolatry is told by Samuel Schoenbaum in *Shakespeare's Lives*, Oxford 1970.

The only substantial book on Johnson as editor of Shakespeare is Arthur Sherbo's *Samuel Johnson, Editor of Shakespeare with an essay on 'The Adventurer'*, Illinois Studies in Language and Literature 42, Urbana 1956. While this contains a wealth of useful information, some of Sherbo's conclusions about Johnson's indebtedness to previous Shakespearian scholars need to be modified. The case against his unacknowledged debt to Benjamin Heath (see above, p. 19) and others has been forcefully made by Arthur M. Eastman in 'In Defense of Dr Johnson', *Shakespeare Quarterly* 8 (1957), 493–500.

There are classic accounts of Johnson's Shakespeare criticism by T. S. Eliot in *A Companion to Shakespeare Studies*, ed. H. Granville-Barker and G. B. Harrison, Cambridge 1934, and by F. R. Leavis in *The Common Pursuit*, 1952. Helen Gardner provides a brief and eminently sensible account of 'Johnson on Shakespeare' in the *New Rambler* (June 1965), 2–12. The only book-length study devoted to the Preface, R. D. Stock's *Samuel Johnson and Neoclassical Dramatic Theory: The Intellectual Context of The Preface to Shakespeare*, Lincoln, Nebraska 1973, is much concerned with the critical background to Johnson's work. A 'post-Kantian' view of the Preface to Shakespeare is given by Murray Krieger in 'Fiction, Nature, and Literary Kinds in Johnson's Criticism of Shakespeare', *Eighteenth-Century Studies* 4 (1970–71), 184–98. Donald T. Siebert Jr makes and perhaps overstates the case for detecting a strong, defensively satirical tone in the Preface in 'The Scholar as Satirist:

Johnson's Edition of Shakespeare', *Studies in English Literature* 15 (1975), 483–503. One of the most vexed passages in the Preface is discussed by W. B. Carnochan in 'Johnsonian Metaphor and the "Adamant of Shakespeare"', *Studies in English Literature* 10 (1970), 541–9. Jacob H. Adler argues strongly that Johnson denies the role of the imagination in reading Shakespeare in 'Johnson's "He That Imagines This"', *Shakespeare Quarterly* 11 (1960), 225–8. In 'The Rise of the Novel', in *Samuel Johnson: New Critical Essays*, ed. Isobel Grundy, London and Totowa, NJ 1984, pp. 70–85, Mark Kinkead-Weekes suggests that Johnson's later admiration for the novel developed out of his interest in character and plot in Shakespeare. Isobel Grundy's *Samuel Johnson and the Scale of Greatness*, Leicester 1986, contains some interesting ideas about Johnson's comparative criticism.

The history of Shakespeare scholarship in the eighteenth century has received some welcome attention in Arthur Sherbo's *The Birth of Shakespeare Studies: Commentators from Rowe (1709) to Boswell–Malone (1821)*, East Lansing, MI, 1986. A classic account of the subject, 'The Treatment of Shakespeare's Text by his Earlier Editors', was contributed to the *Proceedings of the British Academy* 19 (1933) by R. B. McKerrow: this was conveniently reprinted in *Studies in Shakespeare*, ed. Peter Alexander, Oxford 1964. A useful account of the background to Johnson's practice as an editor is given by Robert E. Scholes in 'Dr Johnson and the Bibliographical Criticism of Shakespeare', *Shakespeare Quarterly* 11 (1960), 163–71.

Arthur Sherbo argues for the continuity of 'Johnson's *Shakespeare* and the Dramatic Criticism in the *Lives of the English Poets*' in *Shakespeare: Aspects of Influence*, ed. G. B. Evans, Harvard English Studies 7, Cambridge, Mass. and London 1976, pp. 55–69.

A NOTE ON THE TEXT

For ease of use, quotations (except where the point of Johnson's commentaries would be obscured) and act, scene and line references to Shakespeare's works have been taken from the New Penguin Shakespeare editions. For the two plays which have not yet appeared in this series – *Cymbeline* and *Titus Andronicus* – quotations and references have been taken from the one-volume edition of the works edited by Peter Alexander (1951). In act, scene and line references, only the first line of what is being referred to has been indicated: all references within square brackets have been supplied by the editor.

The definitions of words which have been glossed are taken from the first edition of the *Dictionary* published in 1755; the words are only glossed on their first occurrence.

MISCELLANEOUS OBSERVATIONS ON THE TRAGEDY OF *MACBETH*
(1745)

Miscellaneous Observations on the Tragedy of Macbeth; With Remarks on Sir Thomas Hanmer's Edition of Shakespeare. To which is Affixed Proposals for a New Edition of Shakespeare, With a Specimen

NOTE I
ACT I SCENE I[I.1]

Enter three Witches.

In order to make a true estimate of the abilities and merit of a writer it is always necessary to examine the genius of his age and the opinions of his contemporaries. A poet who should now make the whole action of his tragedy depend upon enchantment and produce the chief events by the assistance of supernatural agents would be censured as transgressing the bounds of probability, he would be banished from the theatre to the nursery and condemned to write fairy-tales instead of tragedies; but a survey of the notions that prevailed at the time when this play was written will prove that Shakespeare was in no danger of such censures since he only turned the system that was then universally admitted to his advantage and was far from overburdening the credulity of his audience.

The reality of witchcraft or enchantment which, though not strictly the same, are confounded in this play has in all ages and countries been credited by the common people and in most by the learned themselves. These phantoms have indeed appeared more frequently in proportion as the darkness of ignorance has been more gross; but it cannot be shown that the brightest gleams of knowledge have at any time been sufficient to drive them out of the world. The time in which this kind of credulity was at its height seems to have been that of the holy war, in which the Christians imputed all their defeats to enchantments or diabolical opposition as they ascribed their success to the assistance of their military saints, and the learned Mr Warburton appears to believe (*Supplement to the Introduction to Don Quixote*) that the first accounts of enchantments were brought into this part of the world by those who returned from their eastern expeditions.[1] But there is always some distance between the birth and maturity of folly as of wickedness: this opinion had long existed though perhaps the application of it had in no foregoing age been so frequent, nor the reception so general. Olympiodorus in Photius's *Extracts*[2] tells us of one Libanius, who practised this kind of military magic and having promised χώρις ὁπλιτῶν κατὰ βαρβάρων ἐνεργεῖν, 'to perform great things against the barbarians without soldiers', was at the instances of the empress Placidia put to death when he was about to have given proofs of his abilities. The Empress showed some kindness in her anger by cutting him off at a time so convenient for his reputation.

But a more remarkable proof of the antiquity of this notion may be found in St Chrysostom's book *De Sacerdotio*, which exhibits a scene of enchantments not exceeded by any romance of the middle age; he supposes a spectator overlooking a field of battle attended by one that points out all the various objects of horror, the engines of destruction and the arts of slaughter. Δεικνύτο δὲ ἔτι παρὰ τοῖς ἐναντίοις καὶ πετομένους ἵππους διά τινος μαγγανείας, καὶ ὁπλίτας δι' ἀέρος φερομένους, καὶ πάσην γοητείας δύναμιν καὶ ἰδέαν: 'Let him then proceed to show him in the opposite armies horses flying by enchantment, armed men transported through the air, and every power and form of magic.' Whether St Chrysostom believed that such performances were really to be seen in a day of battle, or only endeavoured to enliven his description by adopting the notions of the vulgar, it is equally certain that such notions were in his time received and that therefore they were not imported from the Saracens in a later age; the wars with the Saracens however gave occasion to their propagation, not only as bigotry naturally discovers prodigies, but as the scene of action was removed to a great distance and distance either of time or place is sufficient to reconcile weak minds to wonderful relations.

The Reformation did not immediately arrive at its meridian, and though day was gradually increasing upon us, the goblins of witchcraft still continued to hover in the twilight. In the time of Queen Elizabeth was the remarkable trial of the witches of Warboys whose conviction is still commemorated in an annual sermon at Huntingdon.[3] But in the reign of King James in which this tragedy was written many circumstances concurred to propagate and confirm this opinion. The King, who was much celebrated for his knowledge, had before his arrival in England not only examined in person a woman accused of witchcraft, but had given a very formal account of the practices and illusions of evil spirits, the compacts of witches, the ceremonies used by them, the manner of detecting them and the justice of punishing them in his dialogues of *Demonology*, written in the Scottish dialect and published at Edinburgh.[4] This book was, soon after his accession, reprinted at London and as the ready way to gain King James's favour was to flatter his speculations the system of *Demonology* was immediately adopted by all who desired either to gain preferment or not to lose it. Thus the doctrine of witchcraft was very powerfully inculcated and as the greatest part of mankind have no other reason for their opinions than that they are in fashion, it cannot be doubted but this persuasion made a rapid progress, since vanity and credulity co-operated in its favour and it had a tendency to free cowardice from reproach. The infection soon reached the Parliament, who in the first year of King James made a law by which it was enacted Ch. XII that 'if any person shall use any invocation or conjuration of any evil or wicked spirit; 2. Or shall consult, covenant with, entertain, employ, feed or reward any evil or cursed spirit to or for any intent or purpose; 3. Or take up any dead man, woman or child out of the grave, or the skin, bone or any part of the dead person to be employed or used in any manner of witchcraft, sorcery, charm or enchantment; 4. Or shall use, practise or exercise any sort of witchcraft, sorcery, charm or enchantment; 5. Whereby any person shall be destroyed, killed, wasted, consumed, pined or lamed in any part of the body; 6. That every such person being convicted shall suffer death.'[5]

Thus in the time of Shakespeare was the doctrine of witchcraft at once established by law and by the fashion, and it became not only unpolite but criminal to doubt it; and as prodigies are always seen in proportion as they are expected, witches were every day discovered and multiplied so fast in some places that Bishop Hall mentions a village in Lancashire where their number was greater than that of the houses.[6] The Jesuits and sectaries took advantage of this universal error and endeavoured to promote the interest of their parties by pretended cures of persons afflicted by evil spirits, but they were detected and exposed by the clergy of the established Church.

Upon this general infatuation Shakespeare might be easily allowed to found a play, especially since he has followed with great exactness such histories as were then thought true; nor can it be doubted that the scenes of enchantment, however they may now be ridiculed, were both by himself and his audience thought awful and affecting.

NOTE II
SCENE II [1.2.9]

> The merciless Macdonwald . . .
> . . . from the Western Isles
> Of *kerns* and *galloglasses* is supplied,
> And fortune on his damnèd *quarry* smiling
> Showed like a rebel's whore.

'Kerns' are light-armed and 'galloglasses' heavy-armed soldiers. The word 'quarry' has no sense that is properly applicable in this place and therefore it is necessary to read:

> And fortune on his damnèd *quarrel* smiling.

Quarrel was formerly used for 'cause' or for 'the occasion of a quarrel' and is to be found in that sense in Holinshed's account of the story of Macbeth who upon the creation of the Prince of Cumberland thought, says the historian, that he had 'a just quarrel' to endeavour after the crown. The sense therefore is 'fortune smiling on his execrable cause' *etc*.[7]

NOTE III
[1.2.36]

> If I say sooth I must report they were
> As cannons overcharged with double cracks,
> So they redoubled strokes upon the foe.

Mr Theobald has endeavoured to improve the sense of this passage by altering the punctuation thus:

> . . . they were
> As cannons overcharged, with double cracks
> So they redoubled strokes . . .

He declares with some degree of exultation that he has no idea of a 'cannon charged with double cracks'; but surely the great author will not gain much by an alteration which makes him say of a hero that he 'redoubles strokes with double cracks', an expression not more loudly to be applauded or more easily pardoned than that which is rejected in its favour. That 'a cannon is charged with thunder' or 'with double thunders' may be written not only without nonsense but with elegance and nothing else is here meant by 'cracks', which in the time of this writer was a word of such emphasis and dignity that in this play he terms the general dissolution of nature the 'crack of doom' [IV.1.116].

There are among Mr Theobald's alterations others which I do not approve though I do not always censure them; for some of his amendments are so excellent that even when he has failed he ought to be treated with indulgence and respect.

48 SAMUEL JOHNSON ON SHAKESPEARE

NOTE IV
[1.2.46]

KING
  Who comes here?
MALCOLM   The worthy Thane of Ross.
LENNOX
  What a haste looks through his eyes!
  So should he look that *seems* to speak things strange.

The meaning of this passage as it now stands is, 'so should he look, that looks as if he told things strange'. But Ross neither yet told strange things, nor could look as if he told them; Lennox only conjectured from his air that he had strange things to tell and therefore undoubtedly said:

  What a haste looks through his eyes!
  So should he look that *teems* to speak things strange.

'He looks like one that is big with something of importance'; a metaphor so natural that it is every day used in common discourse.

NOTE V
SCENE III [1.3.4]

Thunder. Enter the three Witches.

FIRST WITCH
  A sailor's wife had chestnuts in her lap,
  And munched and munched and munched. 'Give me,'
    quoth I.
  (1) 'Aroint thee, witch!' the rump-fed ronyon cries . . .
            I myself have all the other.
            And the (2) very ports they blow
            All the quarters that they know
            I' the shipman's card.
            I'll drain him dry as hay;
            Sleep shall neither night nor day
            Hang upon his penthouse lid.
            He shall live a man (3) forbid.

Miscellaneous Observations on Macbeth

(1) *'Aroint thee, witch!'*

In one of the folio editions[8] the reading is 'Anoint thee', in a sense very consistent with the common accounts of witches, who are related to perform many supernatural acts by the means of unguents and particularly to fly through the air to the places where they meet at their hellish festivals. In this sense 'anoint thee, witch' will mean 'Away, witch, to your infernal assembly.' This reading I was inclined to favour because I had met with the word 'aroint' in no other place; till looking into Hearne's *Collections* I found it in a very old drawing that he has published, in which St Patrick is represented visiting Hell and putting the devils into great confusion by his presence, of whom one that is driving the damned before him with a prong has a label issuing out from his mouth with these words **'out out arongt'**, of which the last is evidently the same with 'aroint' and used in the same sense as in this passage.

(2) And the *very* ports they blow.

As the word 'very' is here of no other use than to fill up the verse it is likely that Shakespeare wrote 'various', which might be easily mistaken for 'very', being either negligently read, hastily pronounced or imperfectly heard.

(3) He shall live a man *forbid*.

Mr Theobald has very justly explained 'forbid' by 'accursed', but without giving any reason of his interpretation. To 'bid' is originally 'to pray', as in this Saxon fragment:

> He is wis þat bit and bote, *etc*.
> He is wise that *prays* & improves.

As to 'forbid' therefore implies to 'prohibit' in opposition to the word 'bid' in its present sense, it signifies by the same kind of opposition to 'curse', when it is derived from the same word in its primitive meaning.

NOTE VI
SCENE V [I.5]

The incongruity of all the passages in which the Thane of Cawdor is mentioned is very remarkable; in the second scene the Thanes of Ross and Angus bring the King an account of the battle and inform him that Norway:

> Assisted by that most disloyal traitor,
> The Thane of Cawdor, began a dismal conflict . . .
> [I.2.54]

It appears that Cawdor was taken prisoner, for the King says in the same scene:

> Go pronounce his present death
> And with his former title greet Macbeth.
> [I.2.67]

Yet though Cawdor was thus taken by Macbeth in arms against the King, when Macbeth is saluted in the fourth scene 'Thane of Cawdor' by the weird sisters, he asks:

> But how of Cawdor? The Thane of Cawdor lives
> A prosperous gentleman.
> [I.3.71]

And in the next line considers the promises that he should be Cawdor and King as equally unlikely to be accomplished. How can Macbeth be ignorant of the state of the Thane of Cawdor whom he has just defeated and taken prisoner, or call him 'a prosperous gentleman' who has forfeited his title and life by open rebellion? Or why should he wonder that the title of the rebel whom he has overthrown should be conferred upon him? He cannot be supposed to dissemble his knowledge of the condition of Cawdor because he inquires with all the ardour of curiosity and the vehemence of sudden astonishment, and because nobody is present but Banquo who had an equal part in the battle and was equally acquainted with Cawdor's treason. However, in the next scene his ignorance still continues and when Ross and Angus present him from the King with his new title, he cries out:

> The Thane of Cawdor lives. Why do you dress me
> In borrowed robes?
> [I.3.107]

Ross and Angus, who were the messengers that in the second scene informed the King of the assistance given by Cawdor to the invader, having lost as well as Macbeth all memory of what they had so lately seen and related, make this answer:

> Whether he was combined
> With those of Norway, or did line the rebel
> With hidden help and vantage, or that with both
> He laboured in his country's wrack, I know not . . .

Neither Ross knew what he had just reported, nor Macbeth what he had just done. This seems not to be one of the faults that are to be imputed to the transcribers since, though the inconsistency of Ross and Angus might be removed by supposing that their names are erroneously inserted and that only Ross brought the account of the battle and only Angus was sent to compliment Macbeth, yet the forgetfulness of Macbeth cannot be palliated, since what he says could not have been spoken by any other.[9]

NOTE VII
[1.3.138]

> My thought, whose murder yet is but fantastical,
> Shakes so my single state of man . . .

The 'single state of man' seems to be used by Shakespeare for an 'individual', in opposition to a 'commonwealth' or 'conjunct body' of men.

NOTE VIII
[1.3.146]

MACBETH   Come what come may,
   Time and the hour runs through the roughest day.

I suppose every reader is disgusted at the tautology in this passage, 'Time and the hour', and will therefore willingly believe that Shakespeare wrote it thus:

> Come what come may,
> *Time! on!* – the hour runs through the roughest day.

Macbeth is deliberating upon the events which are to befall him, but finding no satisfaction from his own thoughts he grows impatient of reflection and resolves to wait the close without harassing himself with conjectures:

> Come what come may.

But to shorten the pain of suspense he calls upon time in the usual style of ardent desire to quicken his motion:

Time! on!

He then comforts himself with the reflection that all his perplexity must have an end:

> The hour runs through the roughest day.

This conjecture is supported by the passage in the letter to his Lady in which he says, 'They referred me to the *coming on of time* with, "Hail, king that shalt be."'

NOTE IX
SCENE VI [1.4.9]

MALCOLM   He died
> As one that had been studied in his death
> To throw away the dearest thing he *owed*
> As 'twere a careless trifle.

As the word 'owed' affords here no sense but such as is forced and unnatural, it cannot be doubted that it was originally written 'The dearest thing he owned', a reading which needs neither defence nor explication.[10]

NOTE X
[1.4.12]

KING   There's no art
> To find the mind's construction in the face.

Miscellaneous Observations on Macbeth

The 'construction of the mind' is, I believe, a phrase peculiar to Shakespeare; it implies the 'frame' or 'disposition' of the mind by which it is determined to good or ill.

NOTE XI
[1.4.23]

MACBETH
  The service and the loyalty I owe,
  In doing it, pays itself. Your highness' part
  Is to receive our duties; and our duties
  Are to your throne and state, children and servants,
  Which do but what they should by doing *everything*
  Safe toward your love and honour.

Of the last line of this speech which is certainly as it is now read unintelligible, an emendation has been attempted which Mr Warburton and Mr Theobald have admitted as the true reading:

  Our duties
  Are to your throne and state, children and servants,
  Which do but what they should by doing everything
  Fiefs to your love and honour.

My esteem of these critics inclines me to believe that they cannot be much pleased with the expressions 'Fiefs to love', or 'Fiefs to honour', and that they have proposed this alteration rather because no other occurred to them than because they approved it. I shall therefore propose a bolder change, perhaps with no better success, but *sua cuique placent*.[11] I read thus:

  Our duties
  Are to your throne and state, children and servants,
  Which do but what they should by doing *nothing*
  Save toward your love and honour.

We do but perform our duty when we contract all our views to your service, when we act with 'no other' principle than regard to 'your love and honour'.

It is probable that this passage was first corrupted by writing 'safe' for 'save', and the lines then stood thus:

> Doing nothing
> Safe toward your love and honour.

Which the next transcriber observing to be wrong and yet not being able to discover the real fault altered to the present reading.

NOTE XII
SCENE VII [I.5.20]

> Thou'dst have, great Glamis,
> That which cries, 'Thus thou must do' if thou have *it*,
> And that *etc*.

As the object of Macbeth's desire is here introduced speaking of itself it is necessary to read:

> Thoud'st have, great Glamis,
> That which cries, 'Thus thou must do if thou have *me*.'

NOTE XIII
[I.5.23]

> Hie thee hither
> That I may pour my spirits in thine ear,
> And chastise with the valour of my tongue
> All that impedes thee from the golden round
> Which fate and metaphysical aid doth *seem*
> To have thee crowned withal.

For 'seem' the sense evidently directs us to read 'seek'. The crown to which fate destines thee and which preternatural agents 'endeavour' to bestow upon thee. The 'golden round' is the 'diadem'.

NOTE XIV
[1.5.38]

LADY   Come, you spirits
That tend on *mortal thoughts*, unsex me here
And fill me from the crown to the toe top-full
Of direst cruelty. Make thick my blood;
Stop up the access and passage to remorse,
That no compunctious visitings of nature
Shake my fell purpose, nor *keep peace* between
The effect and it.

Mortal thoughts

This expression signifies not 'the thoughts of mortals', but 'murderous, deadly or destructive designs'. So in Act 5th:

> Hold fast the *mortal* sword;
> [IV.3.3]

And in another place:

> With twenty *mortal* murders.
> [III.4.80]

Nor keep peace between
The effect and it.

The intent of Lady Macbeth evidently is to wish that no womanish tenderness or conscientious remorse may hinder her purpose from proceeding to effect, but neither this nor indeed any other sense is expressed by the present reading and therefore it cannot be doubted that Shakespeare wrote differently, perhaps thus:

> That no compunctious visitings of nature
> Shake my fell purpose, nor *keep pace* between
> The effect and it.

To 'keep pace between' may signify 'to pass between', to 'intervene'. 'Pace' is on many occasions a favourite of Shakespeare. This phrase is indeed not usual in this sense,

NOTE XV
SCENE VIII [I.6.I]

KING
  This castle hath a pleasant *seat*; the air
  Nimbly and sweetly recommends itself
  Unto our gentle senses.
BANQUO   This guest of summer,
  The temple-haunting martlet, does approve
  By his loved mansionry that the heaven's breath
  Smells wooingly here; no jutty, frieze,
  Buttress, nor coign of vantage, but this bird
  Hath made his pendent bed and procreant cradle;
  Where they most breed and haunt I have observed
  The air is delicate.

In this short scene, I propose a slight alteration to be made by substituting 'site' for 'seat', as the ancient word for 'situation'; and 'sense' for 'senses' as more agreeable to the measure;[12] for which reason likewise I have endeavoured to adjust this passage:

> Heaven's breath
> Smells wooingly here; no jutty frieze,

by changing the punctuation and adding a syllable thus:

> Heaven's breath
> Smells wooingly. Here is no jutty frieze.

Those who have perused books printed at the time of the first editions of Shakespeare know that greater alterations than these are necessary almost in every page even where it is not to be doubted that the copy was correct.[13]

NOTE XVI
SCENE X [1.7]

The arguments by which Lady Macbeth persuades her husband to commit the murder afford a proof of Shakespeare's knowledge of human nature. She urges the excellence and dignity of courage, a glittering idea which has dazzled mankind from age to age and animated sometimes the housebreaker and sometimes the conqueror; but this sophism Macbeth has for ever destroyed by distinguishing true from false fortitude in a line and a half; of which it may almost be said that they ought to bestow immortality on the author, though all his other productions had been lost:

> I dare do all that may become a man;
> Who dares do more is none.
> [I.7.46]

This topic, which has been always employed with too much success, is used in this scene with peculiar propriety to a soldier by a woman. Courage is the distinguishing virtue of a soldier and the reproach of cowardice cannot be borne by any man from a woman without great impatience.

She then urges the oaths by which he had bound himself to murder Duncan, another art of sophistry by which men have sometimes deluded their consciences and persuaded themselves that what would be criminal in others is virtuous in them; this argument Shakespeare, whose plan obliged him to make Macbeth yield, has not confuted though he might easily have shown that a former obligation could not be vacated by a latter.

NOTE XVII
[1.7.44]

> Letting 'I dare not' wait upon 'I would',
> Like the poor cat i'the adage?

The adage alluded to is, 'The cat loves fish, but dares not wet her foot':

> *Catus amat pisces, sed non vult tingere plantas.*[14]

NOTE XVIII
[1.7.64]

Will I with wine and wassail so convince.

To convince is in Shakespeare to 'overpower' or 'subdue', as in this play:

> Their malady *convinces*
> The great assay of art.
> [IV.3.142]

NOTE XIX
[1.7.71]

> ... who shall bear the guilt
> Of our great *quell*?

'Quell' is 'murder', 'manquellers' being in the old language the term for which 'murderers' is now used.

NOTE XX
ACT II SCENE II [II.1.49]

> Now o'er the one half-world
> (1) *Nature seems dead*, and wicked dreams abuse
> The curtained sleep. Witchcraft celebrates
> Pale Hecat's offerings; and withered Murder,
> Alarumed by his sentinel the wolf,
> Whose howl's his watch, thus with his stealthy pace,
> With (2) *Tarquin's ravishing sides*, towards his design
> Moves like a ghost. Thou sure and firm-set earth,
> Hear not my steps, which way they walk, for fear
> Thy very stones prate of my whereabout
> *And* (3) *take the present horror from the time*
> *That now suits with it.*

>> (1)   Now o'er the one half-world
> Nature seems dead.

That is, 'over our hemisphere all action and motion seem to have ceased'. This image which is perhaps the most striking that poetry can produce has been adopted by Dryden in his *Conquest of Mexico*:

> All things are hushed as Nature's self lay dead,
> The mountains seem to nod their drowsy head;
> The little birds in dreams their songs repeat,
> And sleeping flowers beneath the night-dew sweat;
> Even lust and envy sleep![15]

These lines, though so well known, I have transcribed that the contrast between them and this passage of Shakespeare may be more accurately observed.

Night is described by two great poets, but one describes a night of quiet, the other of perturbation. In the night of Dryden all the disturbers of the world are laid asleep; in that of Shakespeare nothing but sorcery, lust and murder is awake. He that reads Dryden finds himself lulled with serenity and disposed to solitude and contemplation. He that peruses Shakespeare looks round alarmed and starts to find himself alone. One is the night of a lover, the other that of a murderer.

> (2)   Withered Murder . . .
>   . . . thus with his stealthy pace,
> With Tarquin's ravishing sides, towards his design
> Moves like a ghost.

This was the reading of this passage in all the editions before that of Mr Pope, who for 'sides' inserted in the text 'strides', which Mr Theobald has tacitly copied from him, though a more proper alteration might perhaps have been made. A 'ravishing stride' is an action of violence, impetuosity and tumult, like that of a savage rushing on his prey; whereas the poet is here attempting to exhibit an image of secrecy and caution, of anxious circumspection and guilty timidity, the 'stealthy pace' of a 'ravisher' creeping into the chamber of a virgin and of an assassin approaching the bed of him whom he proposes to murder without awaking him; these he describes as 'moving like ghosts', whose progression is so different from 'strides' that it has been in all ages represented to be as Milton expresses it:

> Smooth sliding without step.[16]

This hemistich will afford the true reading of this place which is, I think, to be corrected thus:

> And withered Murder . . .
> . . . thus with his stealthy pace,
> With Tarquin ravishing, slides towards his design,
> Moves like a ghost.

Tarquin is in this place the general name of a ravisher and the sense is, now is the time in which everyone is asleep but those who are employed in wickedness, the witch who is sacrificing to Hecate and the ravisher and the murderer who, like me, are stealing upon their prey.

When the reading is thus adjusted he wishes with great propriety in the following lines that the 'earth' may not 'hear his steps'.

> (3) And take the present horror from the time
> That now suits with it.

I believe everyone that has attentively read this dreadful soliloquy is disappointed at the conclusion which, if not wholly unintelligible, is at least obscure, nor can be explained into any sense worthy of the author. I shall therefore propose a slight alteration:

> Thou sure and firm-set earth,
> Hear not my steps, which way they walk, for fear
> Thy very stones prate of my whereabout
> And *talk* – the present horror of the time!
> *That* now suits with it.

Macbeth has in the foregoing lines disturbed his imagination by enumerating all the terrors of the night, at length he is wrought up to a degree of frenzy that makes him afraid of some supernatural discovery of his design and calls out to the stones not to betray him, not to declare where he walks, nor 'to talk'.

Miscellaneous Observations on Macbeth 61

As he is going to say of what, he discovers the absurdity of his suspicion and pauses but is again overwhelmed by his guilt and concludes that such are the horrors of the present night that the stones may be expected to cry out against him:

That now suits with it.

He observes in a subsequent passage that on such occasions 'Stones have been known to move' [III.4.122]. It is now a very just and strong picture of a man about to commit a deliberate murder under the strongest convictions of the wickedness of his design.

NOTE XXI
SCENE IV [II.3.51]

LENNOX
The night has been unruly. Where we lay,
Our chimneys were blown down, and, as they say,
Lamentings heard i'the air, strange screams of death,
And prophesying, with accents terrible,
Of dire combustion and confused events
New-hatched to the woeful time. The obscure bird
Clamoured the live-long night. Some say the earth
Was feverous and did shake.

These lines I think should be rather regulated thus:

    . . . prophesying, with accents terrible,
Of dire combustion and confused events.
New-hatched to the woeful time, the obscure bird
Clamoured the live-long night. Some say the earth was
    feverous and did shake.

A 'prophecy' of an 'event new-hatched' seems to be 'a prophecy' of an 'event past'. The term 'new-hatched' is properly applicable to 'a bird' and that birds of ill omen should be 'new-hatched to the woeful time' is very consistent with the rest of the prodigies here mentioned and with the universal disorder into which nature is described as thrown by the perpetration of this horrid murder.

NOTE XXII
[II.3.74]

> Up, up, and see
> The Great Doom's image! Malcolm, Banquo,
> As from your graves rise up.

The second line might have been so easily completed that it cannot be supposed to have been left imperfect by the author, who probably wrote:

> Malcolm! Banquo! rise!
> As from your graves rise up.

Many other emendations of the same kind might be made without any greater deviation from the printed copies than is found in each of them from the rest.[17]

NOTE XXIII
[II.3.108]

> MACBETH   Here lay Duncan,
> His silver skin laced with his golden blood,
> And his gashed stabs looked like a breach in nature
> For ruin's wasteful entrance; there the murderers,
> Steeped in the colours of their trade, their daggers
> *Unmannerly breeched with gore*.

An 'unmannerly dagger' and a 'dagger breeched', or as in some editions 'breached with gore', are expressions not easily to be understood, nor can it be imagined that Shakespeare would reproach the murderer of his king only with 'want of manners'. There are undoubtedly two faults in this passage which I have endeavoured to take away by reading:

>   daggers
> Unmanly drenched with gore.

'I saw *drenched* with the King's blood the fatal daggers, not only instruments of murder but evidences of cowardice.'

Each of these words might easily be confounded with that

which I have substituted for it by a hand not exact, a casual blot or a negligent inspection.

Mr Pope has endeavoured to improve one of these lines by substituting 'gory blood' for 'golden blood', but it may easily be admitted that he who could on such an occasion talk of 'lacing the silver skin' would 'lace it' with 'golden blood'. No amendment can be made to this line of which every word is equally faulty but by a general blot.

It is not improbable that Shakespeare put these forced and unnatural metaphors into the mouth of Macbeth as a mark of artifice and dissimulation to show the difference between the studied language of hypocrisy and the natural outcries of sudden passion. This whole speech considered in this light is a remarkable instance of judgement as it consists entirely of antitheses and metaphors.

NOTE XXIV
ACT III SCENE II [III.1.48]

MACBETH   Our fears in Banquo
Stick deep . . .
              . . . and under him
My genius is rebuked (1) *as, it is said,*
Mark Antony's was by Caesar . . .
For Banquo's issue have I filed my mind,
For them the gracious Duncan have I murdered,
Put rancours in the vessel of my peace,
Only for them; and mine eternal jewel
Given to the (2) common enemy of man,
To make them kings, the seeds of Banquo kings!
Rather than so, come fate into the list
(3) And champion me to the utterance!

(1)   As, it is said,
Mark Antony's was by Caesar.

Though I would not often assume the critic's privilege of being confident where certainty cannot be obtained, nor indulge myself too far in departing from the established reading, yet I cannot but propose the rejection of this passage, which I believe was an insertion of some player, that having so much learning as to discover to what Shakespeare alluded was not willing that his audience should be less knowing than himself, and has therefore weakened the author's sense by the intrusion of a remote and useless image into a speech bursting from a man wholly possessed with his own present condition and therefore not at leisure to explain his own allusions to himself. If these words are taken away, by which not only the thought but the numbers[18] are injured, the lines of Shakespeare close together without any traces of a breach:

> My genius is rebuked. He chid the sisters.

(2)   . . . the common enemy of man.

It is always an entertainment to an inquisitive reader to trace a sentiment to its original source and therefore though the term 'enemy of man' applied to the Devil is in itself natural and obvious, yet some may be pleased with being informed that Shakespeare probably borrowed it from the first lines of the *Destruction of Troy*, a book which he is known to have read.[19]

That this remark may not appear too trivial I shall take occasion from it to point out a beautiful passage of Milton evidently copied from a book of no greater authority. In describing the gates of Hell (Book 2, 879) he says:

> On a sudden open fly
> With impetuous recoil and jarring sound
> Th'infernal doors, and on their hinges grate
> Harsh thunder.

In the *History of Don Bellianis*, when one of the knights approaches, as I remember, the castle of Brandezar the gates are said to open 'grating harsh thunder upon their brazen hinges'.[20]

(3)   . . . come fate into the list
And champion me to the utterance!

This passage will be best explained by translating it into the language from whence the only word of difficulty in it is borrowed. *Que la destinée se rende en lice, et qu' elle me donne un défi à l'outrance.* A challenge or a combat *à l'outrance*, 'to extremity', was a fixed term in the law of arms, used when the combatants engaged with an *odium internecinum*, 'an intention to destroy each other', in opposition to trials of skill at festivals or on other occasions where the contest was only for reputation or a prize. The sense therefore is, 'let fate, that has foredoomed the exaltation of the sons of Banquo, enter the lists against me with the utmost animosity in defence of its own decrees, which I will endeavour to invalidate whatever be the danger'.

NOTE XXV

[III. 1.91]

MACBETH

    Ay, in the catalogue ye go for men,
    As hounds and greyhounds, mongrels, spaniels, curs,
    Shoughs, water-rugs, and demi-wolves are clept
    All by the name of dogs.

Though this is not the most sparkling passage in the play and though the name of a dog is of no great importance, yet it may not be improper to remark that there is no such species of dogs as 'shoughs' mentioned by Caius *De Canibus Britannicis* or any other writer that has fallen into my hands, nor is the word to be found in any dictionary which I have examined. I therefore imagined that it is falsely printed for 'slouths', a kind of slow hound bred in the southern parts of England, but was informed by a lady that it is more probably used either by mistake or according to the orthography of that time for 'shocks'.[21]

NOTE XXVI

[III. 1.127]

MACBETH   . . . Within this hour, at most,
    I will advise you where to plant yourselves,
    Acquaint you with the perfect spy o' the time,
    The moment on't; for't must be done tonight;
    And something from the palace . . .

What is meant by 'the spy o' the time' it will be found difficult to explain; and therefore sense will be cheaply gained by a slight alteration. Macbeth is assuring the assassins that they shall not want directions to find Banquo and therefore says:

> I will . . .
> Acquaint you with a *perfect spy* o' the time.

Accordingly a third murderer joins them afterwards at the place of action.

'Perfect' is 'well-instructed', or 'well-informed' as in this play:

> Though in your state of honour I am *perfect*.
> [IV.2.66]

'Though I am *well-acquainted* with your quality and rank.'

NOTE XXVII
SCENE IV [III.3.2]

SECOND MURDERER
> He needs not our mistrust, since he delivers
> Our offices and what we have to do
> To the direction just.

Mr Theobald has endeavoured unsuccessfully to amend this passage in which nothing is faulty but the punctuation. The meaning of this abrupt dialogue is this. The 'perfect spy' mentioned by Macbeth in the foregoing scene has, before they enter upon the stage, given them the directions which were promised at the time of their agreement; and therefore one of the murderers observes that since 'he has given them such exact information he needs not doubt of their performance'. Then by way of exhortation to his associates he cries out:

> To the direction just.

'Now nothing remains but that we conform exactly to Macbeth's directions.'

NOTE XXVIII
SCENE V [III.4.1]

MACBETH
You know your own degrees, sit down:
At first and last, the hearty welcome.

As this passage stands, not only the numbers are very imperfect, but the sense if any can be found weak and contemptible. The numbers will be improved by reading:

> . . . sit down at first,
> And last a hearty welcome.

But for 'last' should then be written 'next'. I believe the true reading is:

> You know your own degrees, sit down. To first
> And last, the hearty welcome.

'All of whatever degree from the highest to the lowest may be assured that their visit is well received.'

NOTE XXIX
[III.4.13]

MACBETH
There's blood upon thy face!
FIRST MURDERER
             'Tis Banquo's then.
MACBETH
'Tis better *thee without than he within*.

The sense apparently requires that this passage should be read thus:

> 'Tis better *thee* without than *him* within.

That is, 'I am more pleased that the blood of Banquo should be on thy face than in his body.'

NOTE XXX
[III.4.62]

LADY   O, these flaws and starts,
Impostures to true fear, would well become
A woman's story at a winter's fire,
Authorized by her grandam.

As 'starts' can neither with propriety nor sense be called 'impostures to true fear', something else was undoubtedly intended by the author, who perhaps wrote:

> Those flaws and starts,
> *Impostures true to fear* would well become,
> A woman's story.

These symptoms of terror and amazement might better become 'impostures true *only* to fear, might become a coward at the recital of such falsehoods as no man could credit whose understanding was not weakened by his terrors; tales told by a woman over a fire on the authority of her grandam'.

NOTE XXXI
[III.4.88]

MACBETH
I drink to the general joy o' the whole table,
And to our dear friend Banquo, whom we miss.
Would he were here! To all – and him – we thirst,
And all to all.

Though this passage is, as it now stands, capable of more meanings than one, none of them are very satisfactory; and therefore I am inclined to read it thus:

> To all and him we thirst,
> And hail to all.

Macbeth, being about to salute his company with a bumper, declares that he includes Banquo, though absent, in this act of kindness and wishes 'health' to all. 'Hail' or 'heil' for 'health' was in such continual use among the good-fellows of ancient times that a drinker was called a *was-heiler* or a 'wisher of health', and the liquor was termed *was-heil* because 'health' was so often 'wished' over it. Thus in the lines of Hanvil the monk:

> *Jamque vagante scypho, discincto gutture* Was-heil
> *Ingeminant* Was-heil: *labor est plus perdere vini*
> *Quam sitis.*[22]

These words were afterwards corrupted into 'wassail' and 'wassailer'.

NOTE XXXII
[III.4.111]

MACBETH   You make me strange
Even to the disposition that *I owe*
When now I think you can behold such sights
And keep the natural ruby of your cheeks . . .

This passage as it now stands is unintelligible, but may be restored to sense by a very slight alteration:

> You make me strange
> Even to the disposition that I *know*.

'Though I had before seen many instances of your courage yet it now appears in a degree altogether *new*. So that my *long acquaintance* with your *disposition* does not hinder me from that astonishment which *novelty* produces.'[23]

NOTE XXXIII
[III.4.121]

It will have blood, they say blood will have blood,
Stones have been known to move and trees to speak;
Augurs, that understood relations have
By maggot-pies, and choughs, and rooks brought forth
The secret'st man of blood.

In this passage the first line loses much of its force by the present punctuation. Macbeth, having considered the prodigy which has just appeared, infers justly from it that the death of Duncan cannot pass unpunished:

> It will have blood.

Then after a short pause declares it as the general observation of mankind that murderers cannot escape:

> . . . they say, blood will have blood.

Murderers, when they have practised all human means of security, are detected by supernatural directions:

> Augurs, that understand relations, *etc*.

By the word 'relation' is understood the 'connection' of effects with causes; to 'understand relations' as 'an augur' is to know how those things 'relate to' each other which have no visible combination or dependence.

NOTE XXXIV
SCENE VII [III.6]

Enter Lennox and another Lord.
As this tragedy like the rest of Shakespeare's is perhaps overstocked with personages it is not easy to assign a reason why a nameless character should be introduced here, since nothing is said that might not with equal propriety have been put into the mouth of any other disaffected man. I believe therefore that in the original copy it was written with a very common form of contraction 'Lennox and An.' for which the transcriber instead of 'Lennox and Angus' set down 'Lennox and another Lord'. The author had indeed been more indebted to the transcriber's fidelity and diligence had he committed no errors of greater importance.

NOTE XXXV
ACT IV SCENE I [IV.1]

As this is the chief scene of enchantment in the play it is proper in this place to observe with how much judgement

Shakespeare has selected all the circumstances of his infernal ceremonies and how exactly he has conformed to common opinions and traditions.

> Thrice the brinded cat hath mewed.

The usual form in which familiar spirits are reported to converse with witches is that of a cat. A witch,[24] who was tried about half a century before the time of Shakespeare, had a cat named Rutterkin, as the spirit of one of those witches was Grimalkin; and when any mischief was to be done she used to bid Rutterkin 'go and fly', but once when she would have sent Rutterkin to torment a daughter of the Countess of Rutland, instead of 'going' or 'flying' he only cried 'Mew', from which she discovered that the lady was out of his power, the power of witches being not universal but limited as Shakespeare has taken care to inculcate:

> Though his bark cannot be lost,
> Yet it shall be tempest-tossed.
> [I.3.24]

The common afflictions which the malice of witches produced were melancholy, fits and loss of flesh, which are threatened by one of Shakespeare's witches:

> Weary sev'n-nights nine times nine
> Shall he dwindle, peak, and pine.
> [I.3.22]

It was likewise their practice to destroy the cattle of their neighbours and the farmers have to this day many ceremonies to secure their cows and other cattle from witchcraft; but they seem to have been most suspected of malice against swine. Shakespeare has accordingly made one of his witches declare that she has been 'Killing swine' [I.3.2] and Dr Harsnett observes[25] that about that time, 'a sow could not be ill of the measles, nor a girl of the sullens, but some old woman was charged with witchcraft'.

> Toad that under cold stone
> Days and nights has thirty-one.
> Sweltered venom, sleeping got,
> Boil thou first i'the charmèd pot.
> [IV.1.6]

Toads have likewise long lain under the reproach of being by some means accessary to witchcraft, for which reason Shakespeare in the first scene of this play calls one of the spirits 'Padock' or 'Toad' [I.1.8], and now takes care to put a toad first into the pot. When Vaninus[26] was seized at Tolouse, there was found at his lodgings *ingens bufo vitro inclusus*, 'a great toad shut in a vial', upon which those that prosecuted him *veneficium exprobrabant*, charged him, I suppose, with witchcraft.

> Fillet of a fenny snake
> In the cauldron boil and bake;
> Eye of newt, and toe of frog . . .
> For a charm, *etc.*
> [IV.1.12]

The propriety of these ingredients may be known by consulting the books *De Viribus Animalium* and *De Mirabilibus Mundi* ascribed to Albertus Magnus,[27] in which the reader who has time and credulity may discover very wonderful secrets.

> Finger of birth-strangled babe,
> Ditch-delivered by a drab . . .
> [IV.1.30]

It has been already mentioned in the law against witches that they are supposed to take up dead bodies to use in enchantments, which was confessed by the woman whom King James examined and who had of a dead body, that was divided in one of their assemblies, two fingers for her share. It is observable that Shakespeare, on this great occasion which involves the fate of a king, multiplies all the circumstances of horror. The babe whose finger is used must be strangled in its birth, the grease must not only be human but must have dropped from a gibbet, the gibbet of a murderer, and even the sow whose blood is used must have offended nature by devouring her own farrow. These are touches of judgement and genius.

> And now about the cauldron sing . . .
> Black spirits, and white,
> Red spirits, and grey,
> Mingle, mingle, mingle,
> You that mingle may.[28]
>
> [IV.1.41]

And in a former part:

> The Weird Sisters, hand in hand . . .
> Thus do go, about, about;
> Thrice to thine, and thrice to mine,
> And thrice again, to make up nine.
>
> [I.3.31]

These two passages I have brought together because they both seem subject to the objection of too much levity for the solemnity of enchantment and may both be shown, by one quotation from Camden's *Account of Ireland*[29] to be founded upon a practice really observed by the uncivilized natives of that country. 'When any one gets a fall,' says the informer of Camden, 'he starts up, and *turning three times to the right* digs a hole in the earth; for they imagine that there is a spirit in the ground, and if he falls sick in two or three days they send one of their women that is skilled in that way to the place, where she says, I call thee from the East, West, North and South, from the groves, the woods, the rivers and the fens, from the *Fairies red, black, white.*' There was likewise a book written before the time of Shakespeare describing, amongst other properties, the 'colours' of spirits.[30]

Many other circumstances might be particularized in which Shakespeare has shown his judgement and his knowledge.

NOTE XXXVI
SCENE II [IV.I.III]

MACBETH
Thou art too like the spirit of Banquo. Down!
Thy crown does (1) sear mine eye-balls. And thy (2) *hair*,
Thou other gold-bound brow, is like the first.
A third is like the former.

(1) The expression of Macbeth that the 'crown sears his eye-balls' is taken from the method formerly practised of destroying the sight of captives or competitors by holding a burning basin before the eye, which dried up its humidity.

(2) As Macbeth expected to see a train of kings and was only enquiring from what race they would proceed, he could not be surprised that the 'hair' of the second was 'bound with gold' like that of the first; he was offended only that the second resembled the first, as the first resembled Banquo and therefore said:

And thy *air*,
Thou other gold-bound brow, is like the first.

NOTE XXXVII
[IV.I.149]

I will . . . give to the edge o'the sword
His wife, his babes, and all unfortunate souls
That *trace him in his line* – no boasting, like a fool;
This deed I'll do before this purpose cool.

Both the sense and measure of the third line which, as it rhymes, ought according to the practice of this author to be regular, are at present injured by two superfluous syllables which may easily be removed by reading:

. . . souls,
That trace his line – no boasting like a fool.[31]

Miscellaneous Observations on Macbeth

NOTE XXXVIII
SCENE III [IV.2.19]

ROSS   . . . when we (1) *hold rumour*
From what we fear, yet know not what we fear,
But float upon a wild and violent sea,
Each way, and (2) *move.* I'll take my leave of you;
Shall not be long but I'll be here again.

(1) . . . when we hold rumour
From what we fear, yet know not what we fear.

The present reading seems to afford no sense; and therefore some critical experiments may be properly tried upon it, though the verses being without any connection there is room for suspicion that some intermediate lines are lost and that the passage is therefore irretrievable. If it be supposed that the fault arises only from the corruption of some words and that the traces of the true reading are still to be found, the passage may be changed thus:

. . . when we *bode ruin*
From what we fear, yet know not what we fear.

Or in a sense very applicable to the occasion of the conference:

. . . when the *bold running*
From what they fear, yet know not what they fear.

(2) But float upon a wild and violent sea,
Each way, and move.

That he who 'floats' upon a 'rough sea' must 'move' is evident, too evident for Shakespeare so emphatically to assert. The line therefore is to be written thus:

Each way, and move – I'll take my leave of you.

Ross is about to proceed, but finding himself overpowered by his tenderness breaks off abruptly, for which he makes a short apology, and retires.[32]

NOTE XXXIX
SCENE IV [IV.3.1]

MALCOLM
  Let us seek out some desolate shade, and there
  Weep our sad bosoms empty.
MACDUFF   Let us rather
  Hold fast the mortal sword; and like good men
  Bestride our *downfal birth-doom*.

He who can discover what is meant by him that earnestly exhorts him to 'bestride' his 'downfal birth-doom' is at liberty to adhere to the present text; but those who are willing to confess that such counsel would to them be unintelligible must endeavour to discover some reading less obscure. It is probable that Shakespeare wrote:

. . . like good men
Bestride our *downfaln birthdom*.

The allusion is to a man from whom something valuable is about to be taken by violence and who, that he may defend it without encumbrance, lays it on the ground and stands over it with his weapon in his hand. Our birthdom, or birthright, says he, lies on the ground, let us like men who are to fight for what is dearest to them not abandon it but stand over it and defend it. This is a strong picture of obstinate resolution.

'Birthdom' for 'birthright' is formed by the same analogy with 'masterdom' in this play, signifying the 'privileges' or 'rights' of a 'master' [I.5.68].

Perhaps it might be 'birth-dame' for 'mother'; let us stand over our mother that lies bleeding on the ground.

NOTE XL
[IV.3.136]

MALCOLM
  Now we'll together; and the *chance of goodness*
  Be like our warranted quarrel!

The 'chance of goodness', as it is commonly read, conveys no sense. If there be not some more important error in the passage it should at least be pointed thus:

> . . . and the chance, of goodness,
> Be like our warranted quarrel.

That is, may the event be of the goodness of Heaven (*pro justitia divina*), answerable to the cause.

But I am inclined to believe that Shakespeare wrote:

> . . . and the chance, O Goodness,
> Be like our warranted quarrel.

This some of his transcribers wrote with a small 'o', which another imagined to mean 'of'. If we adopt this reading the sense will be 'and O thou sovereign goodness, to whom we now appeal, may our fortune answer to our cause.'

NOTE XLI
ACT V SCENE III [V.3.1]

MACBETH
  Bring me no more reports; let them fly all,
  Till Birnan Wood remove to Dunsinane
  I cannot taint with fear. What's the boy Malcolm?
  Was he not born of woman? . . .
          . . . fly, false thanes,
  And mingle with the English epicures.

In the first line of this speech the proper pauses are not observed in the present editions:

> Bring me no more reports – let them fly all –

'Tell me not any more of desertions – Let all my subjects leave me – I am safe till', *etc*.

The reproach of epicurism on which Mr Theobald has bestowed a note is nothing more than a natural invective uttered by an inhabitant of a barren country against those who have more opportunities of luxury.

NOTE XLII
[v.3.22]

MACBETH
I have lived long enough: my *Way* of life
Is fallen into the sere, the yellow leaf . . .

As there is no relation between the 'Way of life' and 'fallen into the sere', I am inclined to think that the 'W' is only an 'M' inverted, and that it was originally written: '. . . my *May* of life'.

'I am now passed from the spring to the autumn of my days, but I am without those comforts that should succeed the sprightliness of bloom and support me in this melancholy season.'

NOTE XLIII
SCENE IV [v.4.10]

MALCOLM   'Tis his main hope.
For where there is *advantage to be given*,
Both more and less have given him the revolt . . .

The impropriety of the expression 'advantage to be given', instead of 'advantage given', and the disagreeable repetition of the word 'given' in the next line, incline me to read:

. . . where there is *a vantage* to be *gone*
Both more and less have given him the revolt.

'Advantage' or 'vantage' in the time of Shakespeare signified 'opportunity'.

'More and less' is the same with 'greater and less'. So in the interpolated Mandeville, a book of that age, there is a chapter of 'India the more and the less'.[33]

NOTE XLIV
SCENE V [v.5.15]

MACBETH   Wherefore was that cry?

Miscellaneous Observations on Macbeth 79

SEYTON
  The queen, my lord, is dead.
MACBETH
  She should (1) have died hereafter.
  There would have been a time for such a *word* –
  Tomorrow, and tomorrow, and tomorrow,
  Creeps in this petty pace from day to day
  To the last syllable of (2) recorded time . . .

> She should have died hereafter.
> There would have been a time for such a *word*.

This passage has very justly been suspected of being corrupt. It is not apparent for what 'word' there would have been a 'time' and that there would or would not be a 'time' for any 'word' seems not a consideration of importance sufficient to transport Macbeth into the following exclamation. I read therefore:

(1) She should have died hereafter.
There would have been a time for – such a *world*! –
Tomorrow, *etc.*

It is a broken speech in which only part of the thought is expressed and may be paraphrased thus: 'The queen is dead.' Macbeth: 'Her death should have been deferred to some more peaceful hour; had she lived longer *there would at length have been a time for* the honours due to her as a queen and that respect which I owe her for her fidelity and love. Such is the *world* – such is the condition of human life, that we always think *tomorrow* will be happier than today, but tomorrow and tomorrow steals over us unenjoyed and unregarded and we still linger in the same expectation to the moment appointed for our end. All these days which have thus passed away have sent multitudes of fools to the grave, who were engrossed by the same dream of future felicity and, when life was departing from them, were like me reckoning on tomorrow.'

(2) To the last syllable of recorded time;

'Recorded time' seems to signify the time fixed in the decrees of Heaven for the period of life. The 'record' of 'futurity' is indeed no accurate expression, but as we only know transactions past or present the language of men affords no term for the volumes of prescience in which future events may be supposed to be written.

NOTE XLV
[v.5.40]

MACBETH If thy speech be sooth,
I care not if thou dost for me as much.
I pull in resolution, and begin
To doubt the equivocation of the fiend . . .

I *pull* in resolution . . .

Though this is the reading of all the editions, yet as it is a phrase without either example, elegance or propriety it is surely better to read:

I *pall* in resolution . . .

'I languish in my constancy, my confidence begins to forsake me.' It is scarcely necessary to observe how easily 'pall' might be changed into 'pull' by a negligent writer or mistaken for it by an unskilful printer.

NOTE XLVI
SCENE VIII [v.6.87]

SEYWARD
Had I as many sons as I have hairs
I would not wish them to a fairer death.
And so his knell is knolled.

This incident is thus related from Henry of Huntingdon by Camden in his *Remains*, from which our author probably copied it:

When Seyward, the martial Earl of Northumberland, understood that his son, whom he had sent in service against the Scotchmen was slain, he demanded whether his wound were in the fore part or hinder part of his body. When it was answered in the fore part, he replied, 'I am right glad; neither wish I any other death to me or mine.'[34]

After the foregoing pages were printed the late edition of Shakespeare ascribed to Sir Thomas Hanmer fell into my hands and it was therefore convenient for me to delay the publication of my remarks till I had examined whether they were not anticipated by similar observations or precluded by better. I therefore read over this tragedy but found that the editor's apprehension is of a cast so different from mine that he appears to find no difficulty in most of those passages which I have represented as unintelligible and has therefore passed smoothly over them without any attempt to alter or explain them.

Some of the lines with which I had been perplexed have been indeed so fortunate as to attract his regard and it is not without all the satisfaction which it is usual to express on such occasions that I find an entire agreement between us in substituting (see Note II) 'quarrel' for 'quarry' and in explaining the adage of the cat (Note XVII). But this pleasure is like most others, known only to be regretted; for I have the unhappiness to find no such conformity with regard to any other passage.

The line which I have endeavoured to amend (Note XI) is likewise attempted by the new editor and is perhaps the only passage in the play in which he has not submissively admitted the emendations of foregoing critics. Instead of the common reading:

> . . . doing everything
> *Safe* toward your love and honour.

he has published:

> . . . doing everything
> *Shaped* towards your love and honour.

This alteration which, like all the rest attempted by him, the reader is expected to admit without any reason alleged in its defence is in my opinion more plausible than that of Mr Theobald; whether it is right I am not to determine.

In the passage which I have altered in Note XL an emendation is likewise attempted in the late edition where for:

> . . . and the chance *of* goodness
> Be like our warranted quarrel!

is substituted '. . . and the chance *in* goodness . . .' whether with more or less elegance, dignity and propriety than the reading which I have offered I must again decline the province of deciding.

Most of the other emendations which he has endeavoured whether with good or bad fortune are too trivial to deserve mention. For surely the weapons of criticism ought not to be blunted against an editor who can imagine that he is restoring poetry while he is amusing himself with alterations like these;

For
> This is the sergeant
> Who like a good and hardy soldier fought
> [I.2.3]

> This is the sergeant, who
> Like a *right* good and hardy soldier fought.

For
> Dismayed not this
> Our captains, Macbeth and Banquo?
> [I.2.33]

> Dismayed not this
> Our captains, *brave* Macbeth and Banquo?

Such harmless industry may surely be forgiven if it cannot be praised: may he therefore never want a monosyllable who can use it with such wonderful dexterity.

Rumpatur quisquis rumpitur invidia![35]

The rest of this edition I have not read but from the little that I have seen think it not dangerous to declare that, in my opinion, its pomp recommends it more than its accuracy. There is no distinction made between the ancient reading and the innovations of the editor; there is no reason given for any of the alterations which are made; the emendations of former

Miscellaneous Observations on Macbeth

critics are adopted without any acknowledgement and few of the difficulties are removed which have hitherto embarrassed the readers of Shakespeare.

I would not, however, be thought to insult the editor nor to censure him with too much petulance for having failed in little things, of whom I have been told, that he excels in greater. But I may without indecency observe that no man should attempt to teach others what he has never learned himself; and that those who, like Themistocles, have studied the arts of policy and 'can teach a small state how to grow great'[36] should like him disdain to labour in trifles and consider petty accomplishments as below their ambition.

PROPOSALS FOR PRINTING SHAKESPEARE'S PLAYS
(1745)

Proposals for printing a new edition of the plays of William Shakespeare, with notes critical and explanatory, in which the text will be corrected, the various readings remarked, the conjectures of former editors examined, and their omissions supplied. By the author of the *Miscellaneous Observations on the Tragedy of Macbeth*.

I. This work will be printed in ten small volumes of the same paper and print with the following specimen.

II. The price to subscribers will be one pound, five shillings in sheets, of which half a guinea is to be paid at the time of subscribing.

Note. It is hoped the undertakers of this edition will be thought entitled to some regard when it is considered that the price of Mr Pope's was six guineas, Mr Theobald's two and Sir T.H.'s three guineas.[1]

Subscriptions are taken in and receipts signed by E. Cave at St John's Gate and by the editor.

DRURY LANE PROLOGUE
(1747)

*Prologue Spoken by Mr Garrick at the Opening of the
Theatre in Drury Lane, 1747*

When learning's triumph o'er her barbarous foes
First reared the stage, immortal Shakespeare rose;
Each change of many-coloured life he drew,
Exhausted worlds and then imagined new;
Existence saw him spurn her bounded reign, 5
And panting time toiled after him in vain;
His powerful strokes presiding truth impressed,
And unresisted passion stormed the breast.
   Then Jonson came, instructed from the school
To please in method and invent by rule; 10
His studious patience and laborious art,
By regular approach essayed the heart;
Cold approbation gave the lingering bays,
For those who durst not censure, scarce could praise.
A mortal born he met the general doom, 15
But left, like Egypt's kings, a lasting tomb.
   The wits of Charles found easier ways to fame,
Nor wished for Jonson's art or Shakespeare's flame;
Themselves they studied; as they felt, they writ;
Intrigue was plot, obscenity was wit. 20
Vice always found a sympathetic friend;
They pleased their age and did not aim to mend.
Yet bards like these aspired to lasting praise,
And proudly hoped to pimp in future days.

Their cause was general, their supports were strong, 25
Their slaves were willing and their reign was long;
Till shame regained the post that sense betrayed,
And virtue called oblivion to her aid.

    Then crushed by rules and weakened as refined,
For years the power of tragedy declined; 30
From bard to bard the frigid caution crept,
Till declamation roared, while passion slept.
Yet still did virtue deign the stage to tread,
Philosophy remained, though nature fled.
But forced at length her ancient reign to quit, 35
She saw great Faustus[1] lay the ghost of wit;
Exulting folly hailed the joyful day,
And pantomime and song confirmed her sway.

    But who the coming changes can presage,
And mark the future periods of the stage? 40
Perhaps, if skill could distant times explore,
New Behns, new Durfeys[2] yet remain in store.
Perhaps, where Lear has raved and Hamlet died,
On flying cars new sorcerers may ride.
Perhaps, (for who can guess the effects of chance?), 45
Here Hunt may box, or Mahomet[3] may dance.

    Hard is his lot, that here by fortune placed,
Must watch the wild vicissitudes of taste,
With every meteor of caprice must play,
And chase the new-blown bubbles of the day. 50
Ah! Let not censure term our fate our choice:
The stage but echoes back the public voice.
The drama's laws the drama's patrons give,
For we that live to please must please to live.

    Then prompt no more the follies you decry, 55
As tyrants doom their tools of guilt to die;
'Tis yours this night to bid the reign commence
Of rescued nature and reviving sense;
To chase the charms of sound, the pomp of show,
For useful mirth and salutary woe; 60
Bid scenic virtue form the rising age
And truth diffuse her radiance from the stage.

TWO ESSAYS FROM *THE RAMBLER*
(1751)

No. 156. Saturday, 14 September 1751.

Nunquam aliud natura, aliud sapientia dicit.
                    Juvenal, XIV. 321

For wisdom ever echoes nature's voice.

Every government, say the politicians, is perpetually degenerating towards corruption, from which it must be rescued at certain periods by the resuscitation of its first principles and the re-establishment of its original constitution. Every animal body, according to the methodic[1] physicians is, by the predominance of some exuberant[2] quality, continually declining towards disease and death, which must be obviated by a seasonable reduction of the peccant[3] humour to the just equipoise which health requires.

In the same manner the studies of mankind, all at least which not being subject to rigorous demonstration admit the influence of fancy and caprice, are perpetually tending to error and confusion. Of the great principles of truth which the first speculatists[4] discovered, the simplicity is embarrassed by ambitious additions, or the evidence obscured by inaccurate argumentation;[5] and as they descend from one succession of writers to another, like light transmitted from room to room, they lose their strength and splendour and fade at last in total evanescence.

The systems of learning therefore must be sometimes reviewed, complications analysed into principles and knowledge disentangled from opinion. It is not always possible without a close inspection to separate the genuine shoots of consequential reasoning, which grow out of some radical postulate, from the branches which art has engrafted on it. The accidental prescriptions of authority when time has procured them veneration are often confounded with the laws of nature, and those rules are supposed coeval with reason, of which the first rise cannot be discovered.

Criticism has sometimes permitted fancy to dictate the laws by which fancy ought to be restrained, and fallacy to perplex the principles by which fallacy is to be detected; her superintendance of others has betrayed her to negligence of herself; and, like the ancient Scythians, by extending her conquests over distant regions she has left her throne vacant to her slaves.[6]

Among the laws of which the desire of extending authority or ardour of promoting knowledge has prompted the prescription, all which writers have received, had not the same original right to our regard. Some are to be considered as fundamental and indispensable, others only as useful and convenient; some as dictated by reason and necessity, others as enacted by despotic antiquity; some as invincibly supported by their conformity to the order of nature and operations of the intellect; others as formed by accident, or instituted by example and therefore always liable to dispute and alteration.

That many rules have been advanced without consulting nature or reason we cannot but suspect, when we find it peremptorily decreed by the ancient masters that 'only three speaking personages should appear at once upon the stage';[7] a law which, as the variety and intricacy of modern plays has made it impossible to be observed, we now violate without scruple and as experience proves without inconvenience.

The original of this precept was merely accidental. Tragedy was a monody or solitary song in honour of Bacchus, improved afterwards into a dialogue by the addition of another speaker; but the ancients, remembering that the tragedy was at first pronounced only by one, durst not for some time venture beyond two; at last when custom and impunity had made them daring they extended their liberty to the admission of three, but restrained themselves by a critical edict from further exorbitance.

By what accident the number of acts was limited to five, I know not that any author has informed us; but certainly it is not determined by any necessity arising either from the nature of action or propriety of exhibition. An act is only the representation of such a part of the business of the play as proceeds in an unbroken tenor, or without any intermediate pause. Nothing is more evident than that of every real and by consequence of every dramatic action, the intervals may be more or fewer than five; and indeed the rule is upon the English stage every day broken in effect, without any other mischief than that which arises from an absurd endeavour to observe it in appearance. Whenever the scene is shifted the act ceases, since some time is necessarily supposed to elapse while the personages of the drama change their place.

With no greater right to our obedience have the critics confined the dramatic action to a certain number of hours. Probability requires that the time of action should approach somewhat nearly to that of exhibition and those plays will always be thought most happily conducted which crowd the greatest variety into the least space. But since it will frequently happen that some delusion must be admitted, I know not where the limits of imagination can be fixed. It is rarely observed that minds not prepossessed by mechanical criticism feel any offence from the extension of the intervals between the acts; nor can I conceive it absurd or impossible that he who can multiply three hours into twelve or twenty-four might image with equal ease a greater number.

I know not whether he that professes to regard no other laws than those of nature will not be inclined to receive tragi-comedy to his protection whom, however generally condemned, her own laurels have hitherto shaded from the fulminations of criticism. For what is there in the mingled drama which impartial reason can condemn? The connection of important with trivial incidents, since it is not only common but perpetual in the world, may surely be allowed upon the stage, which pretends only to be the mirror of life. The impropriety of suppressing passions before we have raised them to the intended agitation and of diverting the expectation from an event which we keep suspended only to raise it, may be speciously urged. But will not experience show this objection to be rather subtle than just? Is it not certain that the tragic and comic affections have been moved alternately with equal force and that no plays have oftener filled the eye with tears and the breast with palpitation than those which are variegated with interludes of mirth?

I do not however think it safe to judge of works of genius merely by the event. These resistless vicissitudes of the heart, this alternate prevalence of merriment and solemnity, may sometimes be more properly ascribed to the vigour of the writer than the justness of the design: and instead of vindicating tragi-comedy by the success of Shakespeare, we ought perhaps to pay new honours to that transcendent and unbounded genius that could preside over the passions in sport; who, to actuate the affections, needed not the slow gradation of common means, but could fill the heart with instantaneous jollity or sorrow and vary our disposition as he changed his scenes. Perhaps the effects even of Shakespeare's poetry might have been yet greater had he not counteracted himself; and we might have been more interested in the distresses of his heroes had we not been so frequently diverted by the jokes of his buffoons.

There are other rules more fixed and obligatory. It is necessary that of every play the chief action should be single; for since a play represents some transaction, through its regular maturation to its final event, two actions equally important must evidently constitute two plays.

As the design of tragedy is to instruct by moving the passions it must always have a hero, a personage apparently and incontestably superior to the rest, upon whom the attention may be fixed and the anxiety suspended. For though of two persons opposing each other with equal abilities and equal virtue, the auditor will inevitably in time choose his favourite, yet as that choice must be without any cogency of conviction, the hopes or fears which it raises will be faint and languid. Of two heroes acting in confederacy against a common enemy, the virtues or dangers will give little emotion, because each claims our concern with the same right, and the heart lies at rest between equal motives.

It ought to be the first endeavour of a writer to distinguish nature from custom, or that which is established because it is right, from that which is right only because it is established; that he may neither violate essential principles by a desire of novelty, nor debar himself from the attainment of beauties within his view by a needless fear of breaking rules which no literary dictator had authority to enact.

No. 168. Saturday, 26 October 1751.

Decipit
Frons prima multos, rara mens intelligit
Quod interiore condidit cura angulo.
Phaedrus, *Fabulae Aesopiae*,
IV.2.5–7

The tinsel glitter, and the specious mien,
Delude the most; few pry behind the scene.

It has been observed by Boileau that 'a mean or common thought expressed in pompous diction, generally pleases more than a new or noble sentiment delivered in low and vulgar language; because the number is greater of those whom custom has enabled to judge of words, than whom study has qualified to examine things'.[8]

This solution might satisfy, if such only were offended with meanness of expression as are unable to distinguish propriety of thought, and to separate propositions or images from the vehicles by which they are conveyed to the understanding. But this kind of disgust is by no means confined to the ignorant or superficial; it operates uniformly and universally upon readers of all classes; every man, however profound or abstracted, perceives himself irresistibly alienated by low terms; they who profess the most zealous adherence to truth are forced to admit that she owes part of her charms to her ornaments, and loses much of her power over the soul when she appears disgraced by a dress uncouth[9] or ill-adjusted.

We are all offended by low terms, but are not disgusted alike by the same compositions because we do not all agree to censure the same terms as low. No word is naturally or intrinsically meaner than another; our opinion therefore of words, as of other things arbitrarily and capriciously established, depends wholly upon accident and custom. The cottager thinks those apartments splendid and spacious which an inhabitant of palaces will despise for their inelegance; and to him who has passed most of his hours with the delicate and polite, many expressions will seem sordid which another, equally acute, may hear without offence; but a mean term never fails to displease him to whom it appears mean, as poverty is certainly and invariably despised, though he who is poor in the eyes of some may by others be envied for his wealth.

Words become low by the occasions to which they are applied, or the general character of them who use them; and the disgust which they produce arises from the revival of those images with which they are commonly united. Thus if, in the most solemn discourse, a phrase happens to occur which has been successfully employed in some ludicrous narrative, the gravest auditor finds it difficult to refrain from laughter, when they who are not prepossessed by the same accidental association are utterly unable to guess the reason of his merriment. Words which convey ideas of dignity in one age are banished from elegant writing or conversation in another because they are in time debased by vulgar mouths and can be no longer heard without the involuntary recollection of unpleasing images.

When Macbeth is confirming himself in the horrid purpose of stabbing his king, he breaks out amidst his emotions into a wish natural to a murderer:

> Come, thick night,
> And pall thee in the dunnest smoke of hell,
> That my keen knife see not the wound it makes,
> Nor heaven peep through the blanket of the dark
> To cry, 'Hold, hold!'[10]

[I.5.48]

In this passage is exerted all the force of poetry, that force which calls new powers into being, which embodies sentiment and animates matter; yet perhaps scarce any man now peruses it without some disturbance of his attention from the counteraction of the words to the ideas. What can be more dreadful than to implore the presence of night, invested not in common obscurity, but in the smoke of hell? Yet the efficacy of this invocation is destroyed by the insertion of an epithet now seldom heard but in the stable and *dun* night may come or go without any other notice than contempt.

If we start into raptures when some hero of the *Iliad* tells us that δόρυ μάινεται, his lance rages with eagerness to destroy;[11] if we are alarmed at the terror of the soldiers commanded by Caesar to hew down the sacred grove, who dreaded, says Lucan, lest the axe aimed at the oak should fly back upon the striker:

> *Si robora sacra ferirent,*
> *In sua credebant redituras membra secures,*
> Pharsalia, III.430–31

> None dares with impious steel the grove to rend,
> Lest on himself the destined stroke descend.[12]

we cannot surely but sympathize with the horrors of a wretch about to murder his master, his friend, his benefactor, who suspects that the weapon will refuse its office and start back from the breast which he is preparing to violate. Yet this sentiment is weakened by the name of an instrument used by butchers and cooks in the meanest employments; we do not immediately conceive that any crime of importance is to be committed with a *knife*; or who does not, at last, from the long habit of connecting a knife with sordid offices feel aversion rather than terror?

Macbeth proceeds to wish in the madness of guilt that the inspection of heaven may be intercepted and that he may in the involutions of infernal darkness escape the eye of providence. This is the utmost extravagance of determined wickedness; yet this is so debased by two unfortunate words that while I endeavour to impress on my reader the energy of the sentiment

I can scarce check my risibility when the expression forces itself upon my mind; for who without some relaxation of his gravity can hear of the avengers of guilt 'peeping through a blanket'?

These imperfections of diction are less obvious to the reader as he is less acquainted with common usages; they are therefore wholly imperceptible to a foreigner, who learns our language from books and will strike a solitary academic[13] less forcibly than a modish lady.

Among the numerous requisites that must concur to complete an author, few are of more importance than an early entrance into the living world. The seeds of knowledge may be planted in solitude, but must be cultivated in public. Argumentation may be taught in colleges and theories formed in retirement, but the artifice of embellishment and the powers of attraction can be gained only by general converse.

An acquaintance with prevailing customs and fashionable elegance is necessary likewise for other purposes. The injury that grand imagery suffers from unsuitable language, personal merit may fear from rudeness and indelicacy. When the success of Aeneas depended on the favour of the queen upon whose coasts he was driven, his celestial protectress thought him not sufficiently secured against rejection by his piety or bravery, but decorated him for the interview with preternatural beauty.[14] Whoever desires for his writings or himself what none can reasonably contemn, the favour of mankind, must add grace to strength and make his thoughts agreeable as well as useful. Many complain of neglect who never tried to attract regard. It cannot be expected that the patrons of science or virtue should be solicitous to discover excellencies which they who possess them shade and disguise. Few have abilities so much needed by the rest of the world as to be caressed on their own terms; and he that will not condescend to recommend himself by external embellishments must submit to the fate of just sentiments meanly expressed and be ridiculed and forgotten before he is understood.

DEDICATION TO MRS CHARLOTTE LENNOX'S
SHAKESPEARE ILLUSTRATED
(1753)

TO THE RIGHT HONOURABLE JOHN,
EARL OF ORRERY[1]

My Lord,

I have no other pretence to the honour of a patronage so illustrious as that of your Lordship than the merit of attempting what has by some unaccountable neglect been hitherto omitted, though absolutely necessary to a perfect knowledge of the abilities of Shakespeare.

Among the powers that must conduce to constitute a poet, the first and most valuable is invention; and of all the degrees of invention[2] the highest seems to be that which is able to produce a series of events. It is easy when the thread of a story is once drawn to diversify it with variety of colours; and when a train of action is presented to the mind, a little acquaintance with life will supply circumstances and reflections, and a little knowledge of books, furnish parallels and illustrations. To tell over again a story that has been told already, and to tell it better than the first author, is no rare qualification; but to strike out the first hints of a new fable, hence to introduce a set of characters so diversified in their several passions and interests that from the clashing of this variety may result many necessary incidents; to make these incidents surprising, and yet natural, so as to delight the imagination without shocking the judgement of a reader; and finally, to wind up the whole in a pleasing catastrophe[3] produced by those very means which seem most likely to oppose and prevent it, is the utmost effort of the human mind.

To discover how few of those writers who profess to

recount imaginary adventures have been able to produce anything by their own imagination would require too much of that time which your Lordship employs in nobler studies. Of all the novels and romances that wit or idleness, vanity or indigence, have pushed into the world, there are very few of which the end cannot be conjectured from the beginning; or where the authors have done more than to transpose the incidents of other tales, or strip the circumstances from one event for the decoration of another.

In the examination of a poet's character it is therefore first to be inquired what degree of invention has been exerted by him. With this view I have very diligently read the works of Shakespeare and now presume to lay the result of my searches before your Lordship, before that judge whom Pliny himself would have wished for his assessor to hear a literary cause.[4]

How much the translation of the following novels will add to the reputation of Shakespeare or take away from it, you, my Lord, and men learned and candid like you, if any such can be found, must now determine. Some danger, as I am informed, there is lest his admirers should think him injured by this attempt and clamour as at the diminution of the honour of that nation, which boasts herself the parent of so great a poet.

That no such enemies may arise against me (though I am unwilling to believe it) I am far from being too confident, for who can fix bounds to bigotry and folly? My sex, my age, have not given me many opportunities of mingling in the world; there may be in it many a species of absurdity which I have never seen, and among them such vanity as pleases itself with false praise bestowed on another, and such superstition as worships idols, without supposing them to be gods.

But the truth is that a very small part of the reputation of this mighty genius depends upon the naked plot or story of his plays. He lived in an age when the books of chivalry were yet popular, and when therefore the minds of his auditors were not accustomed to balance probabilities, or to examine nicely the proportion between causes and effects. It was sufficient to recommend a story that it was far removed from common life, that its changes were frequent, and its close pathetic.[5]

This disposition of the age concurred so happily with the imagination of Shakespeare that he had no desire to reform it, and indeed to this he was indebted for the licentious variety by which he has made his plays more entertaining than those of any other author.

He had looked with great attention on the scenes of nature, but his chief skill was in human actions, passions, and habits; he was therefore delighted with such tales as afforded numerous incidents and exhibited many characters in many changes of situation. These characters are so copiously diversified, and some of them so justly pursued, that his works may be considered as a map of life, a faithful miniature of human transactions, and he that has read Shakespeare with attention will perhaps find little new in the crowded world.

Among his other excellencies it ought to be remarked, because it has hitherto been unnoticed, that his heroes are men, that the love and hatred, the hopes and fears of his chief personages are such as are common to other human beings and not like those which later times have exhibited, peculiar to phantoms that strut upon the stage.

It is not perhaps very necessary to inquire whether the vehicle of so much delight and instruction be a story probable or unlikely, native or foreign. Shakespeare's excellence is not the fiction of a tale but the representation of life, and his reputation is therefore safe, till human nature shall be changed. Nor can he who has so many just claims to praise suffer by losing that which ignorant admiration has unreasonably given him. To calumniate the dead is baseness and to flatter them is surely folly.

From flattery, my Lord, either of the dead or the living, I wish to be clear and have therefore solicited the countenance of a patron whom, if I knew how to praise him, I could praise with truth and have the world on my side; whose candour and humanity are universally acknowledged, and whose judgement perhaps was then first to be doubted when he condescended to admit this address from,

My Lord, your Lordship's most obliged and most obedient, humble servant,

THE AUTHOR

SELECTIONS FROM THE *DICTIONARY*
(1755)

ABOMINABLE (adj.) 3 In low and ludicrous language it is a word of loose and indeterminate censure. [Quotes *As You Like It*, IV.1.3]

To ACHE (v.n.) 2 It is frequently applied, in an improper sense, to the heart; as, 'the heart aches' to imply grief or fear. Shakespeare has used it still more licentiously of the soul. [Quotes *Coriolanus*, III.1.108]

ANCHOR (n.) Shakespeare seems to have used this word for 'anchoret', or an abstemious recluse person. [Quotes *Hamlet*, III.2.228]

To ANIMADVERT (v.n.) 1 To pass censures upon.

I should not *animadvert on* him [Jonson] who was otherwise a painful observer of the decorum of the stage, if he had not used extreme severity in his judgement of the incomparable Shakespeare for that fault. Dryden, *Essay of Dramatic Poesy*

To ANSWER (v.n.) 15 To appear to any call, or authoritative summons; in which sense, though figuratively, the following passage may be perhaps taken. [Quotes *King Lear*, III.4.98]

ANTHROPOPHAGINIAN (n.) A ludicrous word, formed by Shakespeare from 'anthropophagi' for the sake of a formidable sound. [Quotes *The Merry Wives of Windsor*, IV.5.7]

To BALK (v.a.) 4 To heap, as on a ridge. This or something like this seems to be intended here. [Quotes *1 Henry IV*, I.1.68]

To BODGE (v.n.) (A word in Shakespeare which is perhaps corrupted from 'boggle'.) To boggle; to stop; to fail. [Quotes *3 Henry VI*, I.4.18]

Selections from the Dictionary

To BUDGE (v.n.) To stir; to move off the place; a low word. [Quotes *The Tempest*, V.1.9; *Coriolanus*, I.6.44]

To CANARY (v.a.) A cant word which seems to signify to dance; to frolic. [Quotes *Love's Labour's Lost*, III.1.7][1]

CARCASS (n.) 2 Body; in a ludicrous sense. [Quotes *Cymbeline*, V.3.66]

CASE (n.) 6 In ludicrous language, condition with regard to leanness or fat. 'In case' is 'lusty' or 'fat'. [Quotes *The Tempest*, III.2.24][2]

CATLING (n.) 2 It seems to be used by Shakespeare for catgut; the materials of fiddle strings. [Quotes *Troilus and Cressida*, III.3.301]

CESS (n.) 3 It seems to have been used by Shakespeare for bounds, or limits, though it stands for 'rate', 'reckoning'. [Quotes *1 Henry IV*, II.1.5][3]

CHIMNEYSWEEPER (n.) 2 It is used proverbially for one of a mean and vile occupation. [Quotes *Cymbeline*, IV.2.263]

CICATRICE/CICATRIX (n.) 2 A mark; an impressure; so used by Shakespeare less properly. [Quotes *As You Like It*, III.5.22]

To CLOY (v.a.) 2 It seems to have in the following passage another sense: perhaps to strike the beak together. [Quotes *Cymbeline*, V.4.117]

COMPANY (n.) 5 A number of persons united for the execution or performance of anything; a band.

Shakespeare was an actor when there were seven *companies* of players in the town together. Dennis, *An Essay on the Genius and Writings of Shakespeare* (1712), Letter III

CONCLUSION (n.) 6 In Shakespeare it seems to signify silence; confinement of the thoughts. [Quotes *Antony and Cleopatra*, IV.15.27]

CONSCIENCE (n.) 6 In ludicrous language, reason; reasonableness. [Quotes *Timon of Athens*, II.2.180]

CONSPECTUITY (n.) Sight; view; sense of seeing. The word is, I believe, peculiar to Shakespeare and perhaps corrupt. [Quotes *Coriolanus*, II.1.60]

CONTEMPTIBLE (adj.) 3 Scornful; apt to despise; contemptuous. This is no proper use. [Quotes *Much Ado About Nothing*, II.3.178][4]

CONTINENT (n.) 2 That which contains anything. This sense is perhaps only in Shakespeare. [Quotes *Hamlet*, V.2.110; *Antony and Cleopatra*, IV.14.39; *King Lear*, III.2.57]

To CONVIVE (v.a.) To entertain; to feast. A word I believe not elsewhere used. [Quotes *Troilus and Cressida*, IV.5.271]

COZ (n.) A cant or familiar word contracted from 'cousin'. [Quotes *2 Henry IV*, IV.2.83]

To CRASH (v.a.) To break or bruise. [Quotes *Romeo and Juliet*, I.2.77] Mr Warburton has it, 'crush a cup of wine'. 'To crash,' says Hanmer 'is to be merry'; a 'crash' being a word still used in some counties for a merry bout. It is surely better to read 'crack'.

CROWKEEPER (n.) A scarecrow. The following passage is controverted. [Quotes *King Lear*, IV.6.87][5]

CROWNET (n.) 2 In the following passage it seems to signify chief end; last purpose; probably from *finis coronat opus*. [Quotes *Antony and Cleopatra*, IV.12.25]

DARKLING (A participle as it seems from 'darkle' which yet I have never found; or perhaps a kind of diminutive from 'dark', as 'young', 'youngling'.) Being in the dark; being without light; a word merely poetical. [Quotes *A Midsummer Night's Dream*, II.2.92; *Antony and Cleopatra*, IV.15.10][6]

DEAR (adj.) 4 It seems to be sometimes used in Shakespeare for 'dire'; sad; hateful; grievous. [Quotes *Twelfth Night*, V.1.67; *Timon of Athens*, V.1.224; *King Lear*, IV.3.51; *Hamlet*, I.2.182; *Titus Andronicus*, III.1.257]

To DESPISE (v.a.) 2 In Shakespeare it seems once to signify 'abhor', as from the Italian *despettare*. [Quotes *Macbeth*, IV.3.201]

DEWLAP (n.) 2 It is used in Shakespeare for a lip flaccid with age, in contempt. [Quotes *A Midsummer Night's Dream*, II.1.47]

DIFFUSED (participial adj.) This word seems to have signified in Shakespeare's time the same as wild, uncouth, irregular. [Quotes *The Merry Wives of Windsor*, IV.4.52; *Henry V*, V.2.59]

Selections from the Dictionary

To DISHABIT (v.a.) (This word I have found only in Shakespeare.) To throw out of place; to drive from their habitation. [Quotes *King John*, II.1.216]

To DISPURSE (v.a.) To pay; to disburse. It is not certain that the following passage should not be written 'disburse'. [Quotes *2 Henry VI*, III.1.115]

To DIVERT (v.a.) 5 To subvert; to destroy; in Shakespeare, unless it belong to the first sense. [Quotes *Troilus and Cressida*, I.3.98]⁷

[EDITOR See under NONSENSE]

To EFFACE (v.a.) 2 To make no more legible or visible; to blot out; to strike out.

> Otway failed to polish or refine,
> And fluent Shakespeare scarce *effaced* a line.
> Pope, *Epistles of Horace*, II.i.278

To ENWHEEL (v.a.) To encompass; to encircle. A word probably peculiar to Shakespeare. [Quotes *Othello*, II.1.85]

EPITHET (n.) 3 It is used improperly for 'phrase', 'expression'. [Quotes *Much Ado About Nothing*, V.2.59]

ESSENCE (n.) 7 The cause of existence. This sense is not proper. [Quotes *The Two Gentlemen of Verona*, III.1.182]

EXORCIST (n.) 2 An enchanter; a conjurer. Improperly. [Quotes *Julius Caesar*, II.1.321; *All's Well That Ends Well*, V.3.302]

EXPEDIENCE/EXPEDIENCY (n.) 2 It is used in Shakespeare for expedition; adventure; or attempt. [Quotes *1 Henry IV*, I.1.30]

3 It is also used by Shakespeare for expedition; haste; dispatch. [Quotes *Antony and Cleopatra*, I.2.178; *Richard II*, II.1.286]

EXPEDIENT (adj.) 2 In Shakespeare, quick; expeditious. [Quotes *King John*, II.1.57]

FACINERIOUS (adj.) (Corrupted by Shakespeare from 'facinorous'; 'facinus', 'facinoris', Latin.) Wicked; facinorous. [Quotes *All's Well That Ends Well*, II.3.27]

FAP (adj.) Fuddled; drunk. It seems to have been a cant word in the time of Shakespeare. [Quotes *The Merry Wives of Windsor*, I.1.161]

FAR (adv.) 8 To a great height; magnificently. This is perhaps only in Shakespeare. [Quotes *Cymbeline*, I.1.22]

FASHION (n.) 10 The farcy; a distemper in horses; the horses' leprosy. A barbarous word. [Quotes *The Taming of the Shrew*, III.2.48]

FEDARY (n.) This word, peculiar to Shakespeare, may signify either a confederate; a partner; or a dependant. [Quotes *Cymbeline*, III.2.19]

FEELING (participial adj.) 2 Sensibly felt. This sense is not sufficiently analogical. [Quotes *King Lear*, IV.6.221]

To FLINCH (v.n.) 2 In Shakespeare it signifies to fail. [Quotes *All's Well That Ends Well*, II.1.187]

FUSTILARIAN (n.) A low fellow; a stinkard; a scoundrel. A word used by Shakespeare only. [Quotes *2 Henry IV*, II.1.57]

GAD (n.) 2 It seems to be used by Shakespeare for a style or graver. [Quotes *Titus Andronicus*, IV.1.103]

GALLIMAUFRY (n.) 3 It is used by Shakespeare ludicrously of a woman. [Quotes *The Merry Wives of Windsor*, II.1.104]

GASKINS (n.) Wide hose; wide breeches. An old ludicrous word. [Quotes *Twelfth Night*, I.5.22]

To GOSPEL (v.n.) To fill with sentiments of religion. This word in Shakespeare, in whom alone I have found it, is used, though so venerable in itself, with some degree of irony: I suppose from the gospellers who had long been held in contempt. [Quotes *Macbeth*, III.1.87]

GRIEVOUS (adj.) 5 Sometimes used adverbially in low language. [Quotes *1 Henry IV*, IV.1.16]

To GROWL (v.n.) 2 To murmur; to grumble.

Othello, neighbours – how he would roar about a foolish handkerchief! And then he would *growl* so manfully. John Gay, *The What D'Ye Call It*, preliminary scene

HAVING (n.) 3 Behaviour; regularity. This is still retained in the Scottish dialect. It may possibly be the meaning here. [Quotes *The Merry Wives of Windsor*, III.2.65][8]

Selections from the Dictionary

To HEND (v.a.) 2 To crowd; to surround. Perhaps the following passage is corrupt and should be read 'hemmed'; or it may mean 'to take possession'. [Quotes *Measure for Measure*, IV.6.13]⁹

HERE (adv.) 6 'Here' seems in the following passage to mean this place. [Quotes *King Lear*, I.1.260]

HOMESPUN (adj.) 3 Plain; coarse; rude; homely; inelegant.

> Our *homespun* authors must forsake the field,
> And Shakespeare to the soft Scarlatti yield.
>
> Addison, Prologue to
> Edmund Smith's *Phaedra and Hippolitus*

HYPERBOLE (n.) A figure in rhetoric by which anything is increased or diminished beyond the exact truth: as, 'he runs faster than lightning'. 'His possessions are fallen to dust.' 'He was so gaunt, the case of a flageolet was a mansion for him.' [cf. *2 Henry IV*, III.2.315]

I (persnl. pron.) 3 'I' is more than once in Shakespeare written for 'ay' or 'yes'. [Quotes *Romeo and Juliet*, III.2.45; *King Lear*, IV.3.9]

IMMEDIACY (n.) Personal greatness; power of acting without dependence. This is a harsh word and sense peculiar, I believe, to Shakespeare. [Quotes *King Lear*, V.3.64]

IMMOMENT (adj.) Trifling; of no importance or value. A barbarous word. [Quotes *Antony and Cleopatra*, V.2.165]

IMPORTANCE (n.) 4 Importunity. An improper use peculiar to Shakespeare. [Quotes *Twelfth Night*, V.1.360]

IMPORTANT (adj.) 3 Importunate. A corrupt use of the word. [Quotes *King Lear*, IV.4.25]

To INCARNADINE (v.a.) To dye red. This word I find only once. [Quotes *Macbeth*, II.2.60]

INCONY (adj.) 2 In Scotland it denotes mischievously unlucky: as 'he's an incony fellow'. This seems to be the meaning in Shakespeare. [Quotes *Love's Labour's Lost*, IV.1.143]

To INHERIT (v.a.) 2 To possess; to obtain possession of: in Shakespeare. Not used. [Quotes *Titus Andronicus*, II.3.1]¹⁰

INHERITANCE (n.) 2 In Shakespeare, possession. [Quotes *Coriolanus*, III.2.66]

To INJOIN (v.a.) 2 In Shakespeare, to join. Not used. [Quotes *Othello*, I.3.33][11]

INSISTURE (n.) This word seems in Shakespeare to signify constancy or regularity. [Quotes *Troilus and Cressida*, I.3.85]

To INSTANCE (v.n.) To give or offer an example.

In tragedy and satire this age and the last have excelled the ancients; and I would *instance* in Shakespeare of the former, in Dorset of the latter sort. Dryden, *Discourse of Satire*[12]

INTESTINE (adj.) 3 Domestic, not foreign. I know not whether the word be properly used in the following example of Shakespeare: perhaps for 'mortal' and 'intestine' should be read 'mortal internecine'. [Quotes *The Comedy of Errors*, I.1.11]

INTRENCHANT (adj.) (This word, which is I believe found only in Shakespeare, is thus explained by one of his editors: 'the "intrenchant" air means the air which suddenly encroaches and closes upon the space left by any body which had passed through it' (*Hanmer*). I believe Shakespeare intended rather to express the idea of indivisibility or invulnerableness, and derived 'intrenchant' from 'in', privative, and 'trencher', to cut; 'intrenchant' is indeed properly 'not cutting', rather than 'not to be cut'; but this is not the only instance in which Shakespeare confounds words of active and passive signification.) Not to be divided; not to be wounded; indivisible. [Quotes *Macbeth*, V.6.48]

KIDNEY (n.) 2 Sort; kind; in ludicrous language. [Quotes *The Merry Wives of Windsor*, III.5.104][13]

KNAVERY (n.) 2 Mischievous tricks or practices. In the following passage it seems a general term for anything put to an ill use, or perhaps for trifling things of more cost than use. [Quotes *The Taming of the Shrew*, IV.3.54]

To KNOW (v.n.) 5 To KNOW of. In Shakespeare is to take cognizance of; to examine. [Quotes *A Midsummer Night's Dream*, I.1.67]

LATINITY (n.) Purity of Latin style; the Latin tongue.

If Shakespeare was able to read Plautus with ease, nothing in *Latinity* could be hard to him. Dennis, *An Essay on the Genius and Writings of Shakespeare* (1712), Letter III

LINK (n.) 7 Perhaps in the following passage it may mean lamp-black. [Quotes *The Taming of the Shrew*, IV.1.120]

LOT (n.) 3 It seems in Shakespeare to signify a lucky or wished chance. [Quotes *Coriolanus*, V.2.9]

To LOUT (v.a.) This word seems in Shakespeare to signify to overpower. [Quotes *1 Henry VI*, IV.3.13]

MARCANTANT (n.) This word in Shakespeare seems to signify a foreigner, or foreign trader. [Quotes *The Taming of the Shrew*, IV.2.62]

METAPHYSICAL (adj.) 2 In Shakespeare it means supernatural or preternatural. [Quotes *Macbeth*, I.5.23]

MIGHTILY (adv.) 3 In a great degree; very much. This is a sense scarcely to be admitted but in low language. [Quotes *3 Henry VI*, III.2.74; *Timon of Athens*, V.1.91]

MINNOCK (n.) Of this word I know not the precise meaning. It is not unlikely that 'minnock' and 'minx' are originally the same word. [Quotes *A Midsummer Night's Dream*, III.2.17][14]

MINUTELY (adv.) 2 (In the following passage it seems rather to be an adjective, as 'hourly' is both the adverb and adjective.) Happening every minute. [Quotes *Macbeth*, V.2.18][15]

MODEL (n.) 5 In Shakespeare it seems to have two unexampled senses. Something representative. [Quotes *Henry VIII*, IV.2.131][16]

6 Something small and diminutive; for 'module' a small measure; which perhaps is likewise the meaning of the example affixed to the third sense. [Quotes *Henry V*, II. Chorus 16][17]

MODERN (n.) 2 In Shakespeare, vulgar; mean; common. [Quotes *Antony and Cleopatra*, V.2.165; *As You Like It*, II.7.154; *All's Well That Ends Well*, II.3.1]

MOONSHINE (n.) 2 (In burlesque.) A month. [Quotes *King Lear*, I.2.5]

NONSENSE (n.) 1 Unmeaning or ungrammatical language.

This *nonsense* got into all the following editions by a mistake of the stage editors. Pope, *Notes to Shakespeare*[18]

NOWADAYS (adv.) (This word, though common and used by the best writers, is perhaps barbarous.) In the present age. [Quotes *A Midsummer Night's Dream*, III.1.136]

O 2 'O' is used with no great elegance by Shakespeare for a circle or oval. [Quotes *Henry V*, I. Chorus 11]

OBSEQUIOUS (adj.) 2 In Shakespeare it seems to signify funereal; such as the rites of funerals require. [Quotes *Hamlet*, I.2.89]

OBSEQUIOUSLY (adv.) 2 In Shakespeare it signifies with funeral rites; with reverence for the dead. [Quotes *Richard III*, I.2.3]

OLD (adj.) 9 A word to signify in burlesque language more than enough. [Quotes *2 Henry IV*, II.4.19; *Macbeth*, II.3.1]

OSTENT (n.) 2 Show; token. These senses are peculiar to Shakespeare. [Quotes *The Merchant of Venice*, II.8.43]

To OUTSHINE (v.a.) 2 To excel in lustre.

> By Shakespeare's, Jonson's, Fletcher's lines,
> Our stage's lustre Rome's *outshines*.
> Sir John Denham, 'On Mr Abraham Cowley His Death and Burial Amongst the Ancient Poets'

OVERWROUGHT (p.pl.) 3 It has in Shakespeare a sense which I know not well how to reconcile to the original meaning of the word, and therefore conclude it misprinted for 'over-raught'; that is, 'over-reached' or cheated. [Quotes *The Comedy of Errors*, I.2.95]

To PEAK (v.n.) ('Pequeno', Spanish, 'little', perhaps 'lean': but I believe this word has some other derivation: we say a withered man has a sharp face; Falstaff dying is said to have 'a nose as sharp as a pen' [*Henry V*, II.3.16]: from this observation a sickly man is said to 'peak' or grow acuminated from 'pique'.)[19]

PEAL (n.) 2 It is once used by Shakespeare for a low dull noise, but improperly. [Quotes *Macbeth*, III.2.41]

PELTING (adj.) This word in Shakespeare signifies, I know not why, mean; paltry; pitiful. [Quotes *Measure for Measure*, II.2.110; *A Midsummer Night's Dream*, II.1.90; *King Lear*, II.3.17; *Richard II*, II.1.60]

Selections from the Dictionary

PERILOUS (adj.) 3 Smart; witty. In this sense it is, I think, only applied to children and probably obtained its signification from the notion that children eminent for wit do not live; a witty boy was therefore a 'perilous' boy or a boy in danger. It is vulgarly 'parlous'. [Quotes *Richard III*, III.1.154]

PILGRIMAGE (n.) 2 Shakespeare uses it for time irksomely spent. [Quotes *1 Henry VI*, II.5.116][20]

PLAYHOUSE (n.) House where dramatic performances are represented.

> Shakespeare, whom you and every *playhouse* bill
> Style the divine the matchless what you will,
> For gain not glory winged his roving flight
> And grew immortal in his own despite.
>   Pope, *Epistles of Horace*, II.i.69[21]

To PLUCK (v.a.) 1 To pull with nimbleness or force; to snatch; to pull; to draw; to force on or off; to force up or down; to act upon with violence. It is very generally and licentiously used, particularly by Shakespeare. It has often some particle after it as 'down', 'off', 'on', 'away', 'up', 'into'. [Quotes *King John*, IV.2.4; *2 Henry IV*, IV.5.118; *Macbeth*, V.3.40; *Coriolanus*, I.3.5; *The Merchant of Venice*, V.1.170; *Richard II*, II.1.201; *1 Henry IV*, I.3.201][22]

PRETENCE (n.) 5 Shakespeare uses this word with more affinity to the original Latin for something threatened, or held out to terrify. [Quotes *King Lear*, I.4.67; *Macbeth*, II.3.127]

PROPER (adj.) 8 It seems in Shakespeare to signify mere; pure. [Quotes *King Lear*, IV.2.59]

PROPERTY (n.) 6 Nearness or right. I know not which is the sense in the following lines. [Quotes *King Lear*, I.1.113]

QUARREL (n.) 7 In Shakespeare it seems to signify anyone peevish or malicious. [Quotes *Henry VIII*, II.3.12]

QUIDDITY (n.) A subtlety; an equivocation. A low word. [Quotes *Hamlet*, V.1.97]

QUILLET (n.) Subtlety; nicety; fraudulent distinction; petty cant. [Quotes *Hamlet*, V.1.97][23]

RAWNESS (n.) 3 Hasty manner. This seems to be the meaning in this obscure passage. [Quotes *Macbeth*, IV.3.26]

REGARD (n.) 7 Prospect; object of sight. Not proper, nor in use. [Quotes *Othello*, II.1.38]

RIGOL (n.) A circle. Used in Shakespeare for a diadem. [Quotes *2 Henry IV*, IV.5.36]

RUDESBY (n.) An uncivil, turbulent fellow. A low word, now little used. [Quotes *The Taming of the Shrew*, III.2.8; *Twelfth Night*, IV.1.48]

SALLY (n.) 4 Escape; levity; extravagant flight; frolic; wild gaiety; exorbitance.

The episodical part, made up of the extravagant *sallies* of the Prince of Wales and Falstaff's humour, is of his own invention. Mrs Lennox, *Shakespeare Illustrated*, 'Plan' of *1 Henry IV*

SCROYLE (n.) (This word I remember only in Shakespeare; it seems derived from 'escrouelle', French, a scrofulous swelling; as he calls a mean fellow a 'scab' from his itch, or a 'patch' from his raggedness.) A mean fellow; a rascal; a wretch. [Quotes *King John*, II.1.373]

To SEEM (v.n.) 3 In Shakespeare to 'seem' perhaps signifies to be beautiful. [Quotes *King Lear*, I.1.197]

SELF (pron.) 8 It is much used in composition, which it is proper to explain by a train of examples. It is to be observed that its composition in Shakespeare is often harsh. [Quotes *Macbeth*, III.4.141; *A Midsummer Night's Dream*, I.1.111; *Othello*, II.3.194; *The Comedy of Errors*, V.1.9; *The Winter's Tale*, IV.1.7; *Richard II*, III.2.51; *King Lear*, IV.3.33, I.1.69; *The Merchant of Venice*, I.1.140; *Romeo and Juliet*, IV.2.13; *The Comedy of Errors*, III.2.171; *King Lear*, II.2.116; *Hamlet*, I.2.131; *King Lear*, V.1.1; *Measure for Measure*, III.2.253; *Macbeth*, I.2.56; *Henry V*, II.4.74; *Henry VIII*, I.1.132; *Henry V*, V. Chorus 17; *Richard II*, II.2.2]

SET (v.n.) 10 It is commonly used in conversation for 'sit', which though undoubtedly barbarous, is sometimes found in authors. [Quotes *Coriolanus*, I.2.28]

SHARDBORN (adj.) Born or produced among broken stones or pots. Perhaps 'shard' in Shakespeare may signify the sheaths of the wings of insects. [Quotes *Macbeth*, III.2.41]

SIZE (n.) 2 A settled quantity. In the following passage it seems to signify the allowance of the table; whence they say a 'sizar' at Cambridge. [Quotes *King Lear*, II.4.168]

SLEEVE (n.) 2 'Sleeve' in some provinces signifies a knot or skein of silk, which is by some very probably supposed to be its meaning in the following passage. [Quotes *Macbeth*, II.2.35]

SOOTH (n.) Sweetness; kindness. This seems to be the meaning here. [Quotes *Richard II*, III.3.133][24]

SPECTACLE (n.) 3 (In the plural.) Glasses to assist the sight.

Shakespeare was naturally learned: he needed not the *spectacles* of books to read nature; he looked inwards and found her there. Dryden, *Essay of Dramatic Poesy*

SQUARE (n.) 8 Quaternion; number four. Though perhaps in the following lines 'square' may mean only 'capacity'. [Quotes *King Lear*, I.1.72][25]

STALE (n.) 2 In Shakespeare it seems to signify a prostitute. [Quotes *Much Ado About Nothing*, IV.1.62]

STARRY (adj.) 3 Resembling stars.

Tears had dimmed the lustre of her *starry* eyes. Mrs Lennox, *Shakespeare Illustrated*, 'Story' of *Troilus and Cressida*

STATE (n.) 7 Hence 'single state' in Shakespeare for individuality. [Quotes *Macbeth*, I.3.138]

STIFF (adj.) 8 In Shakespeare it seems to mean strongly maintained, or asserted with good evidence. [Quotes *Antony and Cleopatra*, I.2.101]

STUMBLING-BLOCK (n.) Cause of stumbling; cause of error; cause of offence.

Shakespeare is a *stumbling-block* to these rigid critics. Addison, *Spectator* 592, 10 September 1714

To TANG (v.n.) (This is, I think, mistaken for 'twang'.) To ring with. [Quotes *Twelfth Night*, II.5.144]

To TATTER (v.a.) To tear; to rend; to make ragged. 'Tattered' is perhaps more properly an adjective. [Quotes *King Lear*, IV.6.165; *Romeo and Juliet*, V.1.37]

To TELL (v.a.) 6 To make excuses. A low word. [Quotes *Othello*, I.1.1]

To TEMPORIZE (v.n.) 3 To comply: this is improper. [Quotes *King John*, V.2.124]

TERMAGANT (n.) A scold; a brawling, turbulent woman. It appears in Shakespeare to have been anciently used of men. It was a kind of heathen deity extremely vociferous and tumultuous in the ancient farces and puppet shows. [Quotes *Hamlet*, III.2.12][26]

THENCE (n.) 4 'From thence' is a barbarous expression, 'thence' implying the same, yet it wants not good authorities. [Quotes *The Winter's Tale*, V.1.158][27]

THEW (n.) 2 In Shakespeare it seems to signify brawn or bulk, from the Saxon 'theoh', 'the thigh', or some such meaning. [Quotes *Hamlet*, I.3.11; *2 Henry IV*, III.2.250]

THING (n.) 4 It is used by Shakespeare once in a sense of honour. [Quotes *Coriolanus*, IV.5.117]

TIDY (adj.) 3 It seems to be here put by mistake or irony for 'untidy'. [Quotes *2 Henry IV*, II.4.226][28]

TIKE (n.) 2 It is in Shakespeare the name of a dog, in which sense it is used in Scotland. [Quotes *King Lear*, III.6.63]

TINY (adj.) Little; small; puny. A burlesque word. [Quotes *2 Henry IV*, V.1.22; *Twelfth Night*, V.1.386]

TOO (adv.) 2 It is sometimes doubled to increase its emphasis; but this reduplication always seems harsh and is therefore laid aside. [Quotes *Hamlet*, I.2.129]

TRACT (n.) 4 Course; manner of process; unless it means in this place, rather, discourse; explanation. [Quotes *Henry VIII*, I.1.40]

5 It seems to be used by Shakespeare for 'track'. [Quotes *Richard III*, V.3.19]

TRADESMAN (n.) A shopkeeper. A merchant is called a 'trader', but not a tradesman; and it seems distinguished in Shakespeare from a man that labours with his hands. [Quotes *Julius Caesar*, I.1.21; *Coriolanus*, IV.6.5]

TRADITIONAL (adj.) 2 Observant of traditions or idle rites. Not used, nor proper. [Quotes *Richard III*, III.1.40]

Selections from the Dictionary

To TRANSLATE (v.n.) 6 To explain. A low colloquial use. [Quotes *Hamlet*, IV.1.1]

TRISTFUL (adj.) Sad; melancholy; gloomy; sorrowful. A bad word. [Quotes *Hamlet*, III.4.49][29]

TROLL-MY-DAMES (n.) (Of this word I know not the meaning.) [Quotes *The Winter's Tale*, IV.3.84]

TUCKET SONANCE (n.) The sound of the tucket. An ancient instrument of music. [Quotes *Henry V*, IV.2.32][30]

UNANELED (adj.) Without the bell rung. This sense I doubt. [Quotes *Hamlet*, I.5.74]

UNCLE (n.) The father's or mother's brother.

Hamlet punishes his *uncle* rather for his own death than the murder of his father. Mrs Lennox, *Shakespeare Illustrated*, 'Observations' on *Hamlet*

UNNECESSARY (adj.) Needless; not wanted; useless.

The reader can easily discover how the plot will be unravelled at last; but the *unnecessary* intricacies in unravelling it still remain to be accounted for. Mrs Lennox, *Shakespeare Illustrated*, 'Fable' of *Measure for Measure*

To UNPAY (v.a.) To undo. A low ludicrous word. [Quotes *2 Henry IV*, II.1.117]

UNQUESTIONABLE (adj.) 2 Such as cannot bear to be questioned without impatience; this seems to be the meaning here. [Quotes *As You Like It*, III.2.357]

To UNRAVEL (v.a.) 3 To clear up the intrigue of a play.

Thus supernaturally is the plot brought to perfection; nor is the *unravelling* of it less happily imagined. Mrs Lennox, *Shakespeare Illustrated*, 'Plan' of *Much Ado About Nothing*

UTIS (n.) A word which probably is corrupted, at least is not now understood. 'Utis' was the octave of a saint's day and may perhaps be taken for any festivity. [Quotes *2 Henry IV*, II.4.19][31]

VAULTY (adj.) Arched; concave. A bad word. [Quotes *King John*, III.4.29; *Romeo and Juliet*, III.5.19]

To VIRGINAL (v.n.) To pat; to strike as on the virginal. A cant word. [Quotes *The Winter's Tale*, I.2.125]

VIRTUE (n.) 1 Moral goodness: opposed to vice.

The character of Prince Henry is improved by Shakespeare; and through the veil of his vices and irregularities we see a dawn of greatness and *virtue*. Mrs Lennox, *Shakespeare Illustrated*, 'Plan' of *1 Henry IV*[32]

To WARP (v.a.) 3 It is used by Shakespeare to express the effect of frost. [Quotes *As You Like It*, II.7.185]
WHEREVER (adv.) At whatsoever place.

Wherever Shakespeare has invented he is greatly below the novelist; since the incidents he has added are neither necessary nor probable. Mrs Lennox, *Shakespeare Illustrated*, 'Fable' of *Measure for Measure*

WHETSTONE (n.) Stone on which anything is whetted or rubbed to make it sharp.

A *whetstone* is not an instrument to carve with; but it sharpens those that do. Mrs Lennox, *Shakespeare Illustrated*, 'Story' of *Troilus and Cressida*

To WHIP (v.a.) To take anything nimbly; always with a particle ascertaining the sense, as 'out', 'on', 'up', 'away'. A ludicrous use. [Quotes *Hamlet*, IV.1.8][33]
WOE (n.) 4 'Woe' seems in phrases of denunciation or imprecation to be a substantive and in exclamation an adjective, as particularly in the following lines, which seem improper and ungrammatical. [Quotes *Antony and Cleopatra*, IV.14.133][34]
WONDERFUL (adj.) Admirable; strange; astonishing.

All this is very *wonderful*, Shakespeare multiplies miracle upon miracle to bring about the same event in the play, which chance with more propriety performs in the novel. Mrs Lennox, *Shakespeare Illustrated*, 'Observations' on *The Winter's Tale*

To WREAK (v.a.) 3 It is corruptly written for 'reck', to heed; to care. [Quotes *As You Like It*, II.4.77]
WREATH (n.) 2 A garland; a chaplet.

To Prince Henry the laurels of his rival are transferred, with the additional *wreath* of having conquered that rival. Mrs Lennox, *Shakespeare Illustrated*, 'Plan' of *1 Henry IV*

YELLOWNESS (n.) 2 It is used in Shakespeare for jealousy. [Quotes *The Merry Wives of Windsor*, I.3.93]

PROPOSALS FOR PRINTING BY SUBSCRIPTION SHAKESPEARE'S PLAYS
(1756)

PROPOSALS FOR PRINTING, BY SUBSCRIPTION, THE DRAMATIC WORKS OF WILLIAM SHAKESPEARE CORRECTED AND ILLUSTRATED BY SAMUEL JOHNSON

CONDITIONS

I. That the book shall be elegantly printed in eight volumes in octavo.
II. That the price to subscribers shall be two guineas; one to be paid at subscribing, the other on the delivery of the book in sheets.
III. That the work shall be published on or before Christmas 1757.

When the works of Shakespeare are, after so many editions, again offered to the public, it will doubtless be inquired why Shakespeare stands in more need of critical assistance than any other of the English writers and what are the deficiencies of the late attempts which another editor may hope to supply.

The business of him that republishes an ancient book is to correct what is corrupt and to explain what is obscure. To have a text corrupt in many places, and in many doubtful, is, among the authors that have written since the use of types, almost peculiar to Shakespeare. Most writers by publishing their own works prevent all various readings and preclude all conjectural criticism. Books indeed are sometimes published after the death of him who produced them, but they are better secured from corruptions than these unfortunate[1] compositions. They subsist in a single copy, written or revised by the author and the faults of the printed volume can be only faults of one descent.

But of the works of Shakespeare the condition has been far different: he sold them not to be printed, but to be played. They were immediately copied for the actors, and multiplied by transcript after transcript, vitiated by the blunders of the penman, or changed by the affectation of the player; perhaps enlarged to introduce a jest, or mutilated to shorten the representation; and printed at last without the concurrence of the author, without the consent of the proprietor, from compilations made by chance or by stealth out of the separate parts written for the theatre; and thus thrust into the world surreptitiously and hastily, they suffered another depravation[2] from the ignorance and negligence of the printers, as every man who knows the state of the press in that age will readily conceive.

It is not easy for invention to bring together so many causes concurring to vitiate a text. No other author ever gave up his works to fortune and time with so little care; no books could be left in hands so likely to injure them as plays frequently acted, yet continued in manuscript; no other transcribers were likely to be so little qualified for their task as those who copied for the stage, at a time when the lower ranks of the people were universally illiterate; no other editions were made from fragments so minutely broken and so fortuitously reunited; and in no other age was the art of printing in such unskilful hands.

With the causes of corruption that make the revisal[3] of Shakespeare's dramatic pieces necessary may be enumerated the causes of obscurity, which may be partly imputed to his age and partly to himself.

When a writer outlives his contemporaries, and remains almost the only unforgotten name of a distant time he is necessarily obscure. Every age has its modes of speech and its cast of thought which, though easily explained when there are many books to be compared with each other, become sometimes unintelligible and always difficult when there are no parallel passages that may conduce to their illustration.

Shakespeare is the first considerable author of sublime[4] or familiar dialogue in our language. Of the books which he read and from which he formed his style, some perhaps have perished and the rest are neglected. His imitations are therefore unnoted, his allusions are undiscovered and many beauties both of pleasantry and greatness are lost with the objects to which they were united, as the figures vanish when the canvas has decayed.

It is the great excellence of Shakespeare that he drew his scenes from nature and from life. He copied the manners of the world then passing before him and has more allusions than other poets to the traditions and superstition of the vulgar, which must therefore be traced before he can be understood.

He wrote at a time when our poetical language was yet unformed, when the meaning of our phrases was yet in fluctuation, when words were adopted at pleasure from the neighbouring languages and while the Saxon was still visibly mingled in our diction. The reader is therefore embarrassed[5] at once with dead and with foreign languages, with obsoleteness and innovation. In that age, as in all others, fashion produced phraseology, which succeeding fashion swept away before its meaning was generally known or sufficiently authorized; and in that age, above all others, experiments were made upon our language which distorted its combinations and disturbed its uniformity.

If Shakespeare has difficulties above other writers it is to be imputed to the nature of his work, which required the use of the common colloquial language and consequently admitted many phrases allusive, elliptical and proverbial, such as we speak and hear every hour without observing them, and of which, being now familiar, we do not suspect that they can ever grow uncouth[6] or that, being now obvious, they can ever seem remote.

These are the principal causes of the obscurity of Shakespeare; to which may be added that fullness of idea, which might sometimes load his words with more sentiment[7] than they could conveniently convey and that rapidity of imagination which might hurry him to a second thought before he had fully explained the first. But my opinion is that very few of his lines were difficult to his audience and that he used such expressions as were then common, though the paucity of contemporary writers makes them now seem peculiar.

Authors are often praised for improvement or blamed for innovation with very little justice by those who read few other books of the same age. Addison himself has been so unsuccessful in enumerating the words with which Milton has enriched our language, as perhaps not to have named one of which Milton was the author; and Bentley has yet more unhappily praised him as the introducer of those elisions into English poetry which had been used from the first essays of versification among us and which Milton was indeed the last that practised.[8]

Another impediment, not the least vexatious to the commentator, is the exactness with which Shakespeare followed his authors. Instead of dilating his thoughts into generalities, and expressing incidents with poetical latitude, he often combines circumstances unnecessary to his main design, only because he happened to find them together. Such passages can be illustrated only by him who has read the same story in the very book which Shakespeare consulted.

He that undertakes an edition of Shakespeare has all these difficulties to encounter and all these obstructions to remove.

The corruptions of the text will be corrected by a careful collation of the oldest copies, by which it is hoped that many restorations may yet be made; at least it will be necessary to collect and note the variations as materials for future critics, for it very often happens that a wrong reading has affinity to the right.

In this part all the present editions are apparently and intentionally defective. The critics did not so much as wish to facilitate the labour of those that followed them. The same books are still to be compared; the work that has been done is to be done again, and no single edition will supply the reader with a text on which he can rely as the best copy of the works of Shakespeare.

The edition now proposed will at least have this advantage

over others. It will exhibit all the observable varieties of all the copies that can be found that, if the reader is not satisfied with the editor's determination, he may have the means of choosing better for himself.

Where all the books are evidently vitiated and collation can give no assistance, then begins the task of critical sagacity, and some changes may well be admitted in a text never settled by the author and so long exposed to caprice and ignorance. But nothing shall be imposed, as in the Oxford edition,[9] without notice of the alteration; nor shall conjecture be wantonly or unnecessarily indulged.

It has been long found that very specious emendations do not equally strike all minds with conviction, nor even the same mind at different times; and therefore, though perhaps many alterations may be proposed as eligible, very few will be obtruded[10] as certain. In a language so ungrammatical as the English, and so licentious as that of Shakespeare, emendatory criticism is always hazardous; nor can it be allowed to any man who is not particularly versed in the writings of that age and particularly studious of his author's diction. There is danger lest peculiarities should be mistaken for corruptions, and passages rejected as unintelligible, which a narrow mind happens not to understand.

All the former critics have been so much employed on the correction of the text that they have not sufficiently attended to the elucidation of passages obscured by accident or time. The editor will endeavour to read the books which the author read, to trace his knowledge to its source, and compare his copies with their originals. If in this part of his design he hopes to attain any degree of superiority to his predecessors, it must be considered that he has the advantage of their labours; that part of the work being already done, more care is naturally bestowed on the other part; and that, to declare the truth, Mr Rowe and Mr Pope were very ignorant of the ancient English literature; Dr Warburton was detained by more important studies; and Mr Theobald, if fame be just to his memory, considered learning only as an instrument of gain, and made no further inquiry after his author's meaning, when once he had notes sufficient to embellish his page with the expected decorations.[11]

With regard to obsolete or peculiar diction, the editor may perhaps claim some degree of confidence, having had more motives to consider the whole extent of our language than any other man from its first formation. He hopes that by comparing the works of Shakespeare with those of writers who lived at the same time, immediately preceded, or immediately followed him, he shall be able to ascertain his ambiguities, disentangle his intricacies and recover the meaning of words now lost in the darkness of antiquity.

When therefore any obscurity arises from an allusion to some other book, the passage will be quoted. When the diction is entangled, it will be cleared by a paraphrase or interpretation. When the sense is broken by the suppression of part of the sentiment in pleasantry or passion, the connection will be supplied. When any forgotten custom is hinted, care will be taken to retrieve and explain it. The meaning assigned to doubtful words will be supported by the authorities of other writers or by parallel passages of Shakespeare himself.

The observation of faults and beauties is one of the duties of an annotator, which some of Shakespeare's editors have attempted, and some have neglected. For this part of his task, and for this only, was Mr Pope eminently and indisputably qualified; nor has Dr Warburton followed him with less diligence or less success. But I have never observed that mankind was much delighted or improved by their asterisks, commas, or double commas, of which the only effect is that they preclude the pleasure of judging for ourselves, teach the young and ignorant to decide without principles, defeat curiosity and discernment by leaving them less to discover, and at last show the opinion of the critic, without the reasons on which it was founded and without affording any light by which it may be examined.[12]

The editor, though he may less delight his own vanity, will probably please his reader more by supposing him equally able with himself to judge of beauties and faults which require no previous acquisition of remote knowledge. A description of the obvious scenes of nature, a representation of general life, a sentiment of reflection or experience, a deduction of conclusive argument, a forcible eruption of effervescent passion, are to be considered as proportionate to common apprehension, unassisted by critical officiousness; since to conceive them nothing more is requisite than acquaintance with the general state of the world and those faculties which he must always bring with him who would read Shakespeare.

But when the beauty arises from some adaptation of the sentiment to customs worn out of use, to opinions not universally prevalent, or to any accidental or minute particularity, which cannot be supplied by common understanding or common observation, it is the duty of a commentator to lend his assistance.

The notice of beauties and faults thus limited will make no distinct part of the design, being reducible to the explanation of obscure passages.

The editor does not however intend to preclude himself from the comparison of Shakespeare's sentiments or expression with those of ancient or modern authors, or from the display of any beauty not obvious to the students of poetry; for as he hopes to leave his author better understood, he wishes likewise to procure him more rational approbation.

The former editors have affected to slight their predecessors; but in this edition all that is valuable will be adopted from every commentator, that posterity may consider it as including all the rest, and exhibiting whatever is hitherto known of the great father of the English drama.

PREFACE TO THE EDITION OF SHAKESPEARE'S PLAYS
(1765)

That praises are without reason lavished on the dead, and that the honours due only to excellence are paid to antiquity, is a complaint likely to be always continued by those who, being able to add nothing to truth, hope for eminence from the heresies of paradox; or those who, being forced by disappointment upon consolatory expedients, are willing to hope from posterity what the present age refuses and flatter themselves that the regard which is yet denied by envy will be at last bestowed by time.

Antiquity, like every other quality that attracts the notice of mankind, has undoubtedly votaries that reverence it, not from reason, but from prejudice. Some seem to admire indiscriminately whatever has been long preserved, without considering that time has sometimes co-operated with chance; all perhaps are more willing to honour past than present excellence; and the mind contemplates genius through the shades of age, as the eye surveys the sun through artificial opacity.[1] The great contention of criticism is to find the faults of the moderns and the beauties of the ancients. While an author is yet living we estimate his powers by his worst performance, and when he is dead we rate them by his best.

To works, however, of which the excellence is not absolute and definite, but gradual and comparative; to works not raised upon principles demonstrative and scientific, but appealing wholly to observation and experience, no other test can be applied than length of duration and continuance of esteem. What mankind have long possessed they have often examined and compared, and if they persist to value the possession, it is because frequent comparisons have confirmed opinion in its favour. As among the works of nature no man can properly call a river deep or a mountain high without the knowledge of many mountains and many rivers; so in the productions of genius, nothing can be styled excellent till it has been compared with other works of the same kind. Demonstration immediately displays its power and has nothing to hope or fear from the flux of years; but works tentative and experimental must be estimated by their proportion to the general and collective ability of man, as it is discovered in a long succession of endeavours. Of the first building that was raised, it might be with certainty determined that it was round or square, but whether it was spacious or lofty must have been referred to time. The Pythagorean scale of numbers[2] was at once discovered to be perfect; but the poems of Homer we yet know not to transcend the common limits of human intelligence, but by remarking that nation after nation, and century after century, has been able to do little more than transpose his incidents, new-name his characters and paraphrase his sentiments.

The reverence due to writings that have long subsisted arises therefore not from any credulous confidence in the superior wisdom of past ages, or gloomy persuasion of the degeneracy of mankind, but is the consequence of acknowledged and indubitable positions, that what has been longest known has been most considered and what is most considered is best understood.

The poet of whose works I have undertaken the revision[3] may now begin to assume the dignity of an ancient and claim the privilege of established fame and prescriptive veneration. He has long outlived his century,[4] the term commonly fixed as the test of literary merit. Whatever advantages he might once derive from personal allusions, local customs or temporary opinions have for many years been lost; and every topic of merriment or motive of sorrow, which the modes of artificial life afforded him, now only obscure the scenes which they once illuminated. The effects of favour and competition are at an end; the tradition of his friendships and his enmities has perished; his works support no opinion with arguments, nor supply any faction with invectives; they can neither indulge vanity nor gratify malignity, but are read without any other reason than the desire of pleasure and are therefore praised only as pleasure is obtained; yet, thus unassisted by interest or passion, they have passed through variations of taste and changes of manners and, as they devolved[5] from one generation to another, have received new honours at every transmission.

But because human judgement, though it be gradually gaining upon certainty, never becomes infallible; and approbation, though long continued, may yet be only the approbation of prejudice or fashion, it is proper to inquire by what peculiarities of excellence Shakespeare has gained and kept the favour of his countrymen.

Nothing can please many, and please long, but just representations of general nature. Particular manners can be known to few and therefore few only can judge how nearly they are copied. The irregular combinations of fanciful invention may delight awhile by that novelty of which the common satiety of life sends us all in quest; but the pleasures of sudden wonder are soon exhausted and the mind can only repose on the stability of truth.

Shakespeare is above all writers, at least above all modern writers, the poet of nature; the poet that holds up to his readers a faithful mirror of manners and of life. His characters are not modified by the customs of particular places, unpractised by the rest of the world; by the peculiarities of studies or professions, which can operate but upon small numbers; or by the accidents of transient fashions or temporary opinions: they are the genuine progeny of common humanity, such as the world will always supply and observation will always find. His persons act and speak by the influence of those general passions and principles by which all minds are agitated, and the whole system of life is continued in motion. In the writings of other poets a character is too often an individual; in those of Shakespeare it is commonly a species.

It is from this wide extension of design that so much

instruction is derived. It is this which fills the plays of Shakespeare with practical axioms and domestic wisdom. It was said of Euripides, that every verse was a precept;[6] and it may be said of Shakespeare that from his works may be collected a system of civil and economical prudence. Yet his real power is not shown in the splendour of particular passages, but by the progress of his fable and the tenor of his dialogue; and he that tries to recommend him by select quotations will succeed like the pedant in Hierocles who, when he offered his house to sale, carried a brick in his pocket as a specimen.[7]

It will not easily be imagined how much Shakespeare excels in accommodating his sentiments to real life, but by comparing him with other authors. It was observed of the ancient schools of declamation that the more diligently they were frequented, the more was the student disqualified for the world, because he found nothing there which he should ever meet in any other place.[8] The same remark may be applied to every stage but that of Shakespeare. The theatre, when it is under any other direction, is peopled by such characters as were never seen, conversing in a language which was never heard, upon topics which will never arise in the commerce of mankind. But the dialogue of this author is often so evidently determined by the incident which produces it, and is pursued with so much ease and simplicity, that it seems scarcely to claim the merit of fiction, but to have been gleaned by diligent selection out of common conversation and common occurrences.

Upon every other stage the universal agent is love, by whose power all good and evil is distributed and every action quickened or retarded. To bring a lover, a lady and a rival into the fable; to entangle them in contradictory obligations, perplex them with oppositions of interest and harass them with violence of desires inconsistent with each other; to make them meet in rapture and part in agony; to fill their mouths with hyperbolical joy and outrageous sorrow; to distress them as nothing human ever was distressed; to deliver them as nothing human ever was delivered, is the business of a modern dramatist. For this, probability is violated, life is misrepresented and language is depraved. But love is only one of many passions, and as it has no great influence upon the sum of life it has little operation in the dramas of a poet, who caught his ideas from the living world and exhibited only what he saw before him. He knew that any other passion, as it was regular or exorbitant, was a cause of happiness or calamity.

Characters thus ample and general were not easily discriminated and preserved, yet perhaps no poet ever kept his personages more distinct from each other. I will not say with Pope[9] that every speech may be assigned to the proper speaker, because many speeches there are which have nothing characteristical; but perhaps, though some may be equally adapted to every person, it will be difficult to find any that can be properly transferred from the present possessor to another claimant. The choice is right, when there is reason for choice.

Other dramatists can only gain attention by hyperbolical or aggravated characters, by fabulous and unexampled excellence or depravity, as the writers of barbarous romances invigorated the reader by a giant and a dwarf; and he that should form his expectations of human affairs from the play, or from the tale, would be equally deceived. Shakespeare has no heroes; his scenes are occupied only by men, who act and speak as the reader thinks that he should himself have spoken or acted on the same occasion. Even where the agency[10] is supernatural the dialogue is level with life. Other writers disguise the most natural passions and most frequent incidents; so that he who contemplates them in the book will not know them in the world: Shakespeare approximates[11] the remote and familiarizes the wonderful; the event which he represents will not happen, but if it were possible, its effects would probably be such as he has assigned; and it may be said that he has not only shown human nature as it acts in real exigences, but as it would be found in trials to which it cannot be exposed.

This therefore is the praise of Shakespeare, that his drama is the mirror of life; that he who has mazed[12] his imagination in following the phantoms which other writers raise up before him may here be cured of his delirious ecstasies, by reading human sentiments in human language; by scenes from which a

Preface to the Edition of Shakespeare's Plays 125

hermit may estimate the transactions of the world and a confessor predict the progress of the passions.

His adherence to general nature has exposed him to the censure of critics who form their judgements upon narrower principles. Dennis and Rymer think his Romans not sufficiently Roman; and Voltaire censures his kings as not completely royal. Dennis is offended that Menenius, a senator of Rome, should play the buffoon; and Voltaire perhaps thinks decency violated when the Danish usurper is represented as a drunkard.[13] But Shakespeare always makes nature predominate over accident; and, if he preserves the essential character, is not very careful of distinctions superinduced[14] and adventitious.[15] His story requires Romans or kings, but he thinks only on men. He knew that Rome, like every other city, had men of all dispositions; and wanting a buffoon, he went into the senate house for that which the senate house would certainly have afforded him. He was inclined to show an usurper and a murderer not only odious but despicable; he therefore added drunkenness to his other qualities, knowing that kings love wine like other men, and that wine exerts its natural power upon kings. These are the petty cavils of petty minds; a poet overlooks the casual distinction of country and condition, as a painter, satisfied with the figure, neglects the drapery.

The censure which he has incurred by mixing comic and tragic scenes, as it extends to all his works, deserves more consideration. Let the fact be first stated and then examined.

Shakespeare's plays are not in the rigorous and critical sense either tragedies or comedies, but compositions of a distinct kind; exhibiting the real state of sublunary nature, which partakes of good and evil, joy and sorrow, mingled with endless variety of proportion and innumerable modes of combination; and expressing the course of the world, in which the loss of one is the gain of another; in which, at the same time, the reveller is hasting to his wine, and the mourner burying his friend; in which the malignity of one is sometimes defeated by the frolic of another; and many mischiefs and many benefits are done and hindered without design.

Out of this chaos of mingled purposes and casualties the ancient poets, according to the laws which custom had prescribed, selected some the crimes of men, and some their absurdities; some the momentous vicissitudes of life, and some the lighter occurrences; some the terrors of distress, and some the gaieties of prosperity. Thus rose the two modes of imitation, known by the names of 'tragedy' and 'comedy', compositions intended to promote different ends by contrary means, and considered as so little allied that I do not recollect among the Greeks or Romans a single writer who attempted both.

Shakespeare has united the powers of exciting laughter and sorrow not only in one mind but in one composition. Almost all his plays are divided between serious and ludicrous characters and, in the successive evolutions of the design, sometimes produce seriousness and sorrow, and sometimes levity and laughter.

That this is a practice contrary to the rules of criticism will be readily allowed; but there is always an appeal open from criticism to nature. The end of writing is to instruct; the end of poetry is to instruct by pleasing.[16] That the mingled drama may convey all the instruction of tragedy or comedy cannot be denied, because it includes both in its alternations[17] of exhibition and approaches nearer than either to the appearance of life, by showing how great machinations and slender designs may promote or obviate one another, and the high and the low co-operate in the general system by unavoidable concatenation.

It is objected that by this change of scenes the passions are interrupted in their progression and that the principal event, being not advanced by a due gradation of preparatory incidents, wants at last the power to move, which constitutes the perfection of dramatic poetry. This reasoning is so specious that it is received as true even by those who in daily experience feel it to be false. The interchanges of mingled scenes seldom fail to produce the intended vicissitudes of passion. Fiction cannot move so much but that the attention may be easily transferred; and though it must be allowed that pleasing melancholy[18] be sometimes interrupted by unwelcome[19] levity, yet let it be considered likewise[20] that melancholy is often not pleasing, and that the disturbance of one man may be the relief of another; that different auditors have different habitudes; and that, upon the whole, all pleasure consists in variety.

The players,[21] who in their edition divided our author's works into comedies, histories and tragedies, seem not to have distinguished the three kinds by any very exact or definite ideas.

An action which ended happily to the principal persons, however serious or distressful through its intermediate incidents, in their opinion constituted a comedy. This idea of a comedy continued long amongst us and plays were written which, by changing the catastrophe, were tragedies today and comedies tomorrow.[22]

Tragedy was not in those times a poem of more general dignity or elevation than comedy; it required only a calamitous conclusion, with which the common criticism of that age was satisfied, whatever lighter pleasure it afforded in its progress.

History was a series of actions, with no other than chronological succession, independent on each other, and without any tendency to introduce or regulate the conclusion. It is not always very nicely[23] distinguished from tragedy. There is not much nearer approach to unity of action in the tragedy of *Antony and Cleopatra* than in the history of *Richard the Second*. But a history might be continued through many plays; as it had no plan, it had no limits.

Through all these denominations of the drama, Shakespeare's mode of composition is the same; an interchange of seriousness and merriment, by which the mind is softened at one time and exhilarated at another. But whatever be his purpose, whether to gladden or depress, or to conduct the story without vehemence or emotion, through tracts of easy and familiar dialogue, he never fails to attain his purpose; as he commands us, we laugh or mourn, or sit silent with quiet expectation, in tranquillity without indifference.

When Shakespeare's plan is understood most of the

criticisms of Rymer and Voltaire vanish away. The play of *Hamlet* is opened, without impropriety, by two sentinels; Iago bellows at Brabantio's window, without injury to the scheme of the play, though in terms which a modern audience would not easily endure; the character of Polonius is seasonable[24] and useful; and the grave-diggers themselves may be heard with applause.[25]

Shakespeare engaged in dramatic poetry with the world open before him; the rules of the ancients were yet known to few; the public judgement was unformed; he had no example of such fame as might force him upon imitation, nor critics of such authority as might restrain his extravagance; he therefore indulged his natural disposition, and his disposition, as Rymer has remarked, led him to comedy.[26] In tragedy he often writes with great appearance of toil and study what is written at last with little felicity; but in his comic scenes he seems to produce without labour what no labour can improve. In tragedy he is always struggling after some occasion to be comic, but in comedy he seems to repose, or to luxuriate, as in a mode of thinking congenial to his nature. In his tragic scenes there is always something wanting, but his comedy often surpasses expectation or desire. His comedy pleases by the thoughts and the language, and his tragedy for the greater part by incident and action. His tragedy seems to be skill, his comedy to be instinct.

The force of his comic scenes has suffered little diminution from the changes made by a century and a half, in manners or in words. As his personages act upon principles arising from genuine passion, very little modified by particular forms, their pleasures and vexations are communicable to all times and to all places; they are natural, and therefore durable. The adventitious peculiarities of personal habits are only superficial dyes, bright and pleasing for a little while, yet soon fading to a dim tinct, without any remains of former lustre; but the discriminations of true passion are the colours of nature; they pervade the whole mass and can only perish with the body that exhibits them. The accidental compositions of heterogeneous modes are dissolved by the chance which combined them; but the uniform simplicity of primitive qualities neither admits increase, nor suffers decay. The sand heaped by one flood is scattered by another, but the rock always continues in its place. The stream of time, which is continually washing the dissoluble fabrics of other poets,[27] passes without injury by the adamant[28] of Shakespeare.

If there be, what I believe there is in every nation, a style which never becomes obsolete, a certain mode of phraseology so consonant and congenial to the analogy and principles of its respective language as to remain settled and unaltered; this style is probably to be sought in the common intercourse of life, among those who speak only to be understood, without ambition of elegance. The polite are always catching modish innovations, and the learned depart from established forms of speech in hope of finding or making better; those who wish for distinction forsake the vulgar, when the vulgar is right; but there is a conversation above grossness and below refinement, where propriety resides, and where this poet seems to have gathered his comic dialogue. He is therefore more agreeable to the ears of the present age than any other author equally remote and among his other excellencies deserves to be studied as one of the original masters of our language.

These observations are to be considered not as unexceptionably constant, but as containing general and predominant truth. Shakespeare's familiar dialogue is affirmed to be smooth and clear, yet not wholly without ruggedness or difficulty; as a country may be eminently fruitful, though it has spots unfit for cultivation: his characters are praised as natural, though their sentiments are sometimes forced and their actions improbable; as the earth upon the whole is spherical, though its surface is varied with protuberances and cavities.

Shakespeare with his excellencies has likewise faults, and faults sufficient to obscure and overwhelm any other merit. I shall show them in the proportion in which they appear to me, without envious malignity or superstitious veneration. No question can be more innocently discussed than a dead poet's pretensions to renown; and little regard is due to that bigotry which sets candour[29] higher than truth.

His first defect is that to which may be imputed most of the evil in books or in men. He sacrifices virtue to convenience and is so much more careful to please than to instruct that he seems to write without any moral purpose. From his writings indeed a system of social duty may be selected, for he that thinks reasonably must think morally; but his precepts and axioms drop casually from him; he makes no just distribution of good or evil, nor is always careful to show in the virtuous a disapprobation of the wicked; he carries his persons indifferently through right and wrong and at the close dismisses them without further care and leaves their examples to operate by chance. This fault the barbarity of his age cannot extenuate; for it is always a writer's duty to make the world better, and justice is a virtue independent on time or place.

The plots are often so loosely formed that a very slight consideration may improve them, and so carelessly pursued that he seems not always fully to comprehend his own design. He omits opportunities of instructing or delighting which the train of his story seems to force upon him, and apparently rejects those exhibitions which would be more affecting for the sake of those which are more easy.

It may be observed that in many of his plays the latter part is evidently neglected. When he found himself near the end of his work and in view of his reward, he shortened the labour to snatch the profit. He therefore remits his efforts where he should most vigorously exert them, and his catastrophe[30] is improbably produced or imperfectly represented.

He had no regard to distinction of time or place, but gives to one age or nation, without scruple, the customs, institutions and opinions of another, at the expense not only of likelihood but of possibility. These faults Pope has endeavoured, with more zeal than judgement, to transfer to his imagined interpolators.[31] We need not wonder to find Hector quoting Aristotle [*Troilus and Cressida*, II.2.167] when we see the loves of Theseus and Hippolyta combined with the Gothic mythology of fairies. Shakespeare, indeed, was not the only violator of chronology, for in the same age Sidney, who wanted not the advantages of learning, has in his *Arcadia* confounded the

Preface to the Edition of Shakespeare's Plays 131

pastoral with the feudal times, the days of innocence, quiet and security with those of turbulence, violence and adventure.

In his comic scenes he is seldom very successful when he engages his characters in reciprocations of smartness and contests of sarcasm; their jests are commonly gross and their pleasantry licentious; neither his gentlemen nor his ladies have much delicacy, nor are sufficiently distinguished from his clowns by any appearance of refined manners. Whether he represented the real conversation of his time is not easy to determine; the reign of Elizabeth is commonly supposed to have been a time of stateliness, formality and reserve, yet perhaps the relaxations of that severity were not very elegant. There must, however, have been always some modes of gaiety preferable to others, and a writer ought to choose the best.

In tragedy his performance seems constantly to be worse, as his labour is more. The effusions of passion which exigence forces out are for the most part striking and energetic; but whenever he solicits his invention, or strains his faculties, the offspring of his throes is tumour,[32] meanness, tediousness and obscurity.

In narration he affects a disproportionate pomp of diction and a wearisome train of circumlocution, and tells the incident imperfectly in many words, which might have been more plainly delivered in few. Narration in dramatic poetry is naturally tedious, as it is unanimated and inactive and obstructs the progress of the action; it should therefore always be rapid and enlivened by frequent interruption. Shakespeare found it an encumbrance, and instead of lightening it by brevity, endeavoured to recommend it by dignity and splendour.

His declamations or set speeches are commonly cold and weak, for his power was the power of nature; when he endeavoured, like other tragic writers, to catch opportunities of amplification,[33] and instead of inquiring what the occasion demanded, to show how much his stores of knowledge could supply, he seldom escapes without the pity or resentment of his reader.

It is incident to him to be now and then entangled with an

unwieldy sentiment, which he cannot well express and will not reject; he struggles with it a while and if it continues stubborn, comprises it in words such as occur and leaves it to be disentangled and evolved[34] by those who have more leisure to bestow upon it.

Not that always where the language is intricate the thought is subtle, or the image always great where the line is bulky; the equality of words to things is very often neglected, and trivial sentiments and vulgar ideas disappoint the attention to which they are recommended by sonorous epithets and swelling figures.

But the admirers of this great poet have most reason to complain when he approaches nearest to his highest excellence and seems fully resolved[35] to sink them in dejection and mollify them with tender emotions by the fall of greatness, the danger of innocence, or the crosses of love. What he does best, he soon ceases to do.[36] He is not long soft and pathetic without some idle conceit, or contemptible equivocation. He no sooner begins to move than he counteracts himself; and terror and pity, as they are rising in the mind, are checked and blasted by sudden frigidity.[37]

A quibble[38] is to Shakespeare what luminous vapours are to the traveller; he follows it at all adventures, it is sure to lead him out of his way and sure to engulf him in the mire. It has some malignant power over his mind and its fascinations are irresistible. Whatever be the dignity or profundity of his disquisition, whether he be enlarging knowledge or exalting affection, whether he be amusing attention with incidents, or enchaining it in suspense, let but a quibble spring up before him and he leaves his work unfinished. A quibble is the golden apple for which he will always turn aside from his career, or stoop from his elevation.[39] A quibble, poor and barren as it is, gave him such delight that he was content to purchase it by the sacrifice of reason, propriety and truth. A quibble was to him the fatal Cleopatra for which he lost the world and was content to lose it.

It will be thought strange that in enumerating the defects of this writer I have not yet mentioned his neglect of the unities;

his violation of those laws which have been instituted and established by the joint authority of poets and of critics.

For his other deviations from the art of writing, I resign him to critical justice without making any other demand in his favour than that which must be indulged to all human excellence: that his virtues be rated with his failings. But from the censure which this irregularity may bring upon him, I shall, with due reverence to that learning which I must oppose, adventure to try how I can defend him.

His histories, being neither tragedies nor comedies, are not subject to any of their laws; nothing more is necessary to all the praise which they expect than that the changes of action be so prepared as to be understood, that the incidents be various and affecting, and the characters consistent, natural and distinct. No other unity is intended and therefore none is to be sought.

In his other works he has well enough preserved the unity of action. He has not, indeed, an intrigue regularly perplexed and regularly unravelled; he does not endeavour to hide his design only to discover it, for this is seldom the order of real events and Shakespeare is the poet of nature. But his plan has commonly what Aristotle requires, a beginning, a middle and an end; one event is concatenated with another, and the conclusion follows by easy consequence. There are perhaps some incidents that might be spared, as in other poets there is much talk that only fills up time upon the stage; but the general system makes gradual advances, and the end of the play is the end of expectation.

To the unities of time and place he has shown no regard, and perhaps a nearer view of the principles on which they stand will diminish their value and withdraw from them the veneration which, from the time of Corneille,[40] they have very generally received, by discovering that they have given more trouble to the poet than pleasure to the auditor.

The necessity of observing the unities of time and place arises from the supposed necessity of making the drama credible. The critics hold it impossible that an action of months or years can be possibly believed to pass in three hours; or that the spectator can suppose himself to sit in the theatre while ambassadors go and return between distant kings, while armies are levied and towns besieged, while an exile wanders and returns, or till he whom they saw courting his mistress shall lament the untimely fall of his son. The mind revolts from evident falsehood, and fiction loses its force when it departs from the resemblance of reality.

From the narrow limitation of time necessarily arises the contraction of place. The spectator, who knows that he saw the first act at Alexandria, cannot suppose that he sees the next at Rome, at a distance to which not the dragons of Medea[41] could, in so short a time, have transported him; he knows with certainty that he has not changed his place; and he knows that place cannot change itself; that what was a house cannot become a plain; that what was Thebes can never be Persepolis.

Such is the triumphant language with which a critic exults over the misery of an irregular poet, and exults commonly without resistance or reply. It is time therefore to tell him, by the authority of Shakespeare, that he assumes as an unquestionable principle a position which, while his breath is forming it into words, his understanding pronounces to be false. It is false that any representation is mistaken for reality; that any dramatic fable in its materiality was ever credible, or for a single moment was ever credited.

The objection arising from the impossibility of passing the first hour at Alexandria and the next at Rome supposes that when the play opens the spectator really imagines himself at Alexandria, and believes that his walk to the theatre has been a voyage to Egypt and that he lives in the days of Antony and Cleopatra. Surely he that imagines this may imagine more. He that can take the stage at one time for the palace of the Ptolemies may take it in half an hour for the promontory of Actium. Delusion, if delusion be admitted, has no certain limitation; if the spectator can be once persuaded that his old acquaintance are Alexander and Caesar, that a room illuminated with candles is the plain of Pharsalia, or the bank of Granicus, he is in a state of elevation above the reach of reason or of truth, and from the heights of empyrean poetry may despise the circumscriptions of terrestrial nature. There is no

Preface to the Edition of Shakespeare's Plays   135

reason why a mind thus wandering in ecstasy should count the clock, or why an hour should not be a century in that calenture[42] of the brains that can make the stage a field.

The truth is that the spectators are always in their senses, and know from the first act to the last that the stage is only a stage, and that the players are only players. They come to hear a certain number of lines recited with just gesture and elegant modulation. The lines relate to some action, and an action must be in some place; but the different actions that complete a story may be in places very remote from each other; and where is the absurdity of allowing that space to represent first Athens and then Sicily, which was always known to be neither Sicily nor Athens, but a modern theatre?

By supposition, as place is introduced, time may be extended; the time required by the fable elapses for the most part between the acts; for, of so much of the action as is represented, the real and poetical duration is the same. If in the first act preparations for war against Mithridates are represented to be made in Rome, the event of the war may, without absurdity, be represented in the catastrophe as happening in Pontus; we know that there is neither war, nor preparation for war; we know that we are neither in Rome nor Pontus; that neither Mithridates nor Lucullus are before us. The drama exhibits successive imitations of successive actions, and why may not the second imitation represent an action that happened years after the first, if it be so connected with it that nothing but time can be supposed to intervene? Time is, of all modes of existence, most obsequious to the imagination; a lapse of years is as easily conceived as a passage of hours. In contemplation we easily contract the time of real actions, and therefore willingly permit it to be contracted when we only see their imitation.

It will be asked how the drama moves if it is not credited. It is credited with all the credit due to a drama. It is credited, whenever it moves, as a just picture of a real original; as representing to the auditor what he would himself feel, if he were to do or suffer what is there feigned to be suffered or to be done. The reflection that strikes the heart is not that the evils before us are real evils, but that they are evils to which we ourselves may be exposed. If there be any fallacy, it is not that we fancy the players, but that we fancy ourselves unhappy for a moment; but we rather lament the possibility than suppose the presence of misery, as a mother weeps over her babe when she remembers that death may take it from her. The delight of tragedy proceeds from our consciousness of fiction; if we thought murders and treasons real, they would please no more.

Imitations produce pain or pleasure, not because they are mistaken for realities, but because they bring realities to mind. When the imagination is recreated[43] by a painted landscape, the trees are not supposed capable to give us shade, or the fountains coolness; but we consider how we should be pleased with such fountains playing beside us and such woods waving over us. We are agitated in reading the history of *Henry the Fifth*, yet no man takes his book for the field of Agincourt. A dramatic exhibition is a book recited with concomitants that increase or diminish its effect. Familiar comedy is often more powerful on the theatre than in the page; imperial tragedy is always less. The humour of Petruchio may be heightened by grimace; but what voice or what gesture can hope to add dignity or force to the soliloquy of Cato?[44]

A play read affects the mind like a play acted. It is therefore evident that the action is not supposed to be real, and it follows that between the acts a longer or shorter time may be allowed to pass, and that no more account of space or duration is to be taken by the auditor of a drama than by the reader of a narrative, before whom may pass in an hour the life of a hero, or the revolutions of an empire.

Whether Shakespeare knew the unities and rejected them by design, or deviated from them by happy ignorance, it is, I think, impossible to decide and useless to inquire. We may reasonably suppose that when he rose to notice, he did not want the counsels and admonitions of scholars and critics, and that he at last deliberately persisted in a practice which he might have begun by chance. As nothing is essential to the fable but unity of action, and as the unities of time and place arise evidently from false assumptions, and by circumscribing the extent of the drama lessen its variety, I cannot think it much to be lamented that they were not known by him, or not observed. Nor, if such another poet could arise, should I very vehemently reproach him that his first act passed at Venice and his next in Cyprus.[45] Such violations of rules merely positive[46] become the comprehensive genius of Shakespeare, and such censures are suitable to the minute and slender criticism of Voltaire:

> *Non usque adeo permiscuit imis*
> *Longus summa dies, ut non, si voce Metelli*
> *Serventur leges, malint a Caesare tolli.*[47]

Yet when I speak thus slightly of dramatic rules, I cannot but recollect how much wit and learning may be produced against me; before such authorities I am afraid to stand, not that I think the present question one of those that are to be decided by mere authority, but because it is to be suspected that these precepts have not been so easily received but for better reasons than I have yet been able to find. The result of my inquiries, in which it would be ludicrous to boast of impartiality, is that the unities of time and place are not essential to a just drama; that though they may sometimes conduce to pleasure, they are always to be sacrificed to the nobler beauties of variety and instruction; and that a play written with nice observation of critical rules is to be contemplated as an elaborate curiosity, as the product of superfluous and ostentatious art, by which is shown, rather what is possible, than what is necessary.

He that without diminution of any other excellence shall preserve all the unities unbroken deserves the like applause with the architect, who shall display all the orders of architecture in a citadel without any deduction from its strength; but the principal beauty of a citadel is to exclude the enemy; and the greatest graces of a play are to copy nature and instruct life.

Perhaps what I have here not dogmatically but deliberatively[48] written may recall the principles of the drama to a new examination. I am almost frighted at my own temerity; and when I estimate the fame and the strength of those that maintain the contrary opinion, am ready to sink down in reverential silence; as Aeneas withdrew from the defence of Troy when he saw Neptune shaking the wall and Juno heading the besiegers.[49]

Those whom my arguments cannot persuade to give their approbation to the judgement of Shakespeare will easily, if they consider the condition of his life, make some allowance for his ignorance.

Every man's performances, to be rightly estimated, must be compared with the state of the age in which he lived and with his own particular opportunities; and though to the reader a book be not worse or better for the circumstances of the author, yet as there is always a silent reference of human works to human abilities, and as the inquiry how far man may extend his designs, or how high he may rate his native force, is of far greater dignity than in what rank we shall place any particular performance, curiosity is always busy to discover the instruments as well as to survey the workmanship, to know how much is to be ascribed to original powers and how much to casual and adventitious help. The palaces of Peru or Mexico were certainly mean and incommodious habitations if compared to the houses of European monarchs; yet who could forbear to view them with astonishment who remembered that they were built without the use of iron?

The English nation in the time of Shakespeare was yet struggling to emerge from barbarity. The philology[50] of Italy had been transplanted hither in the reign of Henry the Eighth; and the learned languages had been successfully cultivated by Lily, Linacre and More; by Pole, Cheke and Gardiner; and afterwards by Smith, Clerke, Haddon and Ascham.[51] Greek was now taught to boys in the principal schools; and those who united elegance with learning read with great diligence the Italian and Spanish poets. But literature[52] was yet confined to professed scholars, or to men and women of high rank. The public was gross and dark; and to be able to read and write was an accomplishment still valued for its rarity.

Nations, like individuals, have their infancy. A people newly awakened to literary curiosity, being yet unacquainted with the true state of things, knows not how to judge of that which is proposed as its resemblance. Whatever is remote from common appearances is always welcome to vulgar, as to childish, credulity; and of a country unenlightened by learning, the whole people is the vulgar. The study of those who then aspired to plebeian learning was laid out upon adventures, giants, dragons and enchantments. *The Death of Arthur*[53] was the favourite volume.

The mind, which has feasted on the luxurious wonders of fiction, has no taste of the insipidity of truth. A play which imitated only the common occurrences of the world would, upon the admirers of *Palmerin* and *Guy of Warwick*,[54] have made little impression; he that wrote for such an audience was under the necessity of looking round for strange events and fabulous transactions; and that incredibility by which maturer knowledge is offended was the chief recommendation of writings to unskilful curiosity.

Our author's plots are generally borrowed from novels, and it is reasonable to suppose that he chose the most popular, such as were read by many and related by more; for his audience could not have followed him through the intricacies of the drama had they not held the thread of the story in their hands.

The stories which we now find only in remoter authors were in his time accessible and familiar. The fable of *As You Like It*, which is supposed to be copied from Chaucer's *Gamelyn*,[55] was a little pamphlet of those times; and old Mr Cibber[56] remembered the tale of Hamlet in plain English prose, which the critics have now to seek in Saxo Grammaticus.

His English histories he took from English chronicles and English ballads; and as the ancient writers were made known to his countrymen by versions, they supplied him with new subjects; he dilated some of Plutarch's lives into plays, when they had been translated by North.[57]

His plots, whether historical or fabulous, are always crowded with incidents by which the attention of a rude people was more easily caught than by sentiment or argumentation; and such is the power of the marvellous, even over those who despise it, that every man finds his mind more strongly seized by the tragedies of Shakespeare than of any other writer; others please us by particular speeches, but he always makes us anxious for the event and has perhaps excelled all but Homer in securing the first purpose of a writer, by exciting restless and unquenchable curiosity and compelling him that reads his work to read it through.

The shows and bustle with which his plays abound have the same original. As knowledge advances, pleasure passes from the eye to the ear, but returns, as it declines, from the ear to the eye. Those to whom our author's labours were exhibited had more skill in pomps or processions than in poetical language and perhaps wanted some visible and discriminated events as comments on the dialogue. He knew how he should most please; and whether his practice is more agreeable to nature, or whether his example has prejudiced the nation, we still find that on our stage something must be done as well as said, and inactive declamation is very coldly heard, however musical or elegant, passionate or sublime.

Voltaire expresses his wonder that our author's extravagances are endured by a nation which has seen the tragedy of *Cato*.[58] Let him be answered that Addison speaks the language of poets, and Shakespeare of men. We find in *Cato* innumerable beauties which enamour us of its author, but we see nothing that acquaints us with human sentiments or human actions; we place it with the fairest and the noblest progeny which judgement propagates by conjunction with learning; but *Othello* is the vigorous and vivacious offspring of observation impregnated by genius. *Cato* affords a splendid exhibition of artificial and fictitious manners, and delivers just and noble sentiments, in diction easy, elevated and harmonious, but its hopes and fears communicate no vibration to the heart; the composition refers us only to the writer; we pronounce the name of *Cato*, but we think on Addison.

The work of a correct and regular writer is a garden accurately formed and diligently planted, varied with shades and scented with flowers; the composition of Shakespeare is a forest, in which oaks extend their branches, and pines tower in the air, interspersed sometimes with weeds and brambles, and sometimes giving shelter to myrtles and to roses; filling the eye with awful pomp and gratifying the mind with endless diversity. Other poets display cabinets of precious rarities, minutely finished, wrought into shape and polished unto brightness. Shakespeare opens a mine which contains gold and diamonds in unexhaustible plenty, though clouded by incrustations, debased by impurities and mingled with a mass of meaner minerals.

It has been much disputed whether Shakespeare owed his excellence to his own native force, or whether he had the common helps of scholastic education, the precepts of critical science and the examples of ancient authors.

There has always prevailed a tradition that Shakespeare wanted learning, that he had no regular education, nor much skill in the dead languages. Jonson, his friend, affirms that 'he had small Latin, and less Greek';[59] who, besides that he had no imaginable temptation to falsehood, wrote at a time when the character and acquisitions of Shakespeare were known to multitudes. His evidence ought therefore to decide the controversy, unless some testimony of equal force could be opposed.

Some have imagined that they have discovered deep learning in many imitations of old writers; but the examples which I have known urged were drawn from books translated in his time; or were such easy coincidences of thought as will happen to all who consider the same subjects; or such remarks on life or axioms of morality as float in conversation and are transmitted through the world in proverbial sentences.

I have found it remarked that in this important sentence, 'Go before, I'll follow', we read a translation of, *I prae, sequar*.[60] I have been told that when Caliban, after a pleasing dream, says, 'I cried to sleep again',[61] the author imitates Anacreon, who had, like every other man, the same wish on the same occasion.

There are a few passages which may pass for imitations, but so few that the exception only confirms the rule; he obtained them from accidental quotations or by oral communication, and as he used what he had, would have used more if he had obtained it.

The Comedy of Errors is confessedly[62] taken from the *Menaechmi* of Plautus; from the only play of Plautus which was then in English.[63] What can be more probable than that he who copied that would have copied more; but that those which were not translated were inaccessible?

Whether he knew the modern languages is uncertain. That his plays have some French scenes proves but little; he might easily procure them to be written, and probably, even though he had known the language in the common degree, he could not have written it without assistance. In the story of Romeo and Juliet he is observed to have followed the English translation, where it deviates from the Italian;[64] but this on the other part proves nothing against his knowledge of the original. He was to copy, not what he knew himself, but what was known to his audience.

It is most likely that he had learned Latin sufficiently to make him acquainted with construction,[65] but that he never advanced to an easy perusal of the Roman authors. Concerning his skill in modern languages, I can find no sufficient ground of determination; but as no imitations of French or Italian authors have been discovered, though the Italian poetry was then high in esteem, I am inclined to believe that he read little more than English and chose for his fables only such tales as he found translated.

That much knowledge is scattered over his works is very justly observed by Pope,[66] but it is often such knowledge as books did not supply. He that will understand Shakespeare must not be content to study him in the closet, he must look for his meaning sometimes among the sports of the field and sometimes among the manufactures of the shop.

There is, however, proof enough that he was a very diligent reader, nor was our language then so indigent[67] of books but that he might very liberally indulge his curiosity without excursion into foreign literature. Many of the Roman authors were translated, and some of the Greek; the Reformation had filled the kingdom with theological learning; most of the topics of human disquisition had found English writers; and poetry had been cultivated, not only with diligence but success. This was a stock of knowledge sufficient for a mind so capable of appropriating and improving it.

But the greater part of his excellence was the product of his own genius. He found the English stage in a state of the utmost rudeness; no essays either in tragedy or comedy had appeared from which it could be discovered to what degree of delight either one or other might be carried. Neither character nor dialogue were yet understood. Shakespeare may be truly said to have introduced them both amongst us and in some of his happier scenes to have carried them both to the utmost height.

By what gradations of improvement he proceeded is not easily known; for the chronology of his works is yet unsettled. Rowe is of opinion that 'perhaps we are not to look for his beginning, like those of other writers, in his least perfect works; art had so little and nature so large a share in what he did, that for aught I know,' says he, 'the performances of his youth, as they were the most vigorous, were the best.'[68] But the power of nature is only the power of using to any certain purpose the materials which diligence procures or opportunity supplies. Nature gives no man knowledge, and when images are collected by study and experience, can only assist in combining or applying them. Shakespeare, however favoured by nature, could impart only what he had learned; and as he must increase his ideas, like other mortals, by gradual acquisition, he, like them, grew wiser as he grew older, could display life better as he knew it more, and instruct with more efficacy as he was himself more amply instructed.

There is a vigilance of observation and accuracy of distinction which books and precepts cannot confer; from this almost all original and native excellence proceeds. Shakespeare must have looked upon mankind with perspicacity, in the highest degree curious and attentive. Other writers borrow their characters from preceding writers and diversify them only by the accidental appendages of present manners; the dress is a little varied, but the body is the same. Our author had both matter and form to provide; for, except the characters of Chaucer, to whom I think he is not much indebted, there were no writers in English, and perhaps not many in other modern languages, which showed life in its native colours.

The contest about the original benevolence or malignity of man had not yet commenced. Speculation had not yet attempted to analyse the mind, to trace the passions to their sources, to unfold the seminal principles of vice and virtue, or sound the depths of the heart for the motives of action. All those inquiries which, from that time that human nature became the fashionable study, have been made, sometimes with nice discernment, but often with idle subtlety, were yet unattempted. The tales with which the infancy of learning was satisfied exhibited only the superficial appearances of action, related the events but omitted the causes, and were formed for such as delighted in wonders rather than in truth. Mankind was not then to be studied in the closet; he that would know the world was under the necessity of gleaning his own remarks by mingling as he could in its business and amusements.

Boyle congratulated himself upon his high birth, because it favoured his curiosity by facilitating his access.[69] Shakespeare had no such advantage; he came to London a needy adventurer and lived for a time by very mean employments. Many works of genius and learning have been performed in states of life that appear very little favourable to thought or to inquiry; so many, that he who considers them is inclined to think that he sees enterprise and perseverance predominating over all external agency, and bidding help and hindrance vanish before them. The genius of Shakespeare was not to be depressed by the weight of poverty, nor limited by the narrow conversation to which men in want are inevitably condemned; the encumbrances of his fortune were shaken from his mind, 'as dew-drops from a lion's mane'.[70]

Though he had so many difficulties to encounter and so little assistance to surmount them, he has been able to obtain an exact knowledge of many modes of life and many casts of native dispositions; to vary them with great multiplicity; to mark them by nice distinctions; and to show them in full view by proper combinations. In this part of his performances he had none to imitate, but has himself been imitated by all succeeding writers; and it may be doubted whether from all his successors more maxims of theoretical knowledge or more rules of practical prudence can be collected than he alone has given to his country.

Nor was his attention confined to the actions of men; he was an exact surveyor of the inanimate world; his descriptions have always some peculiarities gathered by contemplating things as they really exist. It may be observed that the oldest poets of many nations preserve their reputation, and that the following generations of wit, after a short celebrity, sink into oblivion. The first, whoever they be, must take their sentiments and descriptions immediately from knowledge; the resemblance is therefore just, their descriptions are verified by every eye and their sentiments acknowledged by every breast. Those whom their fame invites to the same studies copy partly them and partly nature, till the books of one age gain such authority as to stand in the place of nature to another, and imitation, always deviating a little, becomes at last capricious and casual. Shakespeare, whether life or nature be his subject, shows plainly that he has seen with his own eyes; he gives the image which he receives, not weakened or distorted by the intervention of any other mind; the ignorant feel his representations to be just and the learned see that they are complete.

Perhaps it would not be easy to find any author, except Homer, who invented so much as Shakespeare, who so much advanced the studies which he cultivated, or effused[71] so much novelty upon his age or country. The form, the characters, the language and the shows of the English drama are his. 'He seems,' says Dennis, 'to have been the very original of our English tragical harmony, that is, the harmony of blank verse, diversified often by disyllable and trisyllable terminations. For the diversity distinguishes it from heroic harmony, and by bringing it nearer to common use makes it more proper to gain attention and more fit for action and dialogue. Such verse we make when we are writing prose; we make such verse in common conversation.'[72]

I know not whether this praise is rigorously just. The disyllable termination which the critic rightly appropriates to the drama is to be found (though, I think, not in *Gorboduc*,[73] which is confessedly before our author) yet in *Hieronimo*,[74] of which the date is not certain, but which there is reason to believe at least as old as his earliest plays. This however is certain, that he is the first who taught either tragedy or comedy to please, there being no theatrical piece of any older writer of which the name is known, except to antiquaries and collectors of books, which are sought because they are scarce, and would not have been scarce had they been much esteemed.

To him we must ascribe the praise, unless Spenser may divide it with him, of having first discovered to how much smoothness and harmony the English language could be softened. He has speeches, perhaps sometimes scenes, which have all the delicacy of Rowe, without his effeminacy. He endeavours indeed commonly to strike by the force and vigour of his dialogue, but he never executes his purpose better than when he tries to soothe by softness.

Yet it must be at last confessed that as we owe everything to him, he owes something to us; that if much of his praise is paid by perception and judgement, much is likewise given by custom and veneration. We fix our eyes upon his graces and turn them from his deformities and endure in him what we should in another loathe or despise. If we endured without praising, respect for the father of our drama might excuse us; but I have seen in the book of some modern critic[75] a collection of anomalies, which show that he has corrupted language by every mode of depravation, but which his admirer has accumulated as a monument of honour.

He has scenes of undoubted and perpetual excellence, but perhaps not one play which, if it were now exhibited as the work of a contemporary writer, would be heard to the conclusion. I am indeed far from thinking that his works were wrought to his own ideas of perfection; when they were such as would satisfy the audience, they satisfied the writer. It is seldom that authors, though more studious of fame than Shakespeare, rise much above the standard of their own age; to add a little to what is best will always be sufficient for present praise, and those who find themselves exalted into fame are willing to credit their encomiasts and to spare the labour of contending with themselves.

It does not appear that Shakespeare thought his works worthy of posterity, that he levied any ideal[76] tribute upon future times, or had any further prospect than of present popularity and present profit. When his plays had been acted, his hope was at an end; he solicited no addition of honour from the reader. He therefore made no scruple to repeat the same jests in many dialogues, or to entangle different plots by the same knot of perplexity, which may be at least forgiven him by those who recollect that of Congreve's four comedies, two[77] are concluded by a marriage in a mask, by a deception which perhaps never happened and which, whether likely or not, he did not invent.

So careless was this great poet of future fame that, though he retired to ease and plenty while he was yet little 'declined into the vale of years' [*Othello* III.3.262], before he could be disgusted with fatigue, or disabled by infirmity, he made no collection of his works, nor desired to rescue those that had been already published from the depravations that obscured them, or secure to the rest a better destiny, by giving them to the world in their genuine state.

Of the plays which bear the name of Shakespeare in the late editions, the greater part were not published till about seven years after his death, and the few which appeared in his life are apparently thrust into the world without the care of the author and therefore probably without his knowledge.

Of all the publishers, clandestine or professed, the[78] negligence and unskilfulness has by the late revisers been sufficiently shown. The faults of all are indeed numerous and gross and have not only corrupted many passages perhaps beyond recovery, but have brought others into suspicion which are only obscured by obsolete phraseology, or by the writer's unskilfulness and affectation. To alter is more easy than to explain, and temerity is a more common quality than diligence. Those who saw that they must employ conjecture to a certain degree were willing to indulge it a little further. Had the author published his own works we should have sat quietly down to disentangle his intricacies and clear his obscurities; but now we tear what we cannot loose and eject what we happen not to understand.

The faults are more than could have happened without the concurrence of many causes. The style of Shakespeare was in itself ungrammatical, perplexed and obscure; his works were transcribed for the players by those who may be supposed to have seldom understood them; they were transmitted by copiers equally unskilful, who still multiplied errors; they were perhaps sometimes mutilated by the actors, for the sake of shortening the speeches; and were at last printed without correction of the press.

In this state they remained, not as Dr Warburton supposes[79] because they were unregarded, but because the editor's art was not yet applied to modern languages, and our ancestors were accustomed to so much negligence of English printers that they could very patiently endure it. At last an edition was undertaken by Rowe; not because a poet was to be published by a poet, for Rowe seems to have thought very little on correction or explanation, but that our author's works might appear like those of his fraternity, with the appendages of a life and recommendatory preface. Rowe has been clamorously blamed for not performing what he did not undertake, and it is time that justice be done him, by confessing that though he seems to have had no thought of corruption beyond the printer's errors, yet he has made many emendations, if they were not made before, which his successors have received without acknowledgement and which, if they had produced them, would have filled pages and pages with censures of the stupidity by which the faults were committed, with displays of the absurdities which they involved, with ostentatious expositions of the new reading and self-congratulations on the happiness of discovering it.

As of the other editors I have preserved the prefaces, I have likewise borrowed the author's life from Rowe,[80] though not written with much elegance or spirit; it relates however what is now to be known, and therefore deserves to pass through all succeeding publications.

Preface to the Edition of Shakespeare's Plays 149

The nation had been for many years content enough with Mr Rowe's performance, when Mr Pope made them acquainted with the true state of Shakespeare's text, showed that it was extremely corrupt, and gave reason to hope that there were means of reforming it. He collated the old copies, which none had thought to examine before, and restored many lines to their integrity; but, by a very compendious[81] criticism, he rejected whatever he disliked and thought more of amputation than of cure.

I know not why he is commended by Dr Warburton for distinguishing the genuine from the spurious plays. In this choice he exerted no judgement of his own; the plays which he received were given by Heming and Condell, the first editors; and those which he rejected, though according to the licentiousness of the press in those times they were printed during Shakespeare's life, with his name, had been omitted by his friends and were never added to his works before the edition of 1664, from which they were copied by the later printers.[82]

This was a work which Pope seems to have thought unworthy of his abilities, being not able to suppress his contempt of 'the dull duty of an editor'.[83] He understood but half his undertaking. The duty of a collator is indeed dull yet, like other tedious tasks, is very necessary; but an emendatory critic would ill discharge his duty without qualities very different from dullness. In perusing a corrupted piece, he must have before him all possibilities of meaning, with all possibilities of expression. Such must be his comprehension of thought and such his copiousness of language. Out of many readings possible, he must be able to select that which best suits with the state, opinions and modes of language prevailing in every age and with his author's particular cast of thought and turn of expression. Such must be his knowledge and such his taste. Conjectural criticism demands more than humanity possesses, and he that exercises it with most praise has very frequent need of indulgence. Let us now be told no more of the dull duty of an editor.

Confidence is the common consequence of success. They whose excellence of any kind has been loudly celebrated are ready to conclude that their powers are universal. Pope's edition fell below his own expectations, and he was so much offended when he was found to have left anything for others to do that he passed the latter part of his life in a state of hostility with verbal criticism.[84]

I have retained all his notes, that no fragment of so great a writer may be lost; his Preface, valuable alike for elegance of composition and justness of remark, and containing a general criticism on his author so extensive that little can be added and so exact that little can be disputed, every editor has an interest to suppress, but that every reader would demand its insertion.

Pope was succeeded by Theobald, a man of narrow comprehension and small acquisitions, with no native and intrinsic splendour of genius, with little of the artificial light of learning, but zealous for minute accuracy and not negligent in pursuing it. He collated the ancient copies and rectified many errors. A man so anxiously scrupulous might have been expected to do more, but what little he did was commonly right.

In his reports of copies and editions he is not to be trusted without examination. He speaks sometimes indefinitely of copies, when he has only one. In his enumeration of editions he mentions the two first folios as of high, and the third folio as of middle authority; but the truth is that the first is equivalent to all others and that the rest only deviate from it by the printer's negligence. Whoever has any of the folios has all, excepting those diversities which mere reiteration of editions will produce. I collated them all at the beginning, but afterwards used only the first.

Of his notes I have generally retained those which he retained himself in his second edition, except when they were confuted by subsequent annotators, or were too minute to merit preservation. I have sometimes adopted his restoration of a comma, without inserting the panegyric in which he celebrated himself for his achievement. The exuberant excrescence of his diction I have often lopped, his triumphant exultations over Pope and Rowe I have sometimes suppressed, and his contemptible ostentation I have frequently concealed; but I have in some places shown him, as he would have shown himself, for the reader's diversion, that the inflated emptiness of some notes may justify or excuse the contraction of the rest.

Theobald, thus weak and ignorant, thus mean and faithless, thus petulant and ostentatious, by the good luck of having Pope for his enemy, has escaped, and escaped alone, with reputation from this undertaking. So willingly does the world support those who solicit favour against those who command reverence; and so easily is he praised whom no man can envy.

Our author fell then into the hands of Sir Thomas Hanmer, the Oxford editor, a man in my opinion eminently qualified by nature for such studies. He had, what is the first requisite to emendatory criticism, that intuition by which the poet's intention is immediately discovered, and that dexterity of intellect which despatches its work by the easiest means. He had undoubtedly read much; his acquaintance with customs, opinions and traditions seems to have been large; and he is often learned without show. He seldom passes what he does not understand without an attempt to find or to make a meaning, and sometimes hastily makes what a little more attention would have found. He is solicitous to reduce to grammar what he could not be sure that his author intended to be grammatical. Shakespeare regarded more the series of ideas than of words; and his language, not being designed for the reader's desk, was all that he desired it to be if it conveyed his meaning to the audience.

Hanmer's care of the metre has been too violently censured.[85] He found the measures reformed in so many passages by the silent labours of some editors, with the silent acquiescence of the rest, that he thought himself allowed to extend a little further the licence, which had already been carried so far without reprehension; and of his corrections in general it must be confessed that they are often just, and made commonly with the least possible violation of the text.

But by inserting his emendations, whether invented or borrowed, into the page without any notice of varying copies, he has appropriated the labour of his predecessors and made his own edition of little authority. His confidence indeed, both in himself and others, was too great; he supposes all to be right that was done by Pope and Theobald; he seems not to suspect a critic of fallibility, and it was but reasonable that he should claim what he so liberally granted.

As he never writes without careful inquiry and diligent consideration, I have received all his notes and believe that every reader will wish for more.

Of the last editor it is more difficult to speak.[86] Respect is due to high place, tenderness to living reputation, and veneration to genius and learning; but he cannot be justly offended at that liberty of which he has himself so frequently given an example, nor very solicitous what is thought of notes which he ought never to have considered as part of his serious employments and which, I suppose, since the ardour of composition is remitted, he no longer numbers among his happy effusions.

The original and predominant error of his commentary is acquiescence in his first thoughts; that precipitation which is produced by consciousness of quick discernment; and that confidence which presumes to do, by surveying the surface, what labour only can perform, by penetrating the bottom. His notes exhibit sometimes perverse interpretations and sometimes improbable conjectures; he at one time gives the author more profundity of meaning than the sentence admits, and at another discovers absurdities where the sense is plain to every other reader. But his emendations are likewise often happy and just; and his interpretation of obscure passages learned and sagacious.

Of his notes, I have commonly rejected those against which the general voice of the public has exclaimed, or which their own incongruity immediately condemns, and which, I suppose, the author himself would desire to be forgotten. Of the rest, to part I have given the highest approbation by inserting the offered reading in the text; part I have left to the judgement of the reader, as doubtful, though specious; and part I have censured without reserve, but I am sure without bitterness of malice and, I hope, without wantonness of insult.

It is no pleasure to me, in revising my volumes, to observe how much paper is wasted in confutation. Whoever considers the revolutions of learning and the various questions of greater or less importance upon which wit and reason have exercised their powers, must lament the unsuccessfulness of inquiry and the slow advances of truth, when he reflects that great part of the labour of every writer is only the destruction of those that went before him. The first care of the builder of a new system is to demolish the fabrics which are standing. The chief desire of him that comments an author is to show how much other commentators have corrupted and obscured him. The opinions prevalent in one age, as truths above the reach of controversy, are confuted and rejected in another, and rise again to reception in remoter times. Thus the human mind is kept in motion without progress. Thus sometimes truth and error, and sometimes contrarieties of error, take each other's place by reciprocal invasion. The tide of seeming knowledge which is poured over one generation retires and leaves another naked and barren; the sudden meteors of intelligence which for a while appear to shoot their beams into the regions of obscurity, on a sudden withdraw their lustre and leave mortals again to grope their way.

These elevations and depressions of renown and the contradictions to which all improvers of knowledge must for ever be exposed, since they are not escaped by the highest and brightest of mankind, may surely be endured with patience by critics and annotators, who can rank themselves but as the satellites of their authors. 'How canst thou beg for life,' says Homer's hero to his captive, 'when thou knowest that thou art now to suffer only what must another day be suffered by Achilles?'[87]

Dr Warburton had a name sufficient to confer celebrity on those who could exalt themselves into antagonists, and his notes have raised a clamour too loud to be distinct. His chief assailants are the authors of *The Canons of Criticism* and of the *Revisal of Shakespeare's Text*;[88] of whom one ridicules his errors with airy petulance, suitable enough to the levity of the controversy; the other attacks them with gloomy malignity, as if he were dragging to justice an assassin or incendiary. The one stings like a fly, sucks a little blood, takes a gay flutter and returns for more; the other bites like a viper and would be glad to leave inflammations and gangrene behind him. When I think on one, with his confederates, I remember the danger of Coriolanus, who was afraid that 'girls with spits, and boys with stones, should slay him in puny battle'; when the other crosses my imagination, I remember the prodigy in *Macbeth*:

> A falcon towering in his pride of place,
> Was by a mousing owl hawked at and killed.[89]

Let me, however, do them justice. One is a wit, and one a scholar. They have both shown acuteness sufficient in the discovery of faults and have both advanced some probable interpretations of obscure passages; but when they aspire to conjecture and emendation, it appears how falsely we all estimate our own abilities, and the little which they have been able to perform might have taught them more candour to the endeavours of others.

Before Dr Warburton's edition, *Critical Observations on Shakespeare* had been published by Mr Upton,[90] a man skilled in languages and acquainted with books, but who seems to have had no great vigour of genius or nicety of taste. Many of his explanations are curious and useful, but he likewise, though he professed to oppose the licentious confidence of editors and adhere to the old copies, is unable to restrain the rage of emendation, though his ardour is ill seconded by his skill. Every cold empiric,[91] when his heart is expanded by a successful experiment, swells into a theorist and the laborious collator at some unlucky moment frolics in conjecture.

Critical, Historical and Explanatory Notes have been likewise published upon Shakespeare by Dr Grey,[92] whose diligent perusal of the old English writers has enabled him to make some useful observations. What he undertook he has well enough performed, but as he neither attempts judicial nor emendatory criticism, he employs rather his memory than his sagacity. It were to be wished that all would endeavour to imitate his modesty who have not been able to surpass his knowledge.

I can say with great sincerity of all my predecessors, what I hope will hereafter be said of me, that not one has left

Shakespeare without improvement, nor is there one to whom I have not been indebted for assistance and information. Whatever I have taken from them it was my intention to refer to its original author, and it is certain that what I have not given to another, I believed when I wrote it to be my own. In some perhaps I have been anticipated; but if I am ever found to encroach upon the remarks of any other commentator, I am willing that the honour, be it more or less, should be transferred to the first claimant, for his right and his alone stands above dispute; the second can prove his pretensions only to himself, nor can himself always distinguish invention, with sufficient certainty, from recollection.

They have all been treated by me with candour, which they have not been careful of observing to one another. It is not easy to discover from what cause the acrimony of a scholiast[93] can naturally proceed. The subjects to be discussed by him are of very small importance; they involve neither property nor liberty; nor favour the interest of sect or party. The various readings of copies and different interpretations of a passage seem to be questions that might exercise the wit without engaging the passions. But whether it be that 'small things make mean men proud',[94] and vanity catches small occasions; or that all contrariety of opinion, even in those that can defend it no longer, makes proud men angry; there is often found in commentaries a spontaneous strain of invective and contempt, more eager and venomous than is vented by the most furious controvertist[95] in politics against those whom he is hired to defame.

Perhaps the lightness of the matter may conduce to the vehemence of the agency; when the truth to be investigated is so near to inexistence as to escape attention, its bulk is to be enlarged by rage and exclamation. That to which all would be indifferent in its original state may attract notice when the fate of a name is appended to it. A commentator has indeed great temptations to supply by turbulence what he wants of dignity, to beat his little gold to a spacious surface, to work that to foam which no art or diligence can exalt to spirit.

The notes which I have borrowed or written are either

illustrative, by which difficulties are explained; or judicial, by which faults and beauties are remarked; or emendatory, by which depravations are corrected.

The explanations transcribed from others, if I do not subjoin any other interpretation, I suppose commonly to be right, at least I intend by acquiescence to confess that I have nothing better to propose.

After the labours of all the editors, I found many passages which appeared to me likely to obstruct the greater number of readers and thought it my duty to facilitate their passage. It is impossible for an expositor not to write too little for some and too much for others. He can only judge what is necessary by his own experience; and how long soever he may deliberate, will at last explain many lines which the learned will think impossible to be mistaken and omit many for which the ignorant will want his help. These are censures merely relative and must be quietly endured. I have endeavoured to be neither superfluously copious, nor scrupulously reserved, and hope that I have made my author's meaning accessible to many who before were frighted from perusing him, and contributed something to the public, by diffusing innocent and rational pleasure.

The complete explanation of an author not systematic and consequential, but desultory and vagrant, abounding in casual allusions and light hints, is not to be expected from any single scholiast. All personal reflections, when names are suppressed, must be in a few years irrecoverably obliterated; and customs, too minute to attract the notice of law, such as modes of dress, formalities of conversation, rules of visits, disposition of furniture and practices of ceremony, which naturally find places in familiar dialogue, are so fugitive and unsubstantial that they are not easily retained or recovered. What can be known will be collected by chance, from the recesses of obscure and obsolete papers, perused commonly with some other view. Of this knowledge every man has some, and none has much; but when an author has engaged the public attention, those who can add anything to his illustration communicate their discoveries and time produces what had eluded diligence.

To time I have been obliged to resign many passages which, though I did not understand them, will perhaps hereafter be explained, having, I hope, illustrated some which others have neglected or mistaken, sometimes by short remarks, or marginal directions, such as every editor has added at his will and often by comments more laborious[96] than the matter will seem to deserve; but that which is most difficult is not always most important, and to an editor nothing is a trifle by which his author is obscured.

The poetical beauties or defects I have not been very diligent to observe. Some plays have more and some fewer judicial observations, not in proportion to their difference of merit, but because I gave this part of my design to chance and to caprice. The reader, I believe, is seldom pleased to find his opinion anticipated; it is natural to delight more in what we find or make than in what we receive. Judgement, like other faculties, is improved by practice and its advancement is hindered by submission to dictatorial decisions, as the memory grows torpid by the use of a table book.[97] Some initiation is, however, necessary; of all skill, part is infused by precept, and part is obtained by habit; I have therefore shown so much as may enable the candidate of criticism to discover the rest.

To the end of most plays I have added short strictures,[98] containing a general censure of faults or praise of excellence; in which I know not how much I have concurred with the current opinion; but I have not, by any affectation of singularity, deviated from it. Nothing is minutely and particularly examined, and therefore it is to be supposed that in the plays which are condemned there is much to be praised, and in those which are praised much to be condemned.

The part of criticism in which the whole succession of editors has laboured with the greatest diligence, which has occasioned the most arrogant ostentation and excited the keenest acrimony, is the emendation of corrupted passages, to which the public attention having been first drawn by the violence of the contention between Pope and Theobald, has been continued by the persecution which, with a kind of conspiracy, has been since raised against all the publishers of Shakespeare.

That many passages have passed in a state of depravation through all the editions is indubitably certain; of these the restoration is only to be attempted by collation of copies or sagacity of conjecture. The collator's province is safe and easy, the conjecturer's perilous and difficult. Yet as the greater part of the plays are extant only in one copy, the peril must not be avoided nor the difficulty refused.

Of the readings which this emulation of amendment has hitherto produced, some from the labours of every publisher I have advanced into the text; those are to be considered as in my opinion sufficiently supported; some I have rejected without mention, as evidently erroneous; some I have left in the notes without censure or approbation, as resting in equipoise between objection and defence; and some, which seemed specious but not right, I have inserted with a subsequent animadversion.[99]

Having classed the observations of others, I was at last to try what I could substitute for their mistakes and how I could supply their omissions. I collated such copies as I could procure and wished for more, but have not found the collectors of these rarities very communicative.[100] Of the editions which chance or kindness put into my hands I have given an enumeration that I may not be blamed for neglecting what I had not the power to do.

By examining the old copies, I soon found that the later publishers, with all their boasts of diligence, suffered many passages to stand unauthorized and contented themselves with Rowe's regulation of the text, even where they knew it to be arbitrary and with a little consideration might have found it to be wrong. Some of these alterations are only the ejection of a word for one that appeared to him more elegant or more intelligible. These corruptions I have often silently rectified; for the history of our language and the true force of our words can only be preserved by keeping the text of authors free from adulteration. Others, and those very frequent, smoothed the cadence or regulated the measure; on these I have not exercised the same rigour; if only a word was transposed, or a particle inserted or omitted, I have sometimes suffered the line to stand; for the inconstancy of the copies is such that some liberties may be easily permitted. But this practice I have not suffered to proceed far, having restored the primitive diction wherever it could for any reason be preferred.

The emendations which comparison of copies supplied I have inserted in the text; sometimes where the improvement was slight, without notice, and sometimes with an account of the reasons of the change.

Conjecture, though it be sometimes unavoidable, I have not wantonly nor licentiously indulged. It has been my settled principle that the reading of the ancient books is probably true and therefore is not to be disturbed for the sake of elegance, perspicuity[101] or mere improvement of the sense. For though much credit is not due to the fidelity, nor any to the judgement of the first publishers, yet they who had the copy before their eyes were more likely to read it right than we who read it only by imagination. But it is evident that they have often made strange mistakes by ignorance or negligence, and that therefore something may be properly attempted by criticism, keeping the middle way between presumption and timidity.

Such criticism I have attempted to practise, and where any passage appeared inextricably perplexed, have endeavoured to discover how it may be recalled to sense with least violence. But my first labour is always to turn the old text on every side and try if there be any interstice[102] through which light can find its way; nor would Huetius[103] himself condemn me as refusing the trouble of research for the ambition of alteration. In this modest industry I have not been unsuccessful. I have rescued many lines from the violations of temerity and secured many scenes from the inroads of correction. I have adopted the Roman sentiment, that it is more honourable to save a citizen than to kill an enemy, and have been more careful to protect than to attack.

I have preserved the common distribution of the plays into acts, though I believe it to be in almost all the plays void of authority. Some of those which are divided in the later editions have no division in the first folio, and some that are divided in the folio have no division in the preceding copies. The settled mode of the theatre requires four intervals in the play, but few, if any, of our author's compositions can be properly distributed in that manner. An act is so much of the drama as passes without intervention of time or change of place. A pause makes a new act. In every real, and therefore in every imitative action, the intervals may be more or fewer, the restriction of five acts being accidental and arbitrary. This Shakespeare knew, and this he practised; his plays were written and at first printed in one unbroken continuity, and ought now to be exhibited with short pauses, interposed as often as the scene is changed or any considerable time is required to pass. This method would at once quell a thousand absurdities.

In restoring the author's works to their integrity, I have considered the punctuation as wholly in my power; for what could be their care of colons and commas who corrupted words and sentences? Whatever could be done by adjusting points[104] is therefore silently performed, in some plays with much diligence, in others with less; it is hard to keep a busy eye steadily fixed upon evanescent[105] atoms or a discursive mind upon evanescent truth.

The same liberty has been taken with a few particles or other words of slight effect. I have sometimes inserted or omitted them without notice. I have done that sometimes which the other editors have done always, and which indeed the state of the text may sufficiently justify.

The greater part of readers, instead of blaming us for passing trifles, will wonder that on mere trifles so much labour is expended, with such importance of debate and such solemnity of diction. To these I answer with confidence that they are judging of an art which they do not understand; yet cannot much reproach them with their ignorance, nor promise that they would become in general, by learning criticism, more useful, happier or wiser.

As I practised conjecture more, I learned to trust it less; and after I had printed a few plays, resolved to insert none of my own readings in the text. Upon this caution I now congratulate myself, for every day increases my doubt of my emendations.

Since I have confined my imagination to the margin, it must not be considered as very reprehensible if I have suffered it to play some freaks in its own dominion. There is no danger in conjecture if it be proposed as conjecture; and while the text remains uninjured, those changes may be safely offered which are not considered even by him that offers them as necessary or safe.

If my readings are of little value, they have not been ostentatiously displayed or importunately obtruded. I could have written longer notes, for the art of writing notes is not of difficult attainment. The work is performed, first by railing at the stupidity, negligence, ignorance and asinine tastelessness of the former editors, and showing from all that goes before and all that follows the inelegance and absurdity of the old reading; then by proposing something which to superficial readers would seem specious, but which the editor rejects with indignation; then by producing the true reading with a long paraphrase, and concluding with loud acclamations on the discovery and a sober wish for the advancement and prosperity of genuine criticism.

All this may be done, and perhaps done sometimes without impropriety. But I have always suspected that the reading is right which requires many words to prove it wrong; and the emendation wrong that cannot without so much labour appear to be right. The justness of a happy restoration strikes at once, and the moral precept may be well applied to criticism, *quod dubitas ne feceris*.[106]

To dread the shore which he sees spread with wrecks is natural to the sailor. I had before my eye so many critical adventures ended in miscarriage that caution was forced upon me. I encountered in every page Wit struggling with its own sophistry, and Learning confused by the multiplicity of its views. I was forced to censure those whom I admired and could not but reflect, while I was dispossessing their emendations, how soon the same fate might happen to my own, and how many of the readings which I have corrected may be by some other editor defended and established.

> Critics I saw, that others' names deface,
> And fix their own, with labour, in the place;
> Their own, like others, soon their place resigned,
> Or disappeared, and left the first behind.
> POPE[107]

That a conjectural critic should often be mistaken cannot be wonderful, either to others or himself, if it be considered that in his art there is no system, no principal and axiomatical truth that regulates subordinate positions. His chance of error is renewed at every attempt; an oblique view of the passage, a slight misapprehension of a phrase, a casual inattention to the parts connected, is sufficient to make him not only fail, but fail ridiculously; and when he succeeds best, he produces perhaps but one reading of many probable, and he that suggests another will always be able to dispute his claims.

It is an unhappy state in which danger is hid under pleasure. The allurements of emendation are scarcely resistible. Conjecture has all the joy and all the pride of invention,[108] and he that has once started a happy change is too much delighted to consider what objections may rise against it.

Yet conjectural criticism has been of great use in the learned world; nor is it my intention to depreciate a study that has exercised so many mighty minds, from the revival of learning to our own age, from the Bishop of Aleria to English Bentley.[109] The critics on ancient authors have, in the exercise of their sagacity, many assistances which the editor of Shakespeare is condemned to want. They are employed upon grammatical and settled languages, whose construction contributes so much to perspicuity that Homer has fewer passages unintelligible than Chaucer. The words have not only a known regimen[110] but invariable quantities, which direct and confine the choice. There are commonly more manuscripts than one; and they do not often conspire in the same mistakes. Yet Scaliger could confess to Salmasius how little satisfaction his emendations gave him: *Illudunt nobis conjecturae nostrae, quarum nos pudet, posteaquam in meliores codices incidimus.*[111] And Lipsius could complain that critics were making faults by trying to remove them, *Ut olim vitiis, ita nunc remediis laboratur.*[112] And indeed, where mere conjecture is to be used, the emendations of Scaliger and Lipsius, notwithstanding their wonderful sagacity and erudition, are often vague and disputable, like mine or Theobald's.

Perhaps I may not be more censured for doing wrong than for doing little; for raising in the public expectations which at last I have not answered. The expectation of ignorance is indefinite, and that of knowledge is often tyrannical. It is hard to satisfy those who know not what to demand, or those who demand by design what they think impossible to be done. I have indeed disappointed no opinion more than my own; yet I have endeavoured to perform my task with no slight solicitude. Not a single passage in the whole work has appeared to me corrupt which I have not attempted to restore; or obscure which I have not endeavoured to illustrate. In many I have failed like others; and from many, after all my efforts, I have retreated and confessed the repulse. I have not passed over with affected superiority what is equally difficult to the reader and to myself, but where I could not instruct him, have owned my ignorance. I might easily have accumulated a mass of seeming learning upon easy scenes; but it ought not to be imputed to negligence that, where nothing was necessary, nothing has been done, or that, where others have said enough, I have said no more.

Notes are often necessary, but they are necessary evils. Let him that is yet unacquainted with the powers of Shakespeare, and who desires to feel the highest pleasure that the drama can give, read every play from the first scene to the last, with utter negligence of all his commentators. When his fancy is once on the wing, let it not stoop at correction or explanation. When his attention is strongly engaged, let it disdain alike to turn aside to the name of Theobald and of Pope. Let him read on through brightness and obscurity, through integrity and corruption; let him preserve his comprehension of the dialogue and his interest in the fable. And when the pleasures of novelty have ceased, let him attempt exactness and read the commentators.

Particular passages are cleared by notes, but the general effect of the work is weakened. The mind is refrigerated by interruption; the thoughts are diverted from the principal subject; the reader is weary, he suspects not why; and at last throws away the book which he has too diligently studied.

Parts are not to be examined till the whole has been surveyed; there is a kind of intellectual remoteness necessary for the comprehension of any great work in its full design and its true proportions; a close approach shows the smaller niceties, but the beauty of the whole is discerned no longer.

It is not very grateful to consider how little the succession of editors has added to this author's power of pleasing. He was read, admired, studied and imitated while he was yet deformed with all the improprieties which ignorance and neglect could accumulate upon him; while the reading was yet not rectified nor his allusions understood; yet then did Dryden pronounce that:

Shakespeare was the man who of all modern and perhaps ancient poets had the largest and most comprehensive soul. All the images of nature were still present to him, and he drew them not laboriously, but luckily: when he describes anything, you more than see it, you feel it too. Those who accuse him to have wanted learning give him the greater commendation; he was naturally learned: he needed not the spectacles of books to read nature; he looked inwards and found her there. I cannot say he is everywhere alike; were he so, I should do him injury to compare him with the greatest of mankind. He is many times flat and insipid; his comic wit degenerating into clenches, his serious swelling into bombast. But he is always great when some great occasion is presented to him. No man can say he ever had a fit subject for his wit and did not then raise himself as high above the rest of poets.

Quantum lenta solent inter viburna cupressi.[113]

It is to be lamented that such a writer should want a commentary; that his language should become obsolete or his sentiments obscure. But it is vain to carry wishes beyond the condition of human things; that which must happen to all has happened to Shakespeare, by accident and time; and more than has been suffered by any other writer since the use of types has been suffered by him through his own negligence of fame or perhaps by that superiority of mind which despised its own performances when it compared them with its powers, and judged those works unworthy to be preserved which the critics of following ages were to contend for the fame of restoring and explaining.

Among these candidates of inferior fame, I am now to stand the judgement of the public; and wish that I could confidently produce my commentary as equal to the encouragement which I have had the honour of receiving. Every work of this kind is by its nature deficient, and I should feel little solicitude about the sentence were it to be pronounced only by the skilful and the learned.

SELECTIONS FROM THE NOTES TO THE EDITION OF SHAKESPEARE'S PLAYS
(1765)

THE TEMPEST

I.1.1
[Stage direction] *Enter a Shipmaster and a Boatswain*

In this naval dialogue, perhaps the first example of sailor's language exhibited on the stage, there are, as I have been told by a skilful navigator, some inaccuracies and contradictory orders.

I.1.28
GONZALO I have great comfort from this fellow.

It may be observed of Gonzalo that, being the only good man that appears with the king, he is the only man that preserves his cheerfulness in the wreck and his hope on the island.

I.2.250
PROSPERO   Dost thou forget
   From what a torment I did free thee?

That the character and conduct of Prospero may be understood something must be known of the system of enchantment which supplied all the marvellous found in the romances of the middle ages. This system seems to be founded on the opinion that the fallen spirits, having different degrees of guilt, had different habitations allotted them at their expulsion, some being confined in hell, 'some', as Hooker,[1] who delivers the opinion of our poet's age, expresses it, 'dispersed in air, some on earth, some in water, others in caves, dens or minerals under the earth'. Of these, some were more malignant and mischievous than others. The earthy spirits seem to have been thought the most depraved and the aerial the least vitiated. Thus Prospero observes of Ariel:

> . . . thou wast a spirit too delicate
> To act her *earthy* and abhorred commands.
> [I.2.272]

Over these spirits a power might be obtained by certain rites performed or charms learned. This power was called the *Black Art*, or Knowledge of Enchantment. The enchanter being, as King James observes in his *Demonology*, one 'who commands the devil, whereas the witch serves him'. Those who thought best of this art, the existence of which was, I am afraid, believed very seriously, held that certain sounds and characters had a physical power over spirits and compelled their agency; others who condemned the practice, which in reality was surely never practised, were of opinion with more reason that the power of charms arose *only* from compact and was no more than the spirits voluntarily allowed them for the seduction of Man. The art was held by all, though not equally criminal yet unlawful and therefore Casaubon speaking of one who had commerce with spirits blames him though he imagines him 'one of the best kind who dealt with them by way of command'.[2] Thus Prospero repents of his art in the last scene. The spirits were always considered as in some measure enslaved to the enchanter, at least for a time, and as serving with unwillingness; therefore Ariel so often begs for liberty; and Caliban observes that the spirits serve Prospero with no good will, but 'hate him rootedly' [III.2.95]. Of these trifles enough.

I.2.306
MIRANDA
   The strangeness of your story put
   Heaviness in me.

Why should a wonderful story produce sleep? I believe experience will prove that any violent agitation of the mind easily subsides in slumber especially when, as in Prospero's relation, the last images are pleasing.

I.2.321
CALIBAN
  As wicked dew as e'er my mother brushed
  With raven's feather from unwholesome fen
  Drop on you both.

Whence these critics [Bentley and others] derived the notion of a new language appropriated to Caliban I cannot find; they certainly mistook brutality of sentiment for uncouthness of words. Caliban had learned to speak of Prospero and his daughter, he had no names for the sun and moon before their arrival and could not have invented a language of his own without more understanding than Shakespeare has thought it proper to bestow upon him. His diction is indeed somewhat clouded by the gloominess of his temper and the malignity of his purposes; but let any other being entertain the same thoughts and he will find them easily issue in the same expressions.

I.2.397
ARIEL
  Full fathom five thy father lies . . .

I know not whether Dr Warburton has very successfully defended these songs from Gildon's accusation [of triflingness].[3] Ariel's lays, however seasonable and efficacious, must be allowed to be of no supernatural dignity or elegance; they express nothing great, nor reveal anything above mortal discovery.

The reason for which Ariel is introduced thus trifling is that he and his companions are evidently of the fairy kind, an order of beings to which tradition has always ascribed a sort of diminutive agency, powerful but ludicrous, a humorous and frolic controlment of nature, well expressed by the songs of Ariel.

II.1.134
SEBASTIAN   Milan and Naples have
More widows in them of this business' making
Than we bring men to comfort them.

It does not clearly appear whether the king and these lords thought the ship lost. This passage seems to imply that they were themselves confident of returning, but imagined part of the fleet destroyed. Why indeed should Sebastian plot against his brother in the following scene unless he knew how to find the kingdom which he was to inherit?

It is observed of *The Tempest* that its plan is regular; this the author of the *Revisal* thinks, what I think too, an accidental effect of the story, not intended or regarded by our author.[4] But whatever might be Shakespeare's intention in forming or adopting the plot, he has made it instrumental to the production of many characters, diversified with boundless invention and preserved with profound skill in nature, extensive knowledge of opinions and accurate observation of life. In a single drama are here exhibited princes, courtiers and sailors, all speaking in their real characters. There is the agency of airy spirits and of an earthly goblin. The operations of magic, the tumults of a storm, the adventures of a desert island, the native effusion of untaught affection, the punishment of guilt and the final happiness of the pair for whom our passions and reason are equally interested.

A MIDSUMMER NIGHT'S DREAM

I.2
In this scene Shakespeare takes advantage of his knowledge of the theatre to ridicule the prejudices and competitions of the players. Bottom, who is generally acknowledged the principal actor, declares his inclination to be for a tyrant, for a part of

fury, tumult and noise, such as every young man pants to perform when he first steps upon the stage. The same Bottom, who seems bred in a tiring-room, has another histrionical passion. He is for engrossing[5] every part and would exclude his inferiors from all possibility of distinction. He is therefore desirous to play Pyramus, Thisbe and the Lion at the same time.

I.2.43
FLUTE Nay, faith, let not me play a woman – I have a beard coming.
QUINCE That's all one: you shall play it in a mask, and you may speak as small as you will.

This passage shows how the want of women on the old stage was supplied. If they had not a young man who could perform the part with a face that might pass for feminine the character was acted in a mask, which was at that time a part of a lady's dress so much in use that it did not give any unusual appearance to the scene; and he that could modulate his voice in a female tone might play the woman very successfully. It is observed in Downes's *Memoirs of the Playhouse*[6] that one of these counterfeit heroines moved the passions more strongly than the women that have since been brought upon the stage. Some of the catastrophes of the old comedies, which make lovers marry the wrong women, are by recollection of the common use of masks brought nearer to probability.

II.1.40
FAIRY
   Those that 'Hobgoblin' call you, and 'Sweet Puck'...

It will be apparent to him that shall compare Drayton's poem [*Nimphidia*] with this play that either one of the poets copied the other, or as I rather believe that there was then some system of the fairy empire generally received, which they both represented as accurately as they could. Whether Drayton or Shakespeare wrote first I cannot discover.[7]

Selections from Notes to the Plays

II.1.42
PUCK   Thou speakest aright:
  I am that merry wanderer of the night.

It seems that in the fairy mythology Puck, or Hobgoblin, was the trusty servant of Oberon and always employed to watch or detect the intrigues of Queen Mab, called by Shakespeare Titania. For in Drayton's *Nimphidia* the same fairies are engaged in the same business. Mab has an amour with Pigwiggin, Oberon being jealous sends Hobgoblin to catch them and one of Mab's nymphs opposes him by a spell.

II.1.51
PUCK
  The wisest aunt telling the saddest tale
  Sometime for threefoot stool mistaketh me;
  Then slip I from her bum. Down topples she,
  And 'Tailor' cries, and falls into a cough;
  And then the whole choir hold their hips and laugh.

The custom of crying 'tailor' at a sudden fall backwards, I think I remember to have observed. He that slips beside his chair falls as a tailor squats upon his board. The Oxford editor and Dr Warburton after him read 'and rails, or cries', plausibly, but I believe not rightly. Besides, the trick of the fairy is represented as producing rather merriment than anger.

III.1
[Stage direction] *Enter the clowns: Bottom, Quince, Snout, Starveling, Flute, and Snug*

In the time of Shakespeare there were many companies of players, sometimes five at the same time, contending for the favour of the public. Of these some were undoubtedly very unskilful and very poor and it is probable that the design of this scene was to ridicule their ignorance and the odd expedients to which they might be driven by the want of proper decorations. Bottom was perhaps the head of a rival house and is therefore honoured with an ass's head.

III.1.164
TITANIA
  And for night-tapers crop their waxen thighs
  And light them at the fiery glow-worms' eyes...

I know not how Shakespeare, who commonly derived his knowledge of nature from his own observation, happened to place the glow-worm's light in his eyes, which is only in his tail.

IV.1.102
THESEUS
  Go, one of you; find out the forester;
  For now our observation is performed.

The honours due to the morning of May. I know not why Shakespeare calls this play a *Midsummer Night's Dream*, when he so carefully informs us that it happened on the night preceding May day.

Of this play, wild and fantastical as it is, all the parts in their various modes are well written and give the kind of pleasure which the author designed. Fairies in his time were much in fashion; common tradition had made them familiar and Spenser's poem had made them great.[8]

THE TWO GENTLEMEN OF VERONA

[Headnote]
When I read this play I cannot but think that I discover both in the serious and ludicrous scenes the language and sentiments of Shakespeare. It is not indeed one of his most powerful effusions, it has neither many diversities of character, nor striking delineations of life, but it abounds in γνῶμαι [maxims] beyond most of his plays and few have more lines or passages which, singly considered, are eminently beautiful. I am yet inclined to believe that it was not very successful and suspect that it has escaped corruption only because being seldom played it was less exposed to the hazards of transcription.

Selections from Notes to the Plays

I.1.69
[Stage direction] *Enter Speed*

That this, like many other scenes, is mean and vulgar will be universally allowed; but that it was interpolated by the players seems advanced [by Pope] without any proof only to give a greater licence to criticism.

In this play there is a strange mixture of knowledge and ignorance, of care and negligence. The versification is often excellent, the allusions are learned and just; but the author conveys his heroes by sea from one inland town to another in the same country; he places the Emperor at Milan and sends his young men to attend him, but never mentions him more; he makes Proteus, after an interview with Silvia, say he has only seen her picture and if we may credit the old copies he has by mistaking places left his scenery inextricable.[9] The reason of all this confusion seems to be that he took his story from a novel which he sometimes followed and sometimes forsook, sometimes remembered and sometimes forgot.

That this play is rightly attributed to Shakespeare, I have little doubt. If it be taken from him to whom shall it be given? This question may be asked of all the disputed plays except *Titus Andronicus*; and it will be found more credible that Shakespeare might sometimes sink below his highest flights than that any other should rise up to his lowest.[10]

MEASURE FOR MEASURE

[Headnote]
There is perhaps not one of Shakespeare's plays more darkened than this by the peculiarities of its author and the unskilfulness of its editors, by distortions of phrase or negligence of transcription.

II.1.164
ESCALUS Which is the wiser here, Justice or Iniquity?

These were, I suppose, two personages well known to the audience by their frequent appearance in the old moralities.

The words therefore at that time produced a combination of ideas which they have now lost.

III.1.13
DUKE   Thou art not noble,
   For all th' accommodations that thou bear'st
   Are nursed by baseness.

Dr Warburton is undoubtedly mistaken in supposing that by 'baseness' is meant 'self-love' here assigned as the motive of all human actions. Shakespeare meant only to observe that a minute analysis of life at once destroys that splendour which dazzles the imagination. Whatever grandeur can display or luxury enjoy is procured by 'baseness', by offices of which the mind shrinks from the contemplation. All the delicacies of the table may be traced back to the shambles[11] and the dunghill, all magnificence of building was hewn from the quarry and all the pomp of ornaments dug from among the damps and darkness of the mine.

III.1.17
DUKE   Thy best of rest is sleep,
   And that thou oft provok'st, yet grossly fear'st
   Thy death, which is no more.

Here Dr Warburton might have found a sentiment worthy of his animadversion. I cannot without indignation find Shakespeare saying that 'death is only sleep', lengthening out his exhortation by a sentence which in the Friar is impious, in the reasoner is foolish and in the poet trite and vulgar.[12]

III.1.32
DUKE   Thou hast nor youth nor age,
   But as it were an after-dinner's sleep,
   Dreaming on both . . .

Selections from Notes to the Plays

This is exquisitely[13] imagined. When we are young we busy ourselves in forming schemes for succeeding time and miss the gratifications that are before us; when we are old we amuse the languor of age with the recollection of youthful pleasures or performances; so that our life, of which no part is filled with the business of the present time, resembles our dreams after dinner when the events of the morning are mingled with the designs of the evening.

III.1.116
CLAUDIO
> If it were damnable, he being so wise,
> Why would he for the momentary trick
> Be perdurably fined?

Shakespeare shows his knowledge of human nature in the conduct of Claudio. When Isabella first tells him of Angelo's proposal he answers with honest indignation, agreeably to his settled principles, 'Thou shalt not do't' [106]. But the love of life being permitted to operate soon furnishes him with sophistical arguments; he believes it cannot be very dangerous to the soul since Angelo who is so wise will venture it.

III.1.142
ISABELLA
> Is't not a kind of incest to take life
> From thine own sister's shame?

In Isabella's declamation there is something harsh and something forced and far-fetched. But her indignation cannot be thought violent when we consider her not only as a virgin but as a nun.

V.1.350
LUCIO Show your sheep-biting face, and be hanged an hour. Will't not off?

This is intended to be the common language of vulgar indignation. Our phrase on such occasions is simply, 'Show your sheep-biting face and be hanged'. The words 'an hour' have no particular use here, nor are authorized by custom. I suppose it was written thus, 'Show your sheep-biting face and be hanged – an' how? wilt not off.' In the midland counties upon any unexpected obstruction or resistance it is common to exclaim 'an' how?'

V.1.443
ISABELLA
  A due sincerity governèd his deeds
  Till he did look on me.

The Duke has justly observed that Isabella is 'importuned against all sense' [430] to solicit for Angelo, yet here 'against all sense' she solicits for him. Her argument is extraordinary:

> A due sincerity governèd his deeds
> Till he did look on me. Since it is so,
> Let him not die.

That Angelo had committed all the crimes charged against him, as far as he could commit them, is evident. The only 'intent' which 'His act did not o'ertake' [448] was the defilement of Isabella. Of this Angelo was only intentionally guilty.

Angelo's crimes were such as must sufficiently justify punishment, whether its end be to secure the innocent from wrong, or to deter guilt by example; and I believe every reader feels some indignation when he finds him spared. From what extenuation of his crime can Isabella, who yet supposes her brother dead, form any plea in his favour? 'Since he was good till he looked on me, let him not die.' I am afraid our varlet poet intended to inculcate that women think ill of nothing that raises the credit of their beauty and are ready, however virtuous, to pardon any act which they think incited by their own charms.

V.1.491
DUKE
  By this Lord Angelo perceives he's safe . . .

It is somewhat strange that Isabella is not made to express either gratitude, wonder or joy at the sight of her brother.

V.1.496
DUKE

  And yet here's one in place I cannot pardon.

After the pardon of two murderers Lucio might be treated by the good Duke with less harshness; but perhaps the poet intended to show what is too often seen, 'that men easily forgive wrongs which are not committed against themselves'.

  Of this play the light or comic part is very natural and pleasing, but the grave scenes, if a few passages be excepted, have more labour than elegance. The plot is rather intricate than artful. The time of the action is indefinite; some time, we know not how much, must have elapsed between the recess of the Duke and the imprisonment of Claudio; for he must have learned the story of Mariana in his disguise or he delegated his power to a man already known to be corrupted. The unities of action and place are sufficiently preserved.

THE MERCHANT OF VENICE

I.2.43
NERISSA Then is there the County Palatine.

I am always inclined to believe that Shakespeare has more allusions to particular facts and persons than his readers commonly suppose. The Count here mentioned was perhaps Albertus à Lasco, a Polish Palatine, who visited England in our author's time, was eagerly caressed and splendidly entertained, but running in debt at last stole away and endeavoured to repair his fortune by enchantment.[14]

I.2.79
NERISSA How like you the young German, the Duke of Saxony's nephew?

In Shakespeare's time the Duke of Bavaria visited London and was made Knight of the Garter.[15]
  Perhaps in this enumeration of Portia's suitors there may be some covert allusion to those of Queen Elizabeth.

II.7.78
PORTIA

>A gentle riddance. Draw the curtains, go.
>Let all of his complexion choose me so. *Exeunt*

The old quarto edition of 1600 has no distribution of acts but proceeds from the beginning to the end in an unbroken tenor. This play therefore having been probably divided without authority by the publishers of the first folio lies open to a new regulation if any more commodious division can be proposed. The story is itself so wildly incredible and the changes of the scene so frequent and capricious that the probability of action does not deserve much care; yet it may be proper to observe that by concluding the second act here time is given for Bassanio's passage to Belmont.

IV.1.90
SHYLOCK

>You have among you many a purchased slave,
>Which like your asses and your dogs and mules
>You use in abject and in slavish parts,
>Because you bought them. Shall I say to you,
>'Let them be free! Marry them to your heirs!'

This argument, considered as used to the particular persons, seems conclusive. I see not how Venetians or Englishmen, while they practise the purchase and sale of slaves, can much enforce or demand the law of 'doing to others as we would that they should do to us' [Matthew 5:12].

V.1.129
PORTIA

>Let me give light, but let me not be light,
>For a light wife doth make a heavy husband . . .

There is scarcely any word with which Shakespeare so much delights to trifle as with 'light', in its various significations.

Of *The Merchant of Venice* the style is even and easy with few peculiarities of diction or anomalies of construction. The comic part raises laughter and the serious fixes expectation. The probability of either one or the other story cannot be maintained. The union of two actions in one event is in this drama eminently happy. Dryden was much pleased with his own address in connecting the two plots of his *Spanish Friar*, which yet, I believe, the critic will find excelled by this play.

AS YOU LIKE IT

II.7.95
ORLANDO   the thorny point
   Of bare distress hath ta'en from me the show
   Of smooth civility . . .

We might read 'torn' with more elegance, but elegance alone will not justify alteration.

III.4.6
ROSALIND His very hair is of the dissembling colour.
CELIA Something browner than Judas's. Marry, his kisses are Judas's own children.
ROSALIND I' faith, his hair is of a good colour.

There is much of nature in this petty perverseness of Rosalind; she finds faults in her lover in hope to be contradicted and when Celia in sportive malice too readily seconds her accusations, she contradicts herself rather than suffer her favourite to want a vindication.

IV.3.1
ROSALIND How say you now? Is it not past two o'clock?

The foregoing noisy scene [IV.2] was introduced only to fill up an interval, which is to represent two hours. This contraction of the time we might impute to poor Rosalind's impatience, but that a few minutes after we find Orlando sending his excuse. I do not see that by any probable division of the acts this absurdity can be obviated.

V.4.104
[Stage direction] *Enter a masquer representing Hymen, and Rosalind and Celia as themselves*

Rosalind is imagined by the rest of the company to be brought by enchantment and is therefore introduced by a supposed aerial being in the character of Hymen.

Of this play the fable[16] is wild[17] and pleasing. I know not how the ladies will approve the facility with which both Rosalind and Celia give away their hearts. To Celia much may be forgiven for the heroism of her friendship. The character of Jaques is natural and well preserved. The comic dialogue is very sprightly with less mixture of low buffoonery than in some other plays; and the graver part is elegant and harmonious. By hastening to the end of his work Shakespeare suppressed the dialogue between the usurper and the hermit and lost an opportunity of exhibiting a moral lesson in which he might have found matter worthy of his highest powers.

LOVE'S LABOUR'S LOST

I.1.31
DUMAINE
  To love, to wealth, to pomp, I pine and die,
  With all these living in philosophy.

The style of the rhyming scenes in this play is often entangled and obscure. I know not certainly to what 'all these' is to be referred; I suppose he means that he finds 'love, pomp *and* wealth *in* philosophy'.

I.1.147
BEROWNE
  Necessity will make us all forsworn
  Three thousand times within this three years' space . . .

Berowne amidst his extravagancies speaks with great justness against the folly of vows. They are made without sufficient regard to the variations of life and are therefore broken by some unforeseen necessity. They proceed commonly from a presumptuous confidence and a false estimate of human power.

II.1.105
PRINCESS
  'Tis deadly sin to keep that oath, my lord,
  And sin to break it.

Sir T. Hanmer reads 'not' sin to break it. I believe erroneously. The Princess shows an inconvenience very frequently attending rash oaths, which whether kept or broken produce guilt.

IV.2.1
[Stage direction] *Enter Holofernes, Nathaniel, and Dull*

I am not of the learned commentator's [Warburton's] opinion that the satire of Shakespeare is so seldom personal. It is of the nature of personal invectives to be soon unintelligible; and the author that gratifies private malice, *animam in vulnere ponit*,[18] destroys the future efficacy of his own writings and sacrifices the esteem of succeeding times to the laughter of a day. It is no wonder therefore that the sarcasms which perhaps in the author's time 'set the *playhouse* in a roar' [cf. *Hamlet*, V.1.188], are now lost among general reflections. Yet whether the character of Holofernes was pointed at any particular man I am, notwithstanding the plausibility of Dr Warburton's conjecture, inclined to doubt. Every man adheres as long as he can to his own preconceptions. Before I read this note I considered the character of Holofernes as borrowed from the Rhombus of Sir Philip Sidney who, in a kind of pastoral entertainment exhibited to Queen Elizabeth, has introduced a schoolmaster so called, speaking 'a leash of languages at once' and puzzling himself and his auditors with a jargon like that of Holofernes in the present play. Sidney himself might bring the character from Italy; for as Peacham observes, the schoolmaster has long been one of the ridiculous personages in the farces of that country.[19]

V.1.2

NATHANIEL Your reasons at dinner have been sharp and sententious, pleasant without scurrility, witty without affection, audacious without impudency, learned without opinion, and strange without heresy.

I know not well what degree of respect Shakespeare intends to obtain for this vicar, but he has here put into his mouth a finished representation of colloquial excellence. It is very difficult to add anything to this character of the schoolmaster's table-talk and perhaps all the precepts of Castiglione[20] will scarcely be found to comprehend a rule for conversation so justly delineated, so widely dilated and so nicely limited.

V.2.69

PRINCESS
None are so surely caught, when they are catched,
As wit turned fool. Folly, in wisdom hatched,
Hath wisdom's warrant and the help of school
And wit's own grace to grace a learnèd fool.

These are observations worthy of a man who has surveyed human nature with the closest attention.

V.2.440

PRINCESS
Your oath once broke, you force not to forswear.

'You force not' is the same with 'you make no difficulty'. This is a very just observation. The crime which has been once committed is committed again with less reluctance.

In this play, which all the editors have concurred to censure and some have rejected as unworthy of our poet, it must be confessed that there are many passages mean, childish and vulgar; and some which ought not to have been exhibited, as we are told they were, to a maiden queen.[21] But there are scattered through the whole many sparks of genius; nor is there any play that has more evident marks of the hand of Shakespeare.

THE WINTER'S TALE

III.1.1
CLEOMENES
> The climate's delicate, the air most sweet,
> Fertile the isle . . .

[Warburton emended 'isle' to 'soil' to correct the location of Apollo's temple.]

Shakespeare is little careful of geography. There is no need of this emendation in a play of which the whole plot depends upon a geographical error by which Bohemia is supposed to be a maritime country.

III.2.151
LEONTES   Apollo, pardon
> My great profaneness 'gainst thine oracle!

This vehement retractation of Leontes, accompanied with the confession of more crimes than he was suspected of, is agreeable to our daily experience of the vicissitudes of violent tempers and the eruptions of minds oppressed with guilt.

IV.1.7
TIME . . . since it is in my power
> To o'erthrow law, and in one self-born hour
> To plant and o'erwhelm custom. Let me pass
> The same I am ere ancient'st order was
> Or what is now received.

The reasoning of Time is not very clear; he seems to mean that he who has broke so many laws may now break another; that he who introduced everything may introduce Perdita on her sixteenth year; and he entreats that he may pass as of old before any 'order' or succession of objects, ancient or modern, distinguished his periods.

IV.4.21
PERDITA
> How would he look to see his work, so noble,
> Vilely bound up?

It is impossible for any man to rid his mind of his profession. The authorship of Shakespeare has supplied him with a metaphor, which rather than he would lose it, he has put with no great propriety into the mouth of a country maid. Thinking of his own works his mind passed naturally to the binder. I am glad that he has no hint at an editor.

V.1.13
PAULINA
  If one by one you wedded all the world,
  Or from the all that are took something good
  To make a perfect woman, she you killed
  Would be unparalleled.

This is a favourite thought; it was bestowed on Miranda and Rosalind before.

V.2.107
FIRST GENTLEMAN Who would be thence that has the benefit of access? Every wink of an eye some new grace will be born. Our absence makes us unthrifty to our knowledge.

It was I suppose only to spare his own labour that the poet put this whole scene into narrative, for though part of the transaction was already known to the audience and therefore could not properly be shown again, yet the two kings might have met upon the stage and after the examination of the old shepherd, the young lady might have been recognized in sight of the spectators.

This play, as Dr Warburton justly observes, is with all its absurdities very entertaining. The character of Autolycus is very naturally conceived and strongly represented.

TWELFTH NIGHT

I.2.42
VIOLA   O, that I served that lady,
  And might not be delivered to the world . . .

I wish I might not be 'made public' to the world, with regard to the 'state' of my birth and fortune, till I have gained a 'ripe opportunity' for my design.

Viola seems to have formed a very deep design with very little premeditation: she is thrown by shipwreck on an unknown coast, hears that the prince is a bachelor and resolves to supplant the lady whom he courts.

IV.2.114

FESTE But tell me true, are you not mad indeed, or do you but counterfeit?

If he was not mad, what did he counterfeit by declaring that he was not mad? The fool who meant to insult him, I think, asks 'Are you mad, or do you but counterfeit?' That is, 'You look like a madman, you talk like a madman: is your madness real, or have you any secret design in it?' This to a man in poor Malvolio's state was a severe taunt.

V.1.213
ORSINO
One face, one voice, one habit, and two persons!
A natural perspective, that is and is not.

A 'perspective' seems to be taken for shows exhibited through a glass with such lights as make the pictures appear really protuberant. The Duke therefore says that nature has here exhibited such a show where shadows seem realities; where that which 'is not' appears like that which 'is'.

This play is in the graver part elegant and easy and in some of the lighter scenes exquisitely humorous. Aguecheek is drawn with great propriety, but his character is in a great measure that of natural fatuity and is therefore not the proper prey of a satirist. The soliloquy of Malvolio [III.4.65] is truly comic; he is betrayed to ridicule merely by his pride. The marriage of Olivia and the succeeding perplexity, though well enough contrived to divert on the stage, wants credibility and fails to produce the proper instruction required in the drama as it exhibits no just picture of life.

THE MERRY WIVES OF WINDSOR

III.5.138

FORD If I have horns to make one mad, let the proverb go with me – I'll be horn-mad.

There is no image which our author appears so fond of as that of a cuckold's horns. Scarcely a light character is introduced that does not endeavour to produce merriment by some allusion to horned husbands. As he wrote his plays for the stage rather than the press, he perhaps reviewed them seldom and did not observe this repetition, or finding the jest, however frequent, still successful, did not think correction necessary.

IV.1

This is a very trifling scene of no use to the plot and I should think of no great delight to the audience; but Shakespeare best knew what would please.

IV.2.182

EVANS I spy a great peard under his muffler.

As the second stratagem by which Falstaff escapes is much the grosser of the two, I wish it had been practised first. It is very unlikely that Ford having been so deceived before and knowing that he had been deceived would suffer him to escape in so slight a disguise.

IV.5.115

MISTRESS QUICKLY Good hearts, what ado here is to bring you together! Sure, one of you does not serve heaven well, that you are so crossed.

The great fault of this play is the frequency of expressions so profane that no necessity of preserving character can justify them. There are laws of higher authority than those of criticism.

V.5.168

PAGE Yet be cheerful, knight. Thou shalt eat a posset tonight at my house, where I will desire thee to laugh at my wife that now laughs at thee.

The two plots are excellently connected and the transition very artfully made in this speech.

Of this play there is a tradition preserved by Mr Rowe that it was written at the command of Queen Elizabeth, who was so delighted with the character of Falstaff that she wished it to be diffused through more plays; but suspecting that it might pall by continued uniformity directed the poet to diversify his manner by showing him in love. No task is harder than that of writing to the ideas of another. Shakespeare knew what the Queen, if the story be true, seems not to have known, that by any real passion of tenderness, the selfish craft, the careless jollity and the lazy luxury of Falstaff must have suffered so much abatement that little of his former cast would have remained. Falstaff could not love but by ceasing to be Falstaff. He could only counterfeit love and his professions could be prompted not by the hope of pleasure but of money. Thus the poet approached as near as he could to the work enjoined him; yet having perhaps in the former plays completed his own idea seems not to have been able to give Falstaff all his former power of entertainment.

This comedy is remarkable for the variety and number of the personages, who exhibit more characters appropriated and discriminated than perhaps can be found in any other play.

Whether Shakespeare was the first that produced upon the English stage the effect of language distorted and depraved by provincial or foreign pronunciation, I cannot certainly decide. This mode of forming ridiculous characters can confer praise only on him who originally discovered it, for it requires not much of either wit or judgement: its success must be derived almost wholly from the player, but its power in a skilful mouth, even he that despises it, is unable to resist.

The conduct of this drama is deficient; the action begins and ends often before the conclusion and the different parts might change places without inconvenience; but its general power, that power by which all works of genius shall finally be tried, is such that perhaps it never yet had reader or spectator who did not think it too soon at an end.[22]

THE TAMING OF THE SHREW

Of this play the two plots are so well united that they can hardly be called two without injury to the art with which they are interwoven. The attention is entertained with all the variety of a double plot, yet is not distracted by unconnected incidents.

The part between Katherina and Petruchio is eminently sprightly and diverting. At the marriage of Bianca the arrival of the real father [Vincentio] perhaps produces more perplexity than pleasure. The whole play is very popular and diverting.

MUCH ADO ABOUT NOTHING

I.3.12
DON JOHN I cannot hide what I am. I must be sad when I have
  cause, and smile at no man's jests; eat when I have stomach,
  and wait for no man's leisure . . .

This is one of our author's natural touches. An envious and unsocial mind, too proud to give pleasure and too sullen to receive it, always endeavours to hide its malignity from the world and from itself under the plainness of simple honesty or the dignity of haughty independence.

IV.1.247
LEONATO   Being that I flow in grief,
  The smallest twine may lead me.

This is one of our author's observations upon life. Men overpowered with distress eagerly listen to the first offers of relief, close with[23] every scheme and believe every promise. He that has no longer any confidence in himself is glad to repose his trust in any other that will undertake to guide him.

ALL'S WELL THAT ENDS WELL

II.3.85
LAFEW Do all they deny her?

None of them have yet denied her or deny her afterwards but Bertram. The scene must be so regulated that Lafew and

Parolles talk at a distance, where they may see what passes between Helena and the lords, but not hear it so that they know not by whom the refusal is made.

IV.2.73
DIANA   Since Frenchmen are so braid,
   Marry that will, I live and die a maid.

The passage is very unimportant and the old reading reasonable enough. Nothing is more common than for girls on such occasions to say in a pet what they do not think or to think for a time what they do not finally resolve.

IV.3.30
FIRST LORD I would gladly have him see his company anatomized, that he might take a measure of his own judgements . . .

This is a very just and moral reason. Bertram, by finding how erroneously he has judged, will be less confident and more easily moved by admonition.

IV.3.274
FIRST SOLDIER What's his brother, the other Captain Dumaine?
SECOND LORD Why does he ask him of me?

This is nature. Every man is on such occasions more willing to hear his neighbour's character than his own.

IV.5.7
COUNTESS I would I had not known him . . .

This dialogue serves to connect the incidents of Parolles with the main plan of the play.

V.1.34
HELENA
   I will come after you with what good speed
   Our means will make us means.

Shakespeare delights much in this kind of reduplication, sometimes so as to obscure his meaning. Helena says 'they will follow with such speed as the means which they have will give them ability to exert'.

V.2.52
LAFEW Though you are a fool and a knave you shall eat.

Parolles has many of the lineaments of Falstaff and seems to be the character which Shakespeare delighted to draw, a fellow that had more wit than virtue. Though justice required that he should be detected and exposed, yet his vices 'sit so fit in him' [I.1.101] that he is not at last suffered to starve.

V.3.21
KING
   We are reconciled, and the first view shall kill
   All repetition.

'The first interview shall put an end to all recollection of the past.' Shakespeare is now hastening to the end of the play, finds his matter sufficient to fill up his remaining scenes and therefore, as on other such occasions, contracts his dialogue and precipitates his action. Decency required that Bertram's double crime of cruelty and disobedience, joined likewise with some hypocrisy, should raise more resentment; and that though his mother might easily forgive him, his king should more pertinaciously vindicate his own authority and Helena's merit: of all this Shakespeare could not be ignorant, but Shakespeare wanted to conclude his play.

V.3.93
BERTRAM
   In Florence was it from a casement thrown me . . .

Bertram still continues to have too little virtue to deserve Helena. He did not know indeed that it was Helena's ring, but he knew that he had it not from a window.

V.3.298
DIANA
> He knows himself my bed he hath defiled,
> And at that time he got his wife with child.
> Dead though she be she feels her young one kick.
> So there's my riddle: one that's dead is quick.
> And now behold the meaning.

This dialogue is too long since the audience already knew the whole transaction; nor is there any reason for puzzling the King and playing with his passions; but it was much easier than to make a pathetical interview between Helena and her husband, her mother and the King.

This play has many delightful scenes, though not sufficiently probable, and some happy characters, though not new, nor produced by any deep knowledge of human nature. Parolles is a boaster and a coward such as has always been the sport of the stage, but perhaps never raised more laughter or contempt than in the hands of Shakespeare.

I cannot reconcile my heart to Bertram; a man noble without generosity and young without truth; who marries Helena as a coward and leaves her as a profligate: when she is dead by his unkindness, sneaks home to a second marriage, is accused by a woman whom he has wronged, defends himself by falsehood and is dismissed to happiness.

The story of Bertram and Diana had been told before of Mariana and Angelo and, to confess the truth, scarcely merited to be heard a second time.

The story is copied from a novel of Boccaccio, which may be read in *Shakespeare Illustrated*, with remarks not more favourable to Bertram than my own.[24]

KING JOHN

II.1.300
FRENCH HERALD
> You men of Angiers, open wide your gates
> And let young Arthur Duke of Brittaine in . . .

This speech is very poetical and smooth and except the conceit of the 'widow's husband' embracing 'the earth' is just and beautiful.

II.1.325
HUBERT
  Heralds, from off our towers we might behold . . .

These three speeches seem to have been laboured. The citizen's [Hubert's] is the best; yet 'both alike we like' [331] is a poor jingle.

III.1.70
CONSTANCE
  To me and to the state of my great grief
  Let kings assemble . . .

In *Much Ado About Nothing* the father of Hero, depressed by her disgrace, declares himself so subdued by grief that 'a thread may lead him' [cf. IV.1.248]. How is it that grief in Leonato and Lady Constance produces effects directly opposite and yet both agreeable to nature? Sorrow softens the mind while it is yet warmed by hope, but hardens it when it is congealed by despair. Distress, while there remains any prospect of relief, is weak and flexible, but when no succour remains is fearless and stubborn; angry alike at those that injure and at those that do not help; careless to please where nothing can be gained and fearless to offend when there is nothing further to be dreaded. Such was this writer's knowledge of the passions.

III.1.147
KING JOHN
  What earthy name to interrogatories
  Can task the free breath of a sacred king?
  Thou canst not, Cardinal, devise a name
  So slight, unworthy, and ridiculous,
  To charge me to an answer, as the Pope.

This must have been at the time when it was written in our struggles with popery a very captivating scene.

Selections from Notes to the Plays

So many passages remain in which Shakespeare evidently takes his advantage of the facts then recent and of the passions then in motion that I cannot but suspect that time has obscured much of his art and that many allusions yet remain undiscovered which perhaps may be gradually retrieved by succeeding commentators.

III.4.40
CONSTANCE   . . . that fell anatomy
 Which cannot hear a lady's feeble voice,
 Which scorns a modern invocation.

It is hard to say what Shakespeare means by 'modern': it is not opposed to 'ancient'. In *All's Well That Ends Well* speaking of a girl in contempt he uses this word, 'her *modern* grace' [V.3.216]. It apparently means something 'slight' and 'inconsiderable'.

III.4.61
KING PHILIP
 Bind up those tresses!

It was necessary that Constance should be interrupted because a passion so violent cannot be borne long. I wish the following speeches had been equally happy; but they only serve to show how difficult it is to maintain the pathetic long.

III.4.99
CONSTANCE   Had you such a loss as I,
 I could give better comfort than you do.

This is a sentiment which great sorrow always dictates. Whoever cannot help himself casts his eyes on others for assistance and often mistakes their inability for coldness.

III.4.107
LEWIS THE DAUPHIN
 There's nothing in this world can make me joy.

The young prince feels his defeat with more sensibility[25] than his father. Shame operates most strongly in the earlier years and when can disgrace be less welcome than when a man is going to his bride?

IV.1.100
ARTHUR
  Or, Hubert, if you will, cut out my tongue,
  So I may keep mine eyes.

This is according to nature. We imagine no evil so great as that which is near us.

IV.2.197
HUBERT
  Standing on slippers which his nimble haste
  Had falsely thrust upon contrary feet . . .

I know not how the commentators understand this important passage, which in Dr Warburton's edition is marked as eminently beautiful and in the whole not without justice. But Shakespeare seems to have confounded a man's shoes with his gloves. He that is frighted or hurried may put his hand into the wrong glove, but either shoe will equally admit either foot. The author seems to be disturbed by the disorder which he describes.

IV.2.231
KING JOHN
  Hadst thou but shook thy head or made a pause
  When I spake darkly what I purposèd . . .

There are many touches of nature in this conference of John with Hubert. A man engaged in wickedness would keep the profit to himself and transfer the guilt to his accomplice. These reproaches vented against Hubert are not the words of art or policy, but the eruptions of a mind swelling with consciousness of a crime and desirous of discharging its misery on another.

  This account of the timidity of guilt is drawn *ab ipsis recessibus mentis*,[26] from an intimate knowledge of mankind, particularly that line [234–5] in which he says that 'to have bid him tell his tale' in 'express words', would have 'struck him dumb'; nothing is more certain than that bad men use all the arts of fallacy upon themselves, palliate their actions to their own minds by gentle terms, and hide themselves from their own detection in ambiguities and subterfuges.

The tragedy of *King John* though not written with the utmost power of Shakespeare is varied with a very pleasing interchange of incidents and characters. The Lady's grief is very affecting and the character of the Bastard contains that mixture of greatness and levity which this author delighted to exhibit.

There is extant another play of *King John*, published with Shakespeare's name, so different from this and I think from all his other works that there is reason to think his name was prefixed only to recommend it to sale.[27] No man writes upon the same subject twice without concurring in many places with himself.[28]

RICHARD II

I.3.227
JOHN OF GAUNT
  Shorten my days thou canst with sullen sorrow,
  And pluck nights from me, but not lend a morrow.

It is matter of very melancholy consideration that all human advantages confer more power of doing evil than good.

III.2.93
KING RICHARD
  Mine ear is open and my heart prepared.

It seems to be the design of the poet to raise Richard to esteem in his fall and consequently to interest the reader in his favour. He gives him only passive fortitude, the virtue of a confessor rather than of a king. In his prosperity we saw him imperious and oppressive but in his distress he is wise, patient and pious.

III.2.207

KING RICHARD
  By heaven, I'll hate him everlastingly
  That bids me be of comfort any more.

This sentiment is drawn from nature. Nothing is more offensive to a mind convinced that his distress is without a remedy and preparing to submit quietly to irresistible calamity than these petty and conjectured comforts which unskilful officiousness thinks it virtue to administer.

III.3.156

KING RICHARD   . . . where subjects' feet
  May hourly trample on their sovereign's head . . .

Shakespeare is very apt to deviate from the *pathetic* to the *ridiculous*. Had the speech of Richard ended at this line [156] it had exhibited the natural language of submissive misery, conforming its intention to the present fortune and calmly ending its purposes in death.

IV.1.125

BISHOP OF CARLISLE
  And shall the figure of God's majesty . . .
  Be judged by subject and inferior breath
  And he himself not present?

Here is another proof that our author did not learn in King James's court his elevated notions of the right of kings. I know not any flatterer of the Stuarts who has expressed this doctrine in much stronger terms. It must be observed that the poet intends from the beginning to the end to exhibit this bishop as brave, pious and venerable.

IV.1.321

BISHOP OF CARLISLE
  The woe's to come. The children yet unborn
  Shall feel this day as sharp to them as thorn.

This pathetic denunciation shows that Shakespeare intended to impress his auditors with dislike of the deposal of Richard.

V.1.46
KING RICHARD
  For why the senseless brands will sympathize
  The heavy accent of thy moving tongue,
  And in compassion weep the fire out . . .

The poet should have ended this speech with the foregoing line [45] and have spared his childish prattle about the fire.

V.3.5
KING HENRY
  Inquire at London 'mongst the taverns there;
  For there, they say, he daily doth frequent
  With unrestrainèd loose companions . . .

This is a very proper introduction to the future character of Henry the Fifth, to his debaucheries in his youth and his greatness in his manhood.

This play is extracted from the *Chronicle* of Holinshed, in which many passages may be found which Shakespeare has, with very little alteration, transplanted into his scenes; particularly a speech of the Bishop of Carlisle [IV.1.114] in defence of King Richard's unalienable right and immunity from human jurisdiction.

Jonson, who in his *Catiline* and *Sejanus* has inserted many speeches from the Roman historians, was perhaps induced to that practice by the example of Shakespeare, who had condescended sometimes to copy more ignoble writers. But Shakespeare had more of his own than Jonson and, if he sometimes was willing to spare his labour, showed by what he performed at other times that his extracts were made by choice or idleness rather than necessity.

This play is one of those which Shakespeare has apparently revised;[29] but as success in works of invention is not always proportionate to labour, it is not finished at last with the happy

1 HENRY IV

I.1.1
KING HENRY
  So shaken as we are, so wan with care . . .

Shakespeare has apparently designed a regular connection of these dramatic histories from Richard the Second to Henry the Fifth. King Henry at the end of *Richard the Second* declares his purpose to visit the Holy Land, which he resumes in this speech. The complaint made by King Henry in the last act of *Richard the Second* of the wildness of his son prepares the reader for the frolics which are here to be recounted and the characters which are now to be exhibited.

I.2.206
PRINCE HAL
  So when this loose behaviour I throw off . . .

This speech is very artfully introduced to keep the Prince from appearing vile in the opinion of the audience; it prepares them for his future reformation and, what is yet more valuable, exhibits a natural picture of a great mind offering excuses to itself and palliating those follies which it can neither justify nor forsake.

I.3.199
HOTSPUR
  By heaven, methinks it were an easy leap
  To pluck bright honour from the pale-faced moon . . .

Though I am very far from condemning this speech with Gildon and Theobald as 'absolute madness', yet I cannot find in it that profundity of reflection and beauty of allegory which the learned commentator [Warburton] has endeavoured to display. This sally of Hotspur may be, I think, soberly and rationally vindicated as the violent eruption of a mind inflated with ambition and fired with resentment; as the boastful clamour of a man able to do much and eager to do more; as the hasty motion of turbulent desire; as the dark expression of indetermined[30] thoughts.

I.3.280
WORCESTER
   The King will always think him in our debt . . .

This is a natural description of the state of mind between those that have conferred and those that have received obligations too great to be satisfied.

That this would be the event of Northumberland's disloyalty was predicted by King Richard in the former play [*Richard II*, V.1.55].

II.4.35
[Stage direction] *Enter Francis, a Drawer*

This scene, helped by the distraction of the drawer and grimaces of the Prince, may entertain upon the stage but afford not much delight to the reader. The author has judiciously made it short.

II.4.485
PRINCE HAL Go hide thee behind the arras.

The bulk of Falstaff made him not the fittest to be concealed behind the hangings, but every poet sacrifices something to the scenery;[31] if Falstaff had not been hidden he could not have been found asleep, nor had his pockets searched.

II.4.511
PRINCE HAL This oily rascal is known as well as Paul's. Go call him forth.
PETO Falstaff! Fast asleep behind the arras, and snorting like a horse.

The scenery here is somewhat perplexed. When the sheriff came the whole gang retired and Falstaff was hidden. As soon as the sheriff is sent away the Prince orders Falstaff to be called: by whom? – By Peto. But why had not Peto gone upstairs with the rest, and if he had, why did not the rest come down with him? The conversation that follows between the Prince and Peto seems to be apart from the others.

I cannot but suspect that for 'Peto' we should read 'Poins': what had Peto done that 'his place should be honourable' [529], or that he should be trusted with the plot against Falstaff? Poins has the Prince's confidence and is a man of courage.

This alteration clears the whole difficulty; they all retired but Poins who with the Prince, having only robbed the robbers, had no need to conceal himself from the travellers. We may therefore boldly change the scenical direction thus, '*Exeunt* Falstaff, Bardolph, Gadshill *and* Peto; *manent* the Prince *and* Poins.'

III.1.22
HOTSPUR
    O, then the earth shook to see the heavens on fire . . .

The poet has here taken, from the perverseness and contrariousness of Hotspur's temper, an opportunity of raising his character by a very rational and philosophical confutation of superstitious error.

III.3.26
FALSTAFF Thou art the Knight of the Burning Lamp.

This is a natural picture. Every man who feels in himself the pain of deformity, however like this merry knight he may affect to make sport with it among those whom it is his interest to please, is ready to revenge any hint of contempt upon one whom he can use with freedom.

IV.1.97
VERNON   All furnished, all in arms,
    All plumed like estridges that with the wind
    Bated, like eagles having lately bathed . . .

Selections from Notes to the Plays

I read:

> All furnished, all in arms,
> All plumed like estridges that *wing* the wind
> Bated like eagles.

This gives a strong image. They were not only plumed like estridges, but their plumes fluttered like those of an estridge on the wing mounting against the wind. A more lively representation of young men ardent for enterprise perhaps no writer has ever given.

IV.2.11

FALSTAFF I am a soused gurnet.

I believe a 'soused gurnet' is a 'pickled anchovy'. Much of Falstaff's humour consists in comparing himself to somewhat little.[32]

2 HENRY IV

[Headnote]
Mr Upton thinks these two plays improperly called *The First* and *Second Parts of Henry the Fourth*. The first play ends, he says, with the peaceful settlement of Henry in the kingdom by the defeat of the rebels. This is hardly true for the rebels are not yet finally suppressed. The second, he tells us, shows Henry the Fifth in the various lights of a good-natured rake, till on his father's death he assumes a more manly character. This is true; but this representation gives us no idea of a dramatic action. These two plays will appear to every reader who shall peruse them without ambition of critical discoveries to be so connected that the second is merely a sequel to the first; to be two only because they are too long to be one.

Induction, 1

RUMOUR
  Open your ears, for which of you will stop
  The vent of hearing when loud Rumour speaks?

This speech of Rumour is not inelegant or unpoetical but is wholly useless, since we are told nothing which the first scene does not clearly and naturally discover. The only end of such prologues is to inform the audience of some facts previous to the action, of which they can have no knowledge from the persons of the drama.

Induction, 15
RUMOUR   Rumour is a pipe
  Blown by surmises, jealousies, conjectures . . .

Here the poet imagines himself describing Rumour and forgets that Rumour is the speaker.

I.1.157
NORTHUMBERLAND
  But let one spirit of the first-born Cain
  Reign in all bosoms, that, each heart being set
  On bloody courses, the rude scene may end,
  And darkness be the burier of the dead!

The conclusion of this noble speech is extremely striking. There is no need to suppose it exactly philosophical: 'darkness' in poetry may be absence of eyes as well as privation of light. Yet we may remark that by an ancient opinion it has been held that if the human race for whom the world was made were extirpated the whole system of sublunary nature would cease.

II.2.163
PRINCE HENRY How might we see Falstaff bestow himself tonight in his true colours, and not ourselves be seen?
POINS Put on two leathern jerkins and aprons, and wait upon him at his table as drawers.

This was a plot very unlikely to succeed where the Prince and the drawers were all known, but it produces merriment, which our author found more useful than probability.

Selections from Notes to the Plays

IV.3.86
FALSTAFF Good faith, this same young sober-blooded boy
  doth not love me, nor a man cannot make him laugh . . .

Falstaff speaks here like a veteran in life. The young prince did not love him and he despaired to gain his affection for he could not make him laugh. Men only become friends by community of pleasures. He who cannot be softened into gaiety cannot easily be melted into kindness.

IV.5.209
KING HENRY IV
  I cut them off, and had a purpose now
  To lead out many to the Holy Land . . .

This journey to the Holy Land, of which the King very frequently revives the mention, had two motives: religion and policy. He durst not wear the ill-gotten crown without expiation, but in the act of expiation he contrives to make his wickedness successful.

IV.5.218
KING HENRY IV
  How I came by the crown, O God forgive,
  And grant it may with thee in true peace live!

This is a true picture of a mind divided between heaven and earth. He prays for the prosperity of guilt while he deprecates its punishment.

V.5.66
KING HENRY V
  Till then I banish thee, on pain of death . . .

Mr Rowe observes that many readers lament to see Falstaff so hardly used by his old friend. But if it be considered that the fat knight has never uttered one sentiment of generosity and with all his power of exciting mirth has nothing in him that can be esteemed, no great pain will be suffered from the reflection that he is compelled to live honestly, and maintained by the king, with a promise of advancement when he shall deserve it.

I think the poet more blameable for Poins, who is always represented as joining some virtues with his vices, and is therefore treated by the Prince with apparent distinction, yet he does nothing in the time of action and, though after the bustle is over he is again a favourite, at last vanishes without notice. Shakespeare certainly lost him by heedlessness in the multiplicity of his characters, the variety of his action and his eagerness to end the play.

V.5.94
LORD CHIEF JUSTICE
  Go, carry Sir John Falstaff to the Fleet.

I do not see why Falstaff is carried to the Fleet. We have never lost sight of him since his dismission from the King; he has committed no new fault and therefore incurred no punishment; but the different agitations of fear, anger and surprise in him and his company made a good scene to the eye; and our author, who wanted them no longer on the stage, was glad to find this method of sweeping them away.

I fancy every reader when he ends this play cries out with Desdemona, 'O, most lame and impotent conclusion!' [*Othello*, II.1.158]. As this play was not to our knowledge divided into acts by the author, I could be content to conclude it with the death of Henry the Fourth.

> In that Jerusalem shall Harry die.
> [IV.5.239]

These scenes which now make the fifth act of *Henry the Fourth* might then be the first of *Henry the Fifth*; but the truth is that they do unite very commodiously to either play. When these plays were represented I believe they ended as they are now ended in the books; but Shakespeare seems to have designed that the whole series of action from the beginning of *Richard the Second* to the end of *Henry the Fifth* should be considered by the reader as one work, upon one plan, only broken into parts by the necessity of exhibition.

None of Shakespeare's plays are more read than the first and

Selections from Notes to the Plays

second parts of *Henry the Fourth*. Perhaps no author has ever in two plays afforded so much delight. The great events are interesting, for the fate of kingdoms depends upon them; the slighter occurrences are diverting and, except one or two, sufficiently probable; the incidents are multiplied with wonderful fertility of invention and the characters diversified with the utmost nicety of discernment and the profoundest skill in the nature of man.

The Prince, who is the hero both of the comic and tragic part, is a young man of great abilities and violent passions, whose sentiments are right, though his actions are wrong; whose virtues are obscured by negligence and whose understanding is dissipated by levity. In his idle hours he is rather loose than wicked and when the occasion forces out his latent qualities he is great without effort and brave without tumult. The trifler is roused into a hero and the hero again reposes in the trifler. This character is great, original and just.

Percy is a rugged soldier, choleric and quarrelsome, and has only the soldier's virtues, generosity and courage.

But Falstaff unimitated, unimitable Falstaff, how shall I describe thee? Thou compound of sense and vice; of sense which may be admired but not esteemed, of vice which may be despised, but hardly detested. Falstaff is a character loaded with faults, and with those faults which naturally produce contempt. He is a thief and a glutton, a coward and a boaster, always ready to cheat the weak and prey upon the poor; to terrify the timorous and insult the defenceless. At once obsequious and malignant, he satirizes in their absence those whom he lives by flattering. He is familiar with the Prince only as an agent of vice, but of this familiarity he is so proud as not only to be supercilious and haughty with common men, but to think his interest of importance to the Duke of Lancaster. Yet the man thus corrupt, thus despicable, makes himself necessary to the prince that despises him by the most pleasing of all qualities, perpetual gaiety, by an unfailing power of exciting laughter, which is the more freely indulged as his wit is not of the splendid or ambitious kind but consists in easy escapes and sallies of levity, which make sport but raise no envy. It must be observed that he is stained with no enormous or sanguinary crimes, so that his licentiousness is not so offensive but that it may be borne for his mirth.

The moral to be drawn from this representation is that no man is more dangerous than he that with a will to corrupt hath the power to please; and that neither wit nor honesty ought to think themselves safe with such a companion when they see Henry seduced by Falstaff.

HENRY V

I. CHORUS 24
CHORUS
 Into a thousand parts divide one man,
 And make imaginary puissance.

This passage shows that Shakespeare was fully sensible of the absurdity of showing battles on the theatre, which indeed is never done but tragedy becomes farce. Nothing can be represented to the eye but by something like it and 'within a wooden O' [13] nothing very like a battle can be exhibited.

II.2.126
KING HENRY
 O, how hast thou with jealousy infected
 The sweetness of affiance!

Shakespeare urges this aggravation of the guilt of treachery with great judgement. One of the worst consequences of breach of trust is the diminution of that confidence which makes the happiness of life and the dissemination of suspicion, which is the poison of society.

II.3.22
HOSTESS I put my hand into the bed, and felt them, and they were as cold as any stone; then I felt to his knees, and so up'ard and up'ard, and all was as cold as any stone.

Such is the end of Falstaff from whom Shakespeare had promised us in his epilogue to *Henry IV* that we should receive more entertainment. It happened to Shakespeare as to other writers to have his imagination crowded with a tumultuary confusion of images which, while they were yet unsorted and unexamined, seemed sufficient to furnish a long train of incidents and a new variety of merriment, but which when he was to produce them to view shrunk suddenly from him or could not be accommodated to his general design. That he once designed to have brought Falstaff on the scene again, we know from himself; but whether he could contrive no train of adventures suitable to his character, or could match him with no companions likely to quicken his humour, or could open no new vein of pleasantry and was afraid to continue the same strain lest it should not find the same reception, he has here for ever discarded him and made haste to dispatch him, perhaps for the same reason for which Addison killed Sir Roger [de Coverley], that no other hand might attempt to exhibit him.

Let meaner authors learn from this example that it is dangerous to sell the bear which is yet not hunted, to promise to the public what they have not written.

This disappointment probably inclined Queen Elizabeth to command the poet to produce him once again, and to show him in love or courtship. This was indeed a new source of humour and produced a new play from the former characters.

I forgot to note in the proper place, and therefore note here, that Falstaff's courtship, or *The Merry Wives of Windsor*, should be read between *Henry IV* and *Henry V*.[33]

III.4.1
[Stage direction] *Enter Katherine and Alice, an old gentlewoman*

[Warburton wished there was evidence to show that 'this ridiculous scene' was interpolated.]

Sir T. Hanmer has rejected it. The scene is indeed mean enough when it is read, but the grimaces of two French women and the odd accent with which they uttered the English made it divert upon the stage. It may be observed that there is in it not only the French language, but the French spirit. Alice compliments the Princess upon her knowledge of four words and tells her that she pronounces like the English themselves. The Princess suspects no deficiency in her instructress, nor the instructress in herself. Throughout the whole scene there may be found French servility and French vanity.

III.6.100
FLUELLEN . . . and his lips blows at his nose, and it is like a coal of fire, sometimes plue, and sometimes red; but his nose is executed, and his fire's out.

This is the last time that any sport can be made with the red face of Bardolph, which to confess the truth seems to have taken more hold on Shakespeare's imagination than on any other. The conception is very cold to the solitary reader, though it may be somewhat invigorated by the exhibition on the stage. This poet is always more careful about the present than the future, about his audience than his readers.

IV.1.223
KING HENRY
    Upon the King!

There is something very striking and solemn in this soliloquy, into which the King breaks immediately, as soon as he is left alone. Something like this, on less occasions, every breast has felt. Reflection and seriousness rush upon the mind upon the separation of a gay company and especially after forced and unwilling merriment.

IV.3.57
KING HENRY
    And Crispin Crispian shall ne'er go by,
    From this day to the ending of the world,
    But we in it shall be rememberèd . . .

It may be observed that we are apt to promise to ourselves a more lasting memory than the changing state of human things admits. This prediction is not verified; the feast of Crispin passes by without any mention of Agincourt. Late events obliterate the former: the civil wars have left in this nation scarcely any tradition of more ancient history.

IV.3.66
KING HENRY
  And hold their manhoods cheap, whiles any speaks
  That fought with us upon Saint Crispin's day.

This speech like many others of the declamatory kind is too long. Had it been contracted to about half the number of lines it might have gained force and lost none of the sentiments.

IV.7.44
FLUELLEN . . . so also Harry Monmouth . . . turned away the fat knight with the great-belly doublet – he was full of jests, and gipes, and knaveries, and mocks: I have forgot his name.

This is the last time that Falstaff can make sport. The poet was loath to part with him and has continued his memory as long as he could.

IV.7.61
KING HENRY
  Besides, we'll cut the throats of those we have . . .

The King is in a very bloody disposition. He has already cut the throats of his prisoners and threatens now to cut them again. No haste of composition could produce such negligence; neither was this play, which is the second draught of the same design, written in haste. There must be some dislocation of the scenes. If we place these lines at the beginning of the twelfth scene [IV.6] the absurdity will be removed and the action will proceed in a regular series. This transposition might easily happen in copies written for the players. Yet it must not be concealed that in the imperfect play of 1608 the order of the scenes is the same as here.[34]

V.1.83
PISTOL
   To England will I steal, and there I'll – steal . . .

The comic scenes of the history of Henry the Fourth and Fifth are now at an end and all the comic personages are now dismissed. Falstaff and Mistress Quickly are dead; Nym and Bardolph are hanged; Gadshill was lost immediately after the robbery; Poins and Peto have vanished since, one knows not how; and Pistol is now beaten into obscurity. I believe every reader regrets their departure.

V.2.122
KING HENRY I'faith, Kate, my wooing is fit for thy understanding.

I know not why Shakespeare now gives the King nearly such a character as he made him formerly ridicule in Percy. This military grossness and unskilfulness in all the softer arts does not suit very well with the gaieties of his youth, with the general knowledge ascribed to him at his accession or with the contemptuous message sent him by the Dauphin, who represents him as fitter for the ballroom than the field and tells him that he is not 'to revel into duchies', or win provinces 'with a nimble galliard' [I.2.253]. The truth is that the poet's matter failed him in the fifth act and he was glad to fill it up with whatever he could get; and not even Shakespeare can write well without a proper subject. It is a vain endeavour for the most skilful hand to cultivate barrenness, or to paint upon vacuity.

V.2.287
BURGUNDY Pardon the frankness of my mirth, if I answer you for that.

We have here but a mean dialogue for princes; the merriment is very gross and the sentiments are very worthless.

This play has many scenes of high dignity and many of easy merriment. The character of the King is well supported except in his courtship, where he has neither the vivacity of Hal, nor the grandeur of Henry. The humour of Pistol is very happily continued; his character has perhaps been the model of all the bullies that have yet appeared on the English stage.

The lines given to the Chorus have many admirers; but the truth is that in them a little may be praised and much must be forgiven; nor can it be easily discovered why the intelligence given by the Chorus is more necessary in this play than in many others where it is omitted. The great defect of this play is the emptiness and narrowness of the last act, which a very little diligence might have easily avoided.

1 HENRY VI

III.4.38
BASSET
Villain, thou knowest the law of arms is such
That whoso draws a sword 'tis very death . . .

This reading [Warburton had emended to 'sword i'th' presence 't's death'] cannot be right because, as Mr Edwards observed, it cannot be pronounced. It is however a good comment as it shows the author's meaning.[35]

2 HENRY VI

III.2.160
WARWICK
See how the blood is settled in his face.

I cannot but stop a moment to observe that this horrible description is scarcely the work of any pen but Shakespeare's.

III.2.333
SUFFOLK
You bade me ban, and will you bid me leave?

This inconsistency is very common in real life. Those who are vexed to impatience are angry to see others less disturbed than themselves, but when others begin to rave they immediately see in them what they could not find in themselves, the deformity and folly of useless rage.

III.3.32
KING
 Close up his eyes, and draw the curtain close;
 And let us all to meditation.

This is one of the scenes which have been applauded by the critics and which will continue to be admired when prejudice shall cease and bigotry give way to impartial examination. These are beauties that rise out of nature and of truth; the superficial reader cannot miss them, the profound can image nothing beyond them.

IV.7.45
CADE Marry, thou oughtest not to let thy horse wear a cloak, when honester men than thou go in their hose and doublets.

This is a reproach truly characteristical. Nothing gives so much offence to the lower ranks of mankind as the sight of superfluities merely ostentatious.

3 HENRY VI

I.2.49
MESSENGER
 The Queen with all the northern earls and lords
 Intend here to besiege you in your castle.
 She is hard by with twenty thousand men;
 And therefore fortify your hold, my lord.
YORK
 Ay, with my sword.

I know not whether the author intended any moral instruction, but he that reads this has a striking admonition against that precipitancy by which men often use unlawful means to do that which a little delay would put honestly in their power.

Selections from Notes to the Plays   213

Had York stayed but a few moments he had saved his cause from the stain of perjury.

II.5.21
KING
   O God! Methinks it were a happy life
   To be no better than a homely swain . . .

This speech is mournful and soft, exquisitely suited to the character of the King, and makes a pleasing interchange by affording amidst the tumult and horror of the battle an unexpected glimpse of rural innocence and pastoral tranquillity.

II.5.54
[Stage direction] *Alarum. Enter at one door a Son that hath killed his father, with the dead body in his arms*
II.5.78
[Stage direction] *Enter at another door a Father that hath killed his son, with the dead body in his arms*

These two horrible incidents are selected to show the innumerable calamities of civil war.

III.1.16
KING
   Thy place is filled, thy sceptre wrung from thee,
   Thy balm washed off wherewith thou wast anointed . . .

This is an image very frequent in the works of Shakespeare. So again in this scene:

>   I was anointed King.
>   [76]

It is common in these plays to find the same images, whether jocular or serious, frequently recurring.

III.2.16
EDWARD
   Widow, we will consider of your suit;
   And come some other time to know our mind.

This is a very lively and sprightly dialogue; the reciprocation is quicker than is common in Shakespeare.

IV.6.67
SOMERSET
My liege, it is young Henry Earl of Richmond.

He was afterwards Henry VII, a man who put an end to the civil war of the two houses, but not otherwise remarkable for virtue. Shakespeare knew his trade. Henry VII was grandfather to Queen Elizabeth and the king from whom James inherited.

V.4.66
[Stage direction] *Flourish and march. Enter Edward, Richard, George, and soldiers*

This scene is ill contrived, in which the King and Queen appear at once on the stage at the head of opposite armies. It had been easy to make one retire before the other entered.

V.5.65
QUEEN
But if you ever chance to have a child,
Look in his youth to have him so cut off
As, deathsmen, you have rid this sweet young Prince!

The condition of this war-like queen would move compassion could it be forgotten that she gave York, to wipe his eyes in his captivity, a handkerchief stained with his young child's blood.

If we take these plays [*1, 2* and *3 Henry VI*] from Shakespeare, to whom shall they be given? What author of that age had the same easiness of expression and fluency of numbers?

Having considered the evidence given by the plays themselves and found it in their favour, let us now inquire what corroboration can be gained from other testimony. They are ascribed to Shakespeare by the first editors, whose attestation may be received in questions of fact, however unskilfully they superintended their edition. They seem to be declared genuine by the voice of Shakespeare himself, who refers to the second play in his epilogue to *Henry V* and apparently connects the first act of *Richard III* with the last of the third part of *Henry VI*. If it be objected that the plays were popular and therefore he alluded to them as well known, it may be answered with equal probability that the natural passions of a poet would have disposed him to separate his own works from those of an inferior hand. And indeed if an author's own testimony is to be overthrown by speculative criticism, no man can be any longer secure of literary reputation.

Of these three plays I think the second the best. The truth is that they have not sufficient variety of action, for the incidents are too often of the same kind; yet many of the characters are well discriminated. King Henry and his Queen, King Edward, the Duke of Gloucester and the Earl of Warwick are very strongly and distinctly painted.

RICHARD III

I.1.28
RICHARD
> And therefore, since I cannot prove a lover
> To entertain these fair well-spoken days,
> I am determined to prove a villain . . .

Shakespeare very diligently inculcates that the wickedness of Richard proceeded from his deformity, from the envy that rose at the comparison of his own person with others and which incited him to disturb the pleasures that he could not partake.

I.2.179
RICHARD
> Nay, do not pause; for I did kill King Henry –
> But 'twas thy beauty that provokèd me.

Shakespeare countenances the observation that no woman can ever be offended with the mention of her beauty.

IV.4.199
KING RICHARD
  Stay, madam; I must talk a word with you.

On this dialogue 'tis not necessary to bestow much criticism: part of it is ridiculous and the whole improbable.

V.3.178
KING RICHARD
  Give me another horse! Bind up my wounds!

There is in this, as in many of our author's speeches of passion, something very trifling and something very striking. Richard's debate whether he should quarrel with himself is too long continued, but the subsequent exaggeration of his crimes is truly tragical.

This is one of the most celebrated of our author's performances; yet I know not whether it has not happened to him as to others to be praised most when praise is not most deserved. That this play has scenes noble in themselves and very well contrived to strike in the exhibition cannot be denied. But some parts are trifling, others shocking and some improbable.

I have nothing to add to the observations of these learned critics [Warburton and Upton] but that some traces of this antiquated exhibition [of the Vice] are still retained in the rustic puppet plays, in which I have seen the Devil very lustily belaboured by Punch, whom I hold to be the legitimate successor of the old Vice.

HENRY VIII

Prologue 18
PROLOGUE
  To rank our chosen truth with such a show
  As fool and fight is, beside forfeiting
  Our own brains . . .

This is not the only passage in which Shakespeare has discovered his conviction of the impropriety of battles represented on the stage. He knew that five or six men with swords give a very unsatisfactory idea of an army and therefore without much care to excuse his former practice he allows that a theatrical fight would destroy all 'opinion' of 'truth' and 'leave' him 'never an understanding friend'. *Magnis ingeniis et multa nihilominus habituris simplex convenit erroris confessio.*[36] Yet I know not whether the coronation shown in this play may not be liable to all that can be objected against a battle.

III.2.399
WOLSEY
  May have a tomb of orphans' tears wept on him.

The Chancellor is the general guardian of orphans. A 'tomb of tears' is very harsh.

IV.2.1

[Stage direction] *Enter Katherine, Dowager, sick* . . .

This scene is above any other part of Shakespeare's tragedies, and perhaps above any scene of any other poet, tender and pathetic, without gods, or furies, or poisons, or precipices, without the help of romantic circumstances, without improbable sallies of poetical lamentation and without any throes of tumultuous misery.

V.5.39
CRANMER
  Nor shall this peace sleep with her; but as when
  The bird of wonder dies, the maiden phoenix,
  Her ashes new-create another heir . . .

These lines, to the interruption by the King [39–55], seem to have been inserted at some revisal of the play after the accession of King James. If the passage . . . be left out, the speech of Cranmer proceeds in a regular tenor of prediction and continuity of sentiments; but by the interposition of the new lines he first celebrates Elizabeth's successor and then wishes he did not know that she was to die; first rejoices at the consequence and then laments the cause. Our author was at once politic and idle; he resolved to flatter James but neglected to reduce the whole speech to propriety, or perhaps intended that the lines inserted should be spoken in the action and omitted in the publication, if any publication ever was in his thoughts. Mr Theobald has made the same observation.

The play of *Henry the Eighth* is one of those which still keeps possession of the stage by the splendour of its pageantry. The coronation about forty years ago drew the people together in multitudes for a great part of the winter.[37] Yet pomp is not the only merit of this play. The meek sorrows and virtuous distress of Katherine have furnished some scenes which may be justly numbered among the greatest efforts of tragedy. But the genius of Shakespeare comes in and goes out with Katherine. Every other part may be easily conceived and easily written.

[EPILOGUE TO THE HISTORIES]

The historical dramas are now concluded, of which the two parts of *Henry the Fourth* and *Henry the Fifth* are among the happiest of our author's compositions; and *King John*, *Richard the Third* and *Henry the Eighth* deservedly stand in the second class. Those whose curiosity would refer the historical scenes to their original may consult Holinshed and sometimes Hall: from Holinshed Shakespeare has often inserted whole speeches with no more alteration than was necessary to the numbers of his verse. To transcribe them into the margin was unnecessary because the original is easily examined and they are seldom less perspicuous[38] in the poet than in the historian.

To play histories, or to exhibit a succession of events by action and dialogue, was a common entertainment among our rude ancestors upon great festivities. The parish clerks once performed at Clerkenwell a play which lasted three days containing *The History of the World*.[39]

KING LEAR

I.1
There is something of obscurity or inaccuracy in this preparatory scene. The King has already divided his kingdom and yet when he enters he examines his daughters to discover in what proportions he should divide it. Perhaps Kent and Gloucester only were privy to his design, which he still kept in his own hands, to be changed or performed as subsequent reasons should determine him.

I.1.171
LEAR
   Which nor our nature nor our place can bear,
   Our potency made good . . .

Lear, who is characterized as hot, heady and violent, is with very just observation of life made to entangle himself with vows; upon any sudden provocation to vow revenge and then to plead the obligation of a vow in defence of implacability.

II.4.1
[Stage direction] *Enter Lear . . .*

It is not very clearly discovered why Lear comes hither [to Gloucester's castle]. In the foregoing part he sent a letter to Gloucester, but no hint is given of its contents. He seems to have gone to visit Gloucester while Cornwall and Regan might prepare to entertain him.

IV.5.22
REGAN
   Let me unseal the letter.
OSWALD   Madam, I had rather –

I know not well why Shakespeare gives the steward, who is a mere factor[40] of wickedness, so much fidelity. He now refuses the letter and afterwards when he is dying thinks only how it may be safely delivered.

IV.6.11
EDGAR   How fearful
And dizzy 'tis to cast one's eyes so low!

This description has been much admired since the time of Addison,[41] who has remarked with a poor attempt at pleasantry that 'he who can read it without being giddy has a very good head, or a very bad one'. The description is certainly not mean, but I am far from thinking it wrought to the utmost excellence of poetry. He that looks from a precipice finds himself assailed by one great and dreadful image of irresistible destruction. But this overwhelming idea is dissipated and enfeebled from the instant that the mind can restore itself to the observation of particulars and diffuse its attention to distinct objects. The enumeration of the choughs and crows, the samphire-man and the fishers, counteracts the great effect of the prospect as it peoples the desert of intermediate vacuity and stops the mind in the rapidity of its descent through emptiness and horror.

IV.7.85
What is printed in italics [IV.7.85–97] is not in the folio. It is at least proper, if not necessary, and was omitted by the author, I suppose, for no other reason than to shorten the representation.

V.3.164
EDGAR   Let's exchange charity.

Our author by negligence gives his heathens the sentiments and practices of Christianity. In *Hamlet* there is the same solemn act of final reconciliation, but with exact propriety, for the personages are Christians:

> Exchange forgiveness with me, noble Hamlet, *etc.*
>   [V.2.323]

V.3.261
KENT   Is this the promised end?

EDGAR
 Or image of that horror?
ALBANY   Fall and cease!

These two exclamations are given to Edgar and Albany in the folio to animate the dialogue and employ all the persons on the stage, but they are very obscure.

The tragedy of *Lear* is deservedly celebrated among the dramas of Shakespeare. There is perhaps no play which keeps the attention so strongly fixed; which so much agitates our passions and interests our curiosity. The artful involutions[42] of distinct interests, the striking opposition of contrary characters, the sudden changes of fortune and the quick succession of events fill the mind with a perpetual tumult of indignation, pity and hope. There is no scene which does not contribute to the aggravation of the distress or conduct of the action and scarce a line which does not conduce to the progress of the scene. So powerful is the current of the poet's imagination that the mind, which once ventures within it, is hurried irresistibly along.

On the seeming improbability of Lear's conduct it may be observed that he is represented according to histories at that time vulgarly received as true. And perhaps if we turn our thoughts upon the barbarity and ignorance of the age to which this story is referred, it will appear not so unlikely as while we estimate Lear's manners by our own. Such preference of one daughter to another, or resignation of dominion on such conditions, would be yet credible if told of a petty prince of Guinea or Madagascar. Shakespeare, indeed, by the mention of his earls and dukes, has given us the idea of times more civilized and of life regulated by softer manners; and the truth is that though he so nicely discriminates and so minutely describes the characters of men, he commonly neglects and confounds the characters of ages by mingling customs ancient and modern, English and foreign.

My learned friend Mr Warton, who has in the *Adventurer*[43] very minutely criticized this play, remarks that the instances of cruelty are too savage and shocking and that the intervention of

Edmund destroys the simplicity of the story. These objections may, I think, be answered by repeating that the cruelty of the daughters is an historical fact, to which the poet has added little, having only drawn it into a series by dialogue and action. But I am not able to apologize with equal plausibility for the extrusion of Gloucester's eyes, which seems an act too horrid to be endured in dramatic exhibition, and such as must always compel the mind to relieve its distress by incredulity. Yet let it be remembered that our author well knew what would please the audience for which he wrote.

The injury done by Edmund to the simplicity of the action is abundantly recompensed by the addition of variety, by the art with which he is made to co-operate with the chief design, and the opportunity which he gives the poet of combining perfidy with perfidy and connecting the wicked son with the wicked daughters, to impress this important moral that villainy is never at a stop, that crimes lead to crimes and at last terminate in ruin.

But though this moral be incidentally enforced, Shakespeare has suffered the virtue of Cordelia to perish in a just cause, contrary to the natural ideas of justice, to the hope of the reader and, what is yet more strange, to the faith of chronicles. Yet this conduct is justified by the *Spectator*, who blames Tate for giving Cordelia success and happiness in his alteration and declares that, in his opinion, 'the tragedy has lost half its beauty'.[44] Dennis has remarked, whether justly or not, that to secure the favourable reception of *Cato*, 'the town was poisoned with much false and abominable criticism', and that endeavours had been used to discredit and decry poetical justice.[45] A play in which the wicked prosper and the virtuous miscarry may doubtless be good, because it is a just representation of the common events of human life: but since all reasonable beings naturally love justice, I cannot easily be persuaded that the observation of justice makes a play worse; or that if other excellencies are equal the audience will not always rise better pleased from the final triumph of persecuted virtue.

In the present case the public has decided. Cordelia from the time of Tate has always retired with victory and felicity. And if my sensations could add anything to the general suffrage, I might relate that I was many years ago so shocked by Cordelia's death that I know not whether I ever endured to read again the last scenes of the play till I undertook to revise them as an editor.

There is another controversy among the critics concerning this play. It is disputed whether the predominant image in Lear's disordered mind be the loss of his kingdom or the cruelty of his daughters. Mr Murphy, a very judicious critic,[46] has evinced by induction of particular passages that the cruelty of his daughters is the primary source of his distress and that the loss of royalty affects him only as a secondary and subordinate evil; he observes with great justness that Lear would move our compassion but little did we not rather consider the injured father than the degraded king.

The story of this play, except the episode of Edmund, which is derived I think from Sidney, is taken originally from Geoffrey of Monmouth, whom Holinshed generally copied; but perhaps immediately from an old historical ballad of which I shall insert the greater part. My reason for believing that the play was posterior to the ballad rather than the ballad to the play is that the ballad has nothing of Shakespeare's nocturnal tempest, which is too striking to have been omitted and that it follows the chronicle; it has the rudiments of the play but none of its amplifications: it first hinted Lear's madness but did not array it in circumstances. The writer of the ballad added something to the history, which is a proof that he would have added more, if more had occurred to his mind and more must have occurred if he had seen Shakespeare. [Johnson then prints 'A lamentable Song of the Death of King Leir and his Three Daughters'.]

TIMON OF ATHENS

IV.2.1
[Stage direction] *Enter Flavius, with two or three Servants*

Nothing contributes more to the exaltation of Timon's character than the zeal and fidelity of his servants. Nothing but real virtue can be honoured by domestics; nothing but impartial kindness can gain affection from dependants.

IV.3.253
TIMON
  Hadst thou, like us from our first swath, proceeded
  The sweet degrees that this brief world affords . . .

There is in this speech a sullen haughtiness and malignant dignity suitable at once to the lord and the man-hater. The impatience with which he bears to have his luxury reproached by one that never had luxury within his reach is natural and graceful.

IV.3.276
TIMON
  If thou hadst not been born the worst of men,
  Thou hadst been a knave and flatterer.

Dryden has quoted two verses of Virgil to show how well he could have written satires.[47] Shakespeare has here given a specimen of the same power by a line bitter beyond all bitterness, in which Timon tells Apemantus that he had not virtue enough for the vices which he condemns.

Dr Warburton explains 'worst' by 'lowest', which somewhat weakens the sense and yet leaves it sufficiently vigorous.

I have heard Mr Burke commend the subtlety of discrimination with which Shakespeare distinguishes the present character of Timon from that of Apemantus, whom to vulgar eyes he would now resemble.[48]

V.3.4
SOLDIER
  Some beast read this; there does not live a man.

There is something elaborately unskilful in the contrivance of sending a soldier, who cannot read, to take the epitaph in wax, only that it may close the play by being read with more solemnity in the last scene.

The play of *Timon* is a domestic tragedy and therefore strongly fastens on the attention of the reader. In the plan there is not much art, but the incidents are natural and the characters various and exact. The catastrophe affords a very powerful warning against that ostentatious liberality, which scatters bounty, but confers no benefits, and buys flattery, but not friendship.

In this tragedy are many passages perplexed, obscure and probably corrupt, which I have endeavoured to rectify or explain with due diligence; but having only one copy [the first folio], cannot promise myself that my endeavours will be much applauded.

TITUS ANDRONICUS

All the editors and critics agree with Mr Theobald in supposing this play spurious. I see no reason for differing from them; for the colour of the style is wholly different from that of the other plays and there is an attempt at regular versification and artificial closes, not always inelegant yet seldom pleasing. The barbarity of the spectacles and the general massacre which are here exhibited can scarcely be conceived tolerable to any audience; yet we are told by Jonson that they were not only borne but praised.[49] That Shakespeare wrote any part, though Theobald declares it 'incontestable', I see no reason for believing.

The testimony produced at the beginning of this play by which it is ascribed to Shakespeare is by no means equal to the argument against its authenticity, arising from the total difference of conduct, language and sentiments by which it stands apart from all the rest. Meres had probably no other evidence than that of a title-page which, though in our time it be sufficient, was then of no great authority; for all the plays which were rejected by the first collectors of Shakespeare's works and admitted in later editions and again rejected by the critical editors, had Shakespeare's name on the title, as we must suppose, by the fraudulence of the printers who, while there were yet no gazettes, nor advertisements, nor any means of circulating literary intelligence, could usurp at pleasure any celebrated name. Nor had Shakespeare any interest in detecting the imposture as none of his fame or profit was produced by the press.[50]

The chronology of this play does not prove it not to be Shakespeare's. If it had been written twenty-five years in 1614 it might have been written when Shakespeare was twenty-five years old. When he left Warwickshire I know not, but at the age of twenty-five it was rather too late to fly for deer-stealing.[51]

Ravenscroft, who in the reign of Charles II revised this play and restored it to the stage, tells us in his preface, from a theatrical tradition I suppose, which in his time might be of sufficient authority, that this play was touched in different parts by Shakespeare, but written by some other poet.[52] I do not find Shakespeare's touches very discernible.

MACBETH

I.3.146
MACBETH   Come what come may,
Time and the hour runs through the roughest day.

I suppose every reader is disgusted at the tautology in this passage, 'Time and the hour', and will therefore willingly believe that Shakespeare wrote it thus:

> Come what come may,
> *Time! on!* – the hour runs through the roughest day.

Macbeth is deliberating upon the events which are to befall him, but finding no satisfaction from his own thoughts, he grows impatient of reflection and resolves to wait the close without harassing himself with conjectures.

> Come what come may.

But to shorten the pain of suspense he calls upon time in the usual style of ardent desire to quicken his motion:

> Time! on! –

Selections from Notes to the Plays 227

He then comforts himself with the reflection that all his perplexity must have an end:

> the hour runs through the roughest day.

This conjecture is supported by the passage in the letter to his lady in which he says, they '*referred me to the coming on of time, with "Hail, king that shalt be"*' [I. 5. 7].

I.7.1
MACBETH
> If it were done when 'tis done, then 'twere well
> It were done quickly.

Of this soliloquy the meaning is not very clear; I have never found the readers of Shakespeare agreeing about it. I understand it thus:

'If that which I am about to do, when it is once *done* and executed, were *done* and ended without any following effects, it would then be best *to do it quickly*; if the murder could terminate in itself and restrain the regular course of consequences, if *its success* could secure *its surcease*,[53] if being once done *successfully*, without detection, it could *fix a period* to all vengeance and inquiry, so that *this blow* might be all that I have to do and this anxiety all that I have to suffer; if this could be my condition, even *here* in *this world*, in this contracted period of temporal existence, on this narrow *bank* in the ocean of eternity, *I would jump the life to come*, I would venture upon the deed without care of any future state. But this is one of *these cases* in which judgement is pronounced and vengeance inflicted upon us *here* in our present life. We teach others to do as we have done and are punished by our own example.'[54]

II.1
[Stage direction] *[Macbeth's Castle]*

The place is not marked in the old edition, nor is it easy to say where this encounter can be. It is not in the 'hall', as the editors have all supposed it, for Banquo sees the sky; it is not far from the bedchamber as the conversation shows: it must be in the inner court of the castle, which Banquo might properly cross in his way to bed.

II.1.25
MACBETH
   If you shall cleave to my consent when 'tis,
   It shall make honour for you.

Macbeth expresses his thought with affected obscurity; he does not mention the royalty, though he apparently has it in his mind, 'If you shall cleave to my consent', if you shall concur with me when I determine to accept the crown, 'when 'tis', when that happens which the prediction promises, 'it shall make honour for you'.[55]

III.4.59
LADY   O proper stuff!
   This is the very painting of your fear.
   This is the air-drawn dagger which you said
   Led you to Duncan. O, these flaws and starts,
   Impostors to true fear, would well become
   A woman's story at a winter's fire,
   Authorized by her grandam. Shame itself!
   Why do you make such faces? When all's done
   You look but on a stool.

This speech is rather too long for the circumstances in which it is spoken. It had begun better at 'Shame itself!'.

IV.3.195
MACDUFF   What concern they?
   The general cause, or is it a fee-grief
   Due to some single breast?

'Fee-grief.' A peculiar sorrow; a grief that hath a single owner. The expression is, at least to our ears, very harsh.

V.3.22
MACBETH
  I have lived long enough: my Way of life
  Is fallen into the sere, the yellow leaf . . .

As there is no relation between the 'way of life' and 'fallen into the sere', I am inclined to think that the 'W' is only an 'M' inverted, and that it was originally written:

my *May* of life.

'I am now passed from the spring to the autumn of my days, but I am without those comforts that should succeed the sprightliness of bloom, and support me in this melancholy season.'
  The author has 'May' in the same sense elsewhere.[56]

This play is deservedly celebrated for the propriety of its fictions, and solemnity, grandeur and variety of its action; but it has no nice[57] discriminations of character, the events are too great to admit the influence of particular dispositions and the course of the action necessarily determines the conduct of the agents.

The danger of ambition is well described; and I know not whether it may not be said in defence of some parts which now seem improbable, that in Shakespeare's time it was necessary to warn credulity against vain and illusive[58] predictions.

The passions are directed to their true end. Lady Macbeth is merely detested; and though the courage of Macbeth preserves some esteem, yet every reader rejoices at his fall.

CORIOLANUS

III.3.129
CORIOLANUS
  Your ignorance – which finds not till it feels . . .

It is remarkable that among the political maxims of the speculative[59] Harrington there is one which he might have borrowed from this speech. 'The people,' says he, 'cannot see, but they can feel.'[60] It is not much to the honour of the people that they have the same character of stupidity from their enemy and their friend. Such was the power of our author's mind that he looked through life in all its relations private and civil.

The tragedy of *Coriolanus* is one of the most amusing[61] of our author's performances. The old man's merriment in Menenius; the lofty lady's dignity in Volumnia; the bridal modesty in Virgilia; the patrician and military haughtiness in Coriolanus; the plebeian malignity and tribunitian insolence in Brutus and Sicinius make a very pleasing and interesting variety: and the various revolutions of the hero's fortune fill the mind with anxious curiosity. There is, perhaps, too much bustle in the first act and too little in the last.

JULIUS CAESAR

Of this tragedy many particular passages deserve regard and the contention and reconcilement of Brutus and Cassius is universally celebrated; but I have never been strongly agitated in perusing it and think it somewhat cold and unaffecting[62] compared with some other of Shakespeare's plays; his adherence to the real story and to Roman manners seems to have impeded the natural vigour of his genius.

ANTONY AND CLEOPATRA

I.1.9
PHILO
    And is become the bellows and the fan
    To cool a gypsy's lust.

In this passage something seems to be wanting. The 'bellows' and 'fan' being commonly used for contrary purposes were probably opposed by the author, who might perhaps have written:

> is become the bellows and the fan
> *To kindle and* to cool a gypsy's lust.

III.13.1
CLEOPATRA
  What shall we do, Enobarbus?
ENOBARBUS   Think, and die.

This reading ['Drink, and die'] offered by Sir T. Hanmer is received by Dr Warburton and Mr Upton, but I have not advanced it into the page, not being convinced that it is necessary. 'Think, and die'; that is, 'Reflect on your folly, and leave the world', is a natural answer.

IV.9.15
ENOBARBUS   Throw my heart
  Against the flint and hardness of my fault,
  Which, being dried with grief, will break to powder,
  And finish all foul thoughts.

The pathetic of Shakespeare too often ends in the ridiculous. It is painful to find the gloomy dignity of this noble scene destroyed by the intrusion of a conceit so far-fetched and unaffecting.

This play keeps curiosity always busy and the passions always interested. The continual hurry of the action, the variety of incidents and the quick succession of one personage to another call the mind forward without intermission from the first act to the last. But the power of delighting is derived principally from the frequent changes of the scene; for except the feminine arts, some of which are too low, which distinguish Cleopatra, no character is very strongly discriminated. Upton, who did not easily miss what he desired to find, has discovered that the language of Antony is with great skill and learning made pompous and superb according to his real practice. But I think his diction not distinguishable from that of others: the most tumid[63] speech in the play is that which Caesar makes to Octavia [III.6.42–55].

The events, of which the principal are described according to history, are produced without any art of connection or care of disposition.

CYMBELINE

I.5.23
CORNELIUS   Your Highness
  Shall from this practice but make hard your heart ...

There is in this passage nothing that much requires a note, yet I cannot forbear to push it forward into observation. The thought would probably have been more amplified had our author lived to be shocked with such experiments as have been published in later times by a race of men that have practised tortures without pity and related them without shame, and are yet suffered to erect their heads among human beings.

Cape saxa manu, cape robora, pastor.[64]

I.5.33
CORNELIUS
  I do not like her.

This soliloquy is very inartificial.[65] The speaker is under no strong pressure of thought; he is neither resolving, repenting, suspecting, nor deliberating, and yet makes a long speech to tell himself what himself knows.

I.6.150
IMOGEN
  A saucy stranger in his court to mart
  As in a Romish stew ...

The stews of Rome are deservedly censured by the reformed. This is one of many instances in which Shakespeare has mingled the manners of distant ages in this play.

II.3.113
CLOTEN
  The contract you pretend with that base wretch,
  One bred of alms and fostered with cold dishes,
  With scraps o' th' court – it is no contract, none.

Here Shakespeare has not preserved with his common nicety the uniformity of character. The speech of Cloten is rough and harsh, but certainly not the talk of one who:

> Cannot take two from twenty, for his heart,
> And leave eighteen.
>
> [II.1.53]

His argument is just and well enforced and its prevalence is allowed throughout all civil nations: as for rudeness, he seems not to be much undermatched.

II.4.70
IACHIMO
 Proud Cleopatra when she met her Roman
 And Cydnus swelled above the banks, or for
 The press of boats or pride.

[Warburton claimed this was 'an agreeable ridicule on poetical exaggeration' and that Shakespeare was parodying Enobarbus's speech in *Antony and Cleopatra* (II.2.196).]

It is easy to sit down, and give our author meanings which he never had. Shakespeare has no great right to censure poetical exaggeration, of which no poet is more frequently guilty. That he intended to ridicule his own lines is very uncertain, when there are no means of knowing which of the two plays was written first. The commentator has contented himself to suppose that the foregoing play in his book was the play of earlier composition. Nor is the reasoning better than the assertion. If the language of Iachimo be such as shows him to be mocking the credibility of his hearer, his language is very improper when his business was to deceive. But the truth is that his language is such as a skilful villain would naturally use, a mixture of airy triumph and serious deposition. His gaiety shows his seriousness to be without anxiety and his seriousness proves his gaiety to be without art.

III.3.35
ARVIRAGUS   What should we speak of
 When we are old as you?

This dread of an old age, unsupplied with matter for discourse and meditation, is a sentiment natural and noble. No state can be more destitute than that of him who when the delights of sense forsake him has no pleasures of the mind.

III.3.101
BELARIUS
At three and two years old, I stole these babes . . .

Shakespeare seems to intend Belarius for a good character, yet he makes him forget the injury which he has done to the young princes, whom he has robbed of a kingdom only to rob their father of heirs.

The latter part of this soliloquy is very inartificial, there being no particular reason why Belarius should now tell to himself what he could not know better by telling it.

IV.3
This scene is omitted against all authority by Sir T. Hanmer. It is indeed of no great use in the progress of the fable, yet it makes a regular preparation for the next act.

IV.4.9
BELARIUS   Newness
  Of Cloten's death – we being not known, not mustered
  Among the bands – may drive us to a render
  Where we have lived . . .

An account of our place of abode.

This dialogue is a just representation of the superfluous caution of an old man.

V.1.1
POSTHUMUS
Yea, bloody cloth, I'll keep thee . . .

This is a soliloquy of nature, uttered when the effervescence of a mind agitated and perturbed spontaneously and inadvertently discharges itself in words. The speech, throughout all its tenor, if the last conceit be excepted, seems to issue warm from the heart. He first condemns his own violence; then tries to disburden himself by imputing part of the crime to Pisanio; he next soothes his mind to an artificial and momentary tranquillity by trying to think that he has been only an instrument of the gods for the happiness of Imogen. He is now grown reasonable enough to determine that having done so much evil he will do no more; that he will not fight against the country which he has already injured; but as life is not longer supportable, he will die in a just cause and die with the obscurity of a man who does not think himself worthy to be remembered.

V.4.27
POSTHUMUS
   If you will take this audit, take this life,
   And cancel these cold bonds.

This equivocal[66] use of 'bonds' is another instance of our author's infelicity in pathetic speeches.

This play has many just sentiments, some natural dialogues and some pleasing scenes, but they are obtained at the expense of much incongruity.

To remark the folly of the fiction, the absurdity of the conduct, the confusion of the names and manners of different times and the impossibility of the events in any system of life, were to waste criticism upon unresisting imbecility, upon faults too evident for detection and too gross for aggravation.

TROILUS AND CRESSIDA

This play is more correctly written than most of Shakespeare's compositions, but it is not one of those in which either the extent of his views or elevation of his fancy is fully displayed. As the story abounded with materials he has exerted little invention; but he has diversified his characters with great variety and preserved them with great exactness. His vicious characters sometimes disgust but cannot corrupt, for both Cressida and Pandarus are detested and contemned. The comic characters seem to have been the favourites of the writer;

they are of the superficial kind and exhibit more of manners than nature, but they are copiously filled and powerfully impressed.

Shakespeare has in his story followed for the greater part the old book of Caxton, which was then very popular; but the character of Thersites, of which it makes no mention, is a proof that this play was written after Chapman had published his version of Homer.[67]

ROMEO AND JULIET

I.5.31
CAPULET
  Nay, sit, nay, sit, good cousin Capulet . . .

This cousin Capulet is 'uncle' in the paper of invitation [I.2.67], but as Capulet is described as old, 'cousin' is probably the right word in both places. I know not how Capulet and his lady might agree, their ages were very disproportionate; he has been past masking for thirty years and her age, as she tells Juliet [I.3.73], is but eight and twenty.

II. CHORUS

The use of this Chorus is not easily discovered; it conduces[68] nothing to the progress of the play, but relates what is already known, or what the next scenes will show; and relates it without adding the improvement of any moral sentiment.

III.1.176
LADY CAPULET
  He is a kinsman to the Montague.
  Affection makes him false. He speaks not true.

The charge of falsehood on Benvolio, though produced at hazard, is very just. The author, who seems to intend the character of Benvolio as good, meant perhaps to show how the best minds in a state of faction and discord are detorted[69] to criminal partiality.

III.5.85
JULIET
  Ay, madam, from the reach of these my hands.
  Would none but I might venge my cousin's death!

Juliet's equivocations are rather too artful for a mind disturbed by the loss of a new lover.

IV.3.1
JULIET   But, gentle Nurse,
  I pray thee leave me to myself tonight.
  For I have need of many orisons . . .

Juliet plays most of her pranks under the appearance of religion; perhaps Shakespeare meant to punish her hypocrisy.

V.1.3
ROMEO
  My bosom's lord sits lightly in his throne,
  And all this day an unaccustomed spirit
  Lifts me above the ground with cheerful thoughts.

These three lines are very gay and pleasing. But why does Shakespeare give Romeo this involuntary cheerfulness just before the extremity of unhappiness? Perhaps to show the vanity of trusting to those uncertain and casual exaltations or depressions, which many consider as certain foretokens of good and evil.

V.3.229
FRIAR
  I will be brief, for my short date of breath
  Is not so long as is a tedious tale.

It is much to be lamented that the poet did not conclude the dialogue with the action and avoid a narrative of events which the audience already knew.

This play is one of the most pleasing of our author's performances. The scenes are busy and various, the incidents numerous and important, the catastrophe irresistibly affecting and the process of the action carried on with such probability, at least with such congruity to popular opinions, as tragedy requires.

Here is one of the few attempts of Shakespeare to exhibit the conversation of gentlemen, to represent the airy sprightliness of juvenile elegance. Mr Dryden mentions a tradition, which might easily reach his time, of a declaration made by Shakespeare that 'he was obliged to kill Mercutio in the third act, lest he should have been killed by him'. Yet he thinks him 'no such formidable person but that he might have lived through the play and died in his bed', without danger to a poet.[70] Dryden well knew, had he been in quest of truth, that in a pointed sentence more regard is commonly had to the words than the thought and that it is very seldom to be rigorously understood. Mercutio's wit, gaiety and courage will always procure him friends that wish him a longer life; but his death is not precipitated, he has lived out the time allotted him in the construction of the play; nor do I doubt the ability of Shakespeare to have continued his existence, though some of his sallies are perhaps out of the reach of Dryden, whose genius was not very fertile of merriment, nor ductile[71] to humour, but acute, argumentative, comprehensive and sublime.

The Nurse is one of the characters in which the author delighted: he has with great subtlety of distinction drawn her at once loquacious and secret, obsequious and insolent, trusty and dishonest.

His comic scenes are happily wrought, but his pathetic strains are always polluted with some unexpected depravations. His persons, however distressed, 'have a conceit left them in their misery, a miserable conceit'.[72]

HAMLET

I.1.129
HORATIO
  If thou hast any sound or use of voice,
  Speak to me.

Selections from Notes to the Plays

The speech of Horatio to the spectre is very elegant and noble, and congruous to the common traditions of the causes of apparitions.

I.2.125
KING
  No jocund health that Denmark drinks today . . .

The King's intemperance is very strongly impressed; everything that happens to him gives him occasion to drink.

II.1.114
POLONIUS
              . . . it is as proper to our age
  To cast beyond ourselves in our opinions
  As it is common for the younger sort
  To lack discretion.

This is not the remark of a weak man. The vice of age is too much suspicion. Men long accustomed to the wiles of life 'cast' commonly 'beyond themselves', let their cunning go further than reason can attend it. This is always the fault of a little mind made artful by long commerce with the world.

II.2.84
KING
  Go to your rest. At night we'll feast together.

The King's intemperance is never suffered to be forgotten.

II.2.86
POLONIUS
  My liege and madam . . .

[Warburton argued that 'Polonius's character is that of a weak, pedant, minister of state. His declamation is a fine satire on the impertinent oratory then in vogue.']

This account of the character of Polonius, though it sufficiently reconciles the seeming inconsistency of so much wisdom with so much folly, does not perhaps correspond exactly to the ideas of our author. The commentator makes the character of Polonius a character only of manners, discriminated by properties superficial, accidental and acquired. The poet intended a nobler delineation of a mixed character of manners and of nature. Polonius is a man bred in courts, exercised in business, stored with observation, confident of his knowledge, proud of his eloquence, and declining into dotage. His mode of oratory is truly represented as designed to ridicule the practice of those times, of prefaces that made no introduction and of method that embarrassed rather than explained. This part of his character is accidental, the rest is natural. Such a man is positive and confident, because he knows that his mind was once strong and knows not that it is become weak. Such a man excels in general principles but fails in the particular application. He is knowing in retrospect and ignorant in foresight. While he depends upon his memory and can draw from his repositories of knowledge he utters weighty sentences[73] and gives useful counsel; but as the mind in its enfeebled state cannot be kept long busy and intent, the old man is subject to sudden dereliction of his faculties, he loses the order of his ideas and entangles himself in his own thoughts, till he recovers the leading principle and falls again into his former train. This idea of dotage encroaching upon wisdom will solve all the phenomena of the character of Polonius.

III.1.56
HAMLET
   To be, or not to be – that is the question . . .

Of this celebrated soliloquy which, bursting from a man distracted with contrariety of desires and overwhelmed with the magnitude of his own purposes, is connected rather in the speaker's mind than on his tongue, I shall endeavour to discover the train and to show how one sentiment produces another.

   Hamlet, knowing himself injured in the most enormous and atrocious degree and seeing no means of redress but such as must expose him to the extremity of hazard, meditates on his situation in this manner: 'before I can form any rational scheme of action under this pressure of distress', it is necessary to decide whether, 'after our present state, we are *to be or not to be*'. That is the question which, as it shall be answered, will determine, 'whether 'tis nobler', and more suitable to the dignity of reason, 'to suffer the outrages of fortune' patiently, or to take arms against 'them', and by opposing end them, 'though perhaps' with the loss of life. If 'to die' were 'to sleep, no more, and by a sleep to end' the miseries of our nature, such a sleep were 'devoutly to be wished'; but if 'to sleep' in death be 'to dream', to retain our powers of sensibility, we must 'pause' to consider, 'in that sleep of death what dreams may come'. This consideration 'makes calamity' so long endured; 'for who would bear' the vexations of life, which might be ended 'by a bare bodkin', but that he is afraid of something in unknown futurity? This fear it is that gives efficacy to conscience which, by turning the mind upon 'this regard', chills the ardour of 'resolution', checks the vigour of 'enterprise', and makes the 'current' of desire stagnate in inactivity.

We may suppose that he would have applied these general observations to his own case, but that he discovered Ophelia.[74]

III.1.70
HAMLET
For who would bear the whips and scorns of time . . .

It may be remarked that Hamlet in his enumeration of miseries forgets, whether properly or not, that he is a prince and mentions many evils to which inferior stations only are exposed.

III.1.77
HAMLET
To grunt and sweat under a weary life . . .

[Johnson prints 'groan'.]

All the old copies have 'to *grunt* and sweat'. It is undoubtedly the true reading, but can scarcely be borne by modern ears.

III.2.307
GUILDENSTERN The King, sir –
HAMLET Ay, sir, what of him?
GUILDENSTERN Is in his retirement marvellous distempered.
HAMLET With drink, sir?

Hamlet takes particular care that his uncle's love of drink shall not be forgotten.

III.3.93
HAMLET
  Then trip him, that his heels may kick at heaven . . .

This speech in which Hamlet, represented as a virtuous character, is not content with taking blood for blood, but contrives damnation for the man that he would punish, is too horrible to be read or to be uttered.

IV.4.53
HAMLET   Rightly to be great,
  Is not to stir without great argument,
  But greatly to find quarrel in a straw
  When honour's at the stake.

This passage I have printed according to the copy. Mr Theobald had regulated it thus:

> 'Tis not to be great,
>   Never to stir without great argument;
>   But greatly, *etc*.

The sentiment of Shakespeare is partly just and partly romantic.

> Rightly to be great,
>   Is not to stir without great argument,

is exactly philosophical.

> But greatly to find quarrel in a straw
>   When honour's at the stake,

is the idea of a modern hero. 'But then,' says he, 'honour is an argument, or subject of debate sufficiently *great* and *when honour is at stake, we must* find cause of quarrel in a straw.'

V.2.82

HAMLET Dost know this waterfly?

A 'waterfly' skips up and down upon the surface of the water without any apparent purpose or reason and is thence the proper emblem of a busy trifler.

V.2.220
HAMLET
   Give me your pardon, sir. I have done you wrong.

I wish Hamlet had made some other defence; it is unsuitable to the character of a good or a brave man to shelter himself in falsehood.

If the dramas of Shakespeare were to be characterized, each by the particular excellence which distinguishes it from the rest, we must allow to the tragedy of *Hamlet* the praise of variety. The incidents are so numerous that the argument of the play would make a long tale. The scenes are interchangeably diversified with merriment and solemnity; with merriment that includes judicious and instructive observations and solemnity not strained by poetical violence above the natural sentiments of man. New characters appear from time to time in continual succession, exhibiting various forms of life and particular modes of conversation. The pretended madness of Hamlet causes much mirth, the mournful distraction of Ophelia fills the heart with tenderness and every personage produces the effect intended, from the apparition that in the first act chills the blood with horror, to the fop in the last that exposes affectation to just contempt.

   The conduct is perhaps not wholly secure against objections. The action is indeed for the most part in continual progression, but there are some scenes which neither forward nor retard it. Of the feigned madness of Hamlet there appears no adequate cause, for he does nothing which he might not have done with the reputation of sanity. He plays the madman most when he treats Ophelia with so much rudeness, which seems to be useless and wanton cruelty.

Hamlet is through the whole play rather an instrument than an agent. After he has by the stratagem of the play convicted the King, he makes no attempt to punish him and his death is at last effected by an incident which Hamlet has no part in producing.

The catastrophe is not very happily produced; the exchange of weapons is rather an expedient of necessity than a stroke of art. A scheme might easily have been formed to kill Hamlet with the dagger and Laertes with the bowl.

The poet is accused of having shown little regard to poetical justice and may be charged with equal neglect of poetical probability. The apparition left the regions of the dead to little purpose; the revenge which he demands is not obtained but by the death of him that was required to take it; and the gratification which would arise from the destruction of an usurper and a murderer is abated by the untimely death of Ophelia, the young, the beautiful, the harmless and the pious.

OTHELLO

I.2.2
IAGO
  Yet do I hold it very stuff o' th' conscience . . .

This expression to common readers appears harsh. 'Stuff'[75] of the 'conscience' is 'substance', or 'essence', of the conscience. 'Stuff' is a word of great force in the Teutonic languages. The elements are called in Dutch *hoefd stoffen* or 'head stuffs'.

I.3.139
OTHELLO
  Wherein of antres vast and deserts idle,
    Rough quarries, rocks, and hills whose heads touch
      heaven . . .

Selections from Notes to the Plays

Whoever ridicules this account of the progress of love shows his ignorance, not only of history, but of nature and manners. It is no wonder that in any age, or in any nation, a lady, recluse, timorous and delicate, should desire to hear of events and scenes which she could never see, and should admire the man who had endured dangers and performed actions which, however great, were yet magnified by her timidity.

[Pope read 'deserts wild']

Every mind is liable to absence and inadvertency, else Pope could never have rejected a word so poetically beautiful.

III. 3.90
OTHELLO
  Excellent wretch!

The meaning of the word 'wretch' is not generally understood. It is now in some parts of England a term of the softest and fondest tenderness. It expresses the utmost degree of amiableness, joined with an idea, which perhaps all tenderness includes, of feebleness, softness and want of protection. Othello, considering Desdemona as excelling in beauty and virtue, soft and timorous by her sex and by her situation absolutely in his power, calls her 'excellent wretch'. It may be expressed:

> Dear, harmless, helpless excellence.

III. 3.204
IAGO
  She did deceive her father, marrying you . . .

This and the following argument of Iago ought to be deeply impressed on every reader. Deceit and falsehood, whatever conveniences they may for a time promise or produce, are in the sum of life obstacles to happiness. Those who profit by the cheat, distrust the deceiver, and the act by which kindness was sought puts an end to confidence.

The same objection may be made with a lower degree of strength against the imprudent generosity of disproportionate marriages. When the first heat of passion is over it is easily succeeded by suspicion that the same violence of inclination which caused one irregularity may stimulate to another; and those who have shown that their passions are too powerful for their prudence will, with very slight appearances against them, be censured as not very likely to restrain them by their virtue.

III.4.99
EMILIA
'Tis not a year or two shows us a man.

From this line it may be conjectured that the author intended the action of this play to be considered as longer than is marked by any note of time. Since their arrival at Cyprus, to which they were hurried on their wedding-night, the fable seems to have been in one continual progress; nor can I see any vacuity into which a 'year or two', or even a month or two, could be put. On the night of Othello's arrival a feast was proclaimed; at that feast Cassio was degraded and immediately applies to Desdemona to get him restored. Iago indeed advises Othello to hold him off a while, but there is no reason to think that he has been held off long. A little longer interval would increase the probability of the story, though it might violate the rules of the drama.

V.2.21
OTHELLO   this sorrow's heavenly –
  It strikes where it doth love.

This tenderness, with which I lament the punishment which justice compels me to inflict, is a holy passion.
  I wish these two lines could be honestly ejected. It is the fate of Shakespeare to counteract his own pathos.

V.2.210
OTHELLO
  That she with Cassio hath the act of shame
  A thousand times committed.

This is another passage which seems to suppose a longer space comprised in the action of this play than the scenes include.

Selections from Notes to the Plays

The beauties of this play impress themselves so strongly upon the attention of the reader that they can draw no aid from critical illustration. The fiery openness of Othello, magnanimous, artless and credulous, boundless in his confidence, ardent in his affection, inflexible in his resolution and obdurate in his revenge; the cool malignity of Iago, silent in his resentment, subtle in his designs and studious at once of his interest and his vengeance; the soft simplicity of Desdemona, confident of merit and conscious of innocence, her artless perseverance in her suit and her slowness to suspect that she can be suspected are such proofs of Shakespeare's skill in human nature as, I suppose, it is vain to seek in any modern writer. The gradual progress which Iago makes in the Moor's conviction and the circumstances which he employs to inflame him are so artfully natural that, though it will perhaps not be said of him as he says of himself that he is 'a man not easily jealous', yet we cannot but pity him when at last we find him 'perplexed in the extreme' [V.2.341].

There is always danger lest wickedness conjoined with abilities should steal upon esteem, though it misses of approbation; but the character of Iago is so conducted that he is from the first scene to the last hated and despised.

Even the inferior characters of this play would be very conspicuous in any other piece, not only for their justness but their strength. Cassio is brave, benevolent and honest, ruined only by his want of stubbornness to resist an insidious invitation. Roderigo's suspicious credulity and impatient submission to the cheats which he sees practised upon him, and which by persuasion he suffers to be repeated, exhibit a strong picture of a weak mind betrayed by unlawful desires to a false friend; and the virtue of Emilia is such as we often find, worn loosely, but not cast off, easy to commit small crimes, but quickened and alarmed at atrocious villainies.

The scenes from the beginning to the end are busy, varied by happy interchanges and regularly promoting the progression of the story; and the narrative in the end, though it tells but what is known already, yet is necessary to produce the death of Othello.

Had the scene opened in Cyprus and the preceding incidents been occasionally[76] related, there had been little wanting to a drama of the most exact and scrupulous regularity.

MISCELLANEOUS REMARKS, CONVERSATIONS AND ANECDOTES

The text of this essay on good humour, addressed in a letter to the *Rambler* from Philomides, is taken from the fourth edition of 1756.

It is remarked by Prince Henry when he sees Falstaff lying on the ground that he 'could have better spared a better man' [*1 Henry IV*, V.4.103]. He was well acquainted with the vices and follies of him whom he lamented; but while his conviction compelled him to do justice to superior qualities, his tenderness still broke out at the remembrance of Falstaff, of the cheerful companion, the loud buffoon, with whom he had passed his time in all the luxury of idleness, who had gladded him with unenvied merriment and whom he could at once enjoy and despise.[1] *Rambler* 72, 24 November 1750

From the *Lives of the Poets*. These extracts are taken from the 'new edition' in four volumes, published in 1783.

Dryden may be properly considered as the father of English criticism, as the writer who first taught us to determine upon principles the merit of composition. Of our former poets the greatest dramatist wrote without rules, conducted through life and nature by a genius that rarely misled, and rarely deserted him. Of the rest, those who knew the laws of propriety had neglected to teach them. *The Life of Dryden* (*Lives*, i.410)

The dialogue on the drama[2] was one of his first essays of criticism, written when he was yet a timorous candidate for reputation, and therefore laboured with that diligence which he might allow himself somewhat to remit when his name gave sanction to his positions and his awe of the public was abated, partly by custom and partly by success. It will not be easy to find in all the opulence of our language a treatise so artfully variegated with successive representations of opposite probabilities, so enlivened with imagery, so brightened with illustrations. His portraits of the English dramatists are wrought with great spirit and diligence. The account of Shakespeare may stand as a perpetual model of encomiastic criticism; exact without minuteness and lofty without exaggeration. The praise lavished by Longinus, on the attestation of the heroes of Marathon by Demosthenes, fades away before it.[3] In a few lines is exhibited a character, so extensive in its comprehension and so curious in its limitations, that nothing can be added, diminished or reformed; nor can the editors and admirers of Shakespeare in all their emulation of reverence boast of much more than of having diffused and paraphrased this epitome of excellence, of having changed Dryden's gold for baser metal, of lower value though of greater bulk. *The Life of Dryden* (*Lives*, i.412)

From Mrs Piozzi's *Anecdotes of the Late Samuel Johnson*, 1786. The extracts are taken from the second edition, published in 1786.

Somebody was praising Corneille one day in opposition to Shakespeare: 'Corneille is to Shakespeare' replied Mr Johnson, 'as a clipped hedge is to a forest.' (*JM*, i.187)

When at Versailles the people showed us the theatre. As we stood on the stage looking at some machinery for playhouse purposes: 'Now we are here, what shall we act, Mr Johnson – *The Englishman at Paris*?' 'No, no' replied he, 'we will try to act Harry the Fifth.'[4] (*JM*, i.216)

It was not King Lear cursing his daughters or deprecating the storm that I remember his commendations of, but Iago's ingenious malice and subtle revenge; or Prince Hal's gay compliance with the vices of Falstaff, whom he all along despised. Those plays had indeed no rivals in Johnson's favour: 'No man, but Shakespeare' he said, 'could have drawn Sir John.' (*JM*, i.282–3)

From Edmond Malone, *Supplement to the Edition of Shakespeare's Plays Published in 1778 by Samuel Johnson and George Steevens*, 1780.

Dr Johnson once assured me that when he wrote his *Irene* he had never read *Othello*, but meeting with it soon afterwards was surprised to find he had given one of his characters a speech very strongly resembling that in which Cassio describes the effects produced by Desdemona's beauty on such inanimate objects as the 'guttered rocks and congregated sands' [II.1.69]. The Doctor added that on making the discovery for fear of imputed plagiarism he struck out this accidental coincidence from his own tragedy.[5] (ii.168)

From Arthur Murphy, *An Essay on the Life and Genius of Samuel Johnson*, 1792.

The contemplation of his own approaching end was constantly before his eyes; and the prospect of death, he declared, was terrible. For many years when he was not disposed to enter into the conversation going forward, whoever sat near his chair might hear him repeating from Shakespeare [quotes *Measure for Measure*, III.1.121].[6]

(*JM*, i.439)

He [Garrick] was also hurt that his Lichfield friend did not think so highly of his dramatic art as the rest of the world. The fact was, Johnson could not see the passions as they rose and chased one another in the varied features of that expressive face; and by his own manner of reciting verses, which was wonderfully impressive, he plainly showed that he thought there was too much of artificial tone and measured cadence in the declamation of the theatre. The present writer well remembers being in conversation with Dr Johnson near the side of the scenes during the tragedy of *King Lear*; when

Garrick came off the stage, he said, 'You two talk so loud you destroy all my feelings.' 'Prithee' replied Johnson 'do not talk of feelings, Punch has no feelings.' This seems to have been his settled opinion; admirable as Garrick's imitation of nature always was, Johnson thought it no better than mere mimicry. (*JM*, i.457)

From James Boswell, *The Life of Samuel Johnson*. The text of the extracts is based on the third edition of 1799.

16 October 1769

Johnson said that the description of the temple in *The Mourning Bride* was the finest poetical passage he had ever read; he recollected none in Shakespeare equal to it.[7] 'But' said Garrick, all alarmed for 'the god of his idolatry' [*Romeo and Juliet*, II.2.114], 'we know not the extent and variety of his powers. We are to suppose there are such passages in his works. Shakespeare must not suffer from the badness of our memories.' Johnson, diverted by this enthusiastic jealousy, went on with greater ardour: 'No, Sir; Congreve has *nature*' (smiling on the tragic eagerness of Garrick); but composing himself, he added: 'Sir, this is not comparing Congreve on the whole, with Shakespeare on the whole; but only maintaining that Congreve has one finer passage than any that can be found in Shakespeare. Sir, a man may have no more than ten guineas in the world; but he may have those ten guineas in one piece and so may have a finer piece than a man who has ten thousand pounds: but then he has only one ten-guinea piece. What I mean is that you can show me no passage where there is simply a description of material objects, without any intermixture of moral notions, which produces such an effect.' Mr Murphy mentioned Shakespeare's description of the night before the battle of Agincourt [*Henry V*, IV. Chorus]; but it was observed it had *men* in it. Mr Davies suggested the speech of Juliet in which she figures herself awaking in the tomb of her ancestors [*Romeo and Juliet*, IV.3.30]. Someone mentioned the description of Dover Cliff [*King Lear*, IV.6.11]. JOHNSON: 'No, Sir; it should be all precipice, all vacuum. The crows impede your fall. The diminished appearance of the boats and other circumstances are all very good description, but do not impress the mind at once with the horrible idea of immense height. The impression is divided; you pass on by computation from one stage of the tremendous space to another. Had the girl in *The Mourning Bride* said she could not cast her shoe to the top of one of the pillars in the temple, it would not have aided the idea, but weakened it'. . . . 'There is no great merit in telling how many plays have ghosts in them and how this ghost is better than that. You must show how terror is impressed on the human heart. In the description of night in *Macbeth* [III.2.40] the beetle and the bat detract from the general idea of darkness, inspissated gloom,' (*Life*, ii.85–90)

19 October 1769

I complained that he had not mentioned Garrick in his Preface to Shakespeare, and asked him if he did not admire him. JOHNSON: 'Yes as "a poor player, who frets and struts his hour upon the stage" [*Macbeth*, V.5.24] – as a shadow.' BOSWELL: 'But has he not brought Shakespeare into notice?' JOHNSON: 'Sir, to allow that would be to lampoon the age. Many of Shakespeare's plays are the worse for being acted: *Macbeth* for instance.' BOSWELL: 'What, Sir, is nothing gained by decoration and action? Indeed I do wish that you had mentioned Garrick.' JOHNSON: 'My dear Sir, had I mentioned him, I must have mentioned many more: Mrs Pritchard, Mrs Cibber – nay and Mr Cibber too; he too altered Shakespeare.' (*Life*, ii.92)

20 October 1769

He again talked of the passage in Congreve with high commendation and said, 'Shakespeare never has six lines together without a fault. Perhaps you may find seven; but this does not refute my general assertion.' (*Life*, ii.96)

12 April 1776

I observed the great defect of the tragedy of *Othello* was that it had not a moral; for that no man could resist the circumstances of suspicion which were artfully suggested to Othello's mind. JOHNSON: 'In the first place, Sir, we learn from *Othello* this very useful moral, not to make an unequal match; in the second place, we learn not to yield too readily to suspicion. The handkerchief is merely a trick, though a very pretty trick; but there are no other circumstances of reasonable suspicion, except what is related by Iago of Cassio's warm expressions concerning Desdemona in his sleep [III.3.416]; and that depended entirely upon the assertion of one man. No, Sir, I think *Othello* has more moral than almost any play.' (*Life*, iii. 39–40)

8 April 1779

We talked of Shakespeare's witches. JOHNSON: 'They are beings of his own creation; they are a compound of malignity and meanness, without any abilities; and are quite different from the Italian magician. King James says in his *Demonology*, "Magicians command the devils; witches are their servants." The Italian magicians are elegant beings.' RAMSAY: 'Opera witches, not Drury Lane witches.'

(*Life*, iii. 382)

October 1783

Johnson, indeed, had thought more upon the subject of acting than might be generally supposed. Talking of it one day to Mr Kemble[8] he said, 'Are you, Sir, one of those enthusiasts who believe yourself transformed into the very character you represent?' Upon Mr Kemble's answering that he had never felt so strong a persuasion himself: 'To be sure not, Sir,' said Johnson, 'the thing is impossible. And if Garrick really believed himself to be that monster Richard III he deserved to be hanged every time he performed it.'

(*Life*, iv. 243–4)

NOTES

Miscellaneous Observations on the Tragedy of Macbeth (1745)

The text is taken from the first edition of 1745: some of the variations between the notes in that text and the notes Johnson printed in the edition of 1765 are indicated below. A few of the long and often inaccurate quotations from the play have been shortened; they have been modernized except where the point of Johnson's commentary would otherwise be obscured (see 'A Note on the Text', p. 42). Johnson's original scene numbers have been retained and his abbreviations silently expanded.

1. Warburton, who was only identified by the initial 'W' in 1745, contributed 'A Supplement to the Translator's Preface' to Charles Jarvis's 1742 translation of *Don Quixote*.
2. Johnson owned a copy of the Byzantine scholar Photius' *Bibliotheca* (*Sale Catalogue*, lot 610).
3. 'the witches of Warboys': the trial and execution of a husband, wife and daughter at Warboys in 1593 was one of the most famous of Elizabethan witchcraft cases.
4. King James's *Demonology* was issued at Edinburgh in 1597 and at London in 1603.
5. In 1765 Johnson added: 'This law was repealed in our own time.'
6. Joseph Hall (1574–1656) was Bishop of Exeter and later of Norwich.
7. In 1765 Johnson restored the correct reading 'quarrel' to the text.
8. In the third and fourth folios.
9. Johnson acknowledged his error in 1765.
10. This note was omitted in 1765.
11. *sua cuique placent*: 'everyone pleases themselves'.

12. 'measure': 14 'Syllables metrically numbered; metre'.
13. Note xv was omitted in 1765.
14. 'The cat loves fish but would not wet its feet.'
15. Dryden's *The Indian Emperor, or The Conquest of Mexico*, III.2.1.
16. 'Smooth sliding without step': Milton, *Paradise Lost*, VIII.302.
17. Note xxii was omitted in 1765.
18. 'numbers': 8 'Verses; poetry'. In 1773 Johnson reprinted this note in his edition of Shakespeare but added the following paragraph:

    This note was written before I was fully acquainted with Shakespeare's manner and I do not now think it of much weight; for though the words which I was once willing to eject seem interpolated, I believe they may still be genuine and added by the author in his revision. The author of the *Revisal* [Benjamin Heath] cannot admit the measure to be faulty. There is only one foot, he says, put for another. This is one of the effects of literature in minds not naturally perspicacious. Every boy or girl finds the metre imperfect, but the pedant comes to its defence with a tribrachys or an anapaest and sets it right at once by applying to one language the rules of another. If we may be allowed to change feet, like the old comic writers, it will not be easy to write a line not metrical. To hint this once is sufficient.

    In the *Dictionary* Johnson defines 'perspicacious' as 'Quick-sighted; sharp of sight'; a 'tribrachys' and an 'anapaest' are Greek and Latin metres.
19. *Destruction of Troy*: Caxton's translation of Raoul Le Fevre's *Recuyell of the Histories of Troy* was first printed at Bruges, probably in 1475. Shakespeare also drew upon it in *Troilus and Cressida*.
20. The *History of Don Bellianis* by Geronimo Fernandez was translated by John Shirley as *The Honour of Chivalry* and published in 1683. See John Hardy, 'Johnson and *Don Bellianis*', *Review of English Studies* new series 17 (1966), 297–9.
21. Note xxv was omitted in 1765. John Caius's book on dogs was first published in 1570; Johnson owned a copy of the 1729 reprint edited by Samuel Jebb (*Sale Catalogue*, lot 446).
22. 'Hanvil the monk': a twelfth-century French poet called Joannes de Altavilla, author of the *Architrenius* (*Archweeper*). The lines Johnson quotes (which describe an English drinking party in Book II), may be translated as 'Now with circulating goblet and ungirded throat "Wassail" they repeat, "Wassail"; the task is more to diminish the wine than the thirst.'
23. Note xxxii was omitted in 1765.
24. Margaret Flower was tried as a witch in 1618–19.

25. Samuel Harsnett's *A Declaration of Egregious Popish Impostures*, 1603; Theobald had first pointed out Shakespeare's use of this work for the devils' names in *King Lear*.
26. Lucilio Vanini (1585-1619), an Italian free-thinker who called himself Giulio Cesare Vanini, was executed as an atheist at Toulouse.
27. Albertus Magnus, a prolific thirteenth-century theologian and writer on scientific subjects.
28. 'Black spirits, and white': these lines derive from Sir William Davenant's version of *Macbeth* published in 1674.
29. William Camden in his *Britannia*, 1586; the translation is by Edmund Gibson (1695). Johnson owned a copy of the *Britannia* (*Sale Catalogue*, lot 605).
30. 'the "colours" of spirits': not identified.
31. Note XXXVII was omitted in 1765.
32. Note XXXVIII was omitted in 1765.
33. An anonymously edited version of Sir John Mandeville's *Travels* was published at London in 1725. Johnson quotes two passages of Mandeville in 'The History of the English Language' prefixed to the *Dictionary*.
34. The antiquary William Camden's *Remains* were published in 1605; Johnson's annotated copy of the 1636 edition is now in the Folger Shakespeare Library (*Books Associated with Johnson* no. 37).
35. From Martial, IX.97: 'Let anyone bursting with jealousy, burst.'
36. The quotation is from Plutarch's life of Themistocles.

Proposals for Printing Shakespeare's Plays (1745)

The text is taken from the folded leaf appended to the *Miscellaneous Observations*, 1745. For the history of these *Proposals* see above, pp. 3-6.

1. The specimen passage which Johnson prints and annotates is *Macbeth*, III.1.44-71. The annotation consists of a reprint with minor variants of almost all of Note XXIV from the *Miscellaneous Observations*.

Drury Lane Prologue (1747)

The text is taken from the first edition of 1747, *Prologue and Epilogue Spoken at the Opening of the Theatre in Drury Lane, 1747*; the Epilogue was by Garrick, under whose management the Drury Lane Theatre came on 15 September 1747. Johnson's poem surveys English theatrical history from Shakespeare to Jonson, to the Restoration dramatists of Charles II's reign and on to the first part of the eighteenth century.

1. 'Faustus' was the hero of the farces or after-pieces which were popular in the 1720s; Pope refers slightingly to Faustus in the three-book *Dunciad* of 1729, iii.229 and 306.
2. Aphra Behn (1640–89) and Thomas Durfey (1653–1723), respectively authors of London comedies and melodramas and farces.
3. Edward Hunt was a lightweight boxer; Mahomet was a ropedancer.

Two Essays from The Rambler *(1751)*

The text of these essays is taken from the fourth edition of 1756 which first printed Johnson's last major revision of the work.

1. 'methodic': not in Johnson's *Dictionary*, but the OED, citing this passage, defines it as 'The distinctive epithet of one of the three ancient schools of physicians, holding views intermediate between those of the Dogmatic and the Empiric school'.
2. 'exuberant': 1 'Growing with superfluous shoots; overabundant; superfluously plenteous; luxuriant'.
3. 'peccant': 2 'Ill-disposed; corrupt; bad; offensive to the body; injurious to health. It is chiefly used in medical writers'.
4. 'speculatists': not in Johnson's *Dictionary*, but defined in the OED as 'One who speculates, or indulges in abstract reasoning; a professed or habitual speculator; a theorist'.
5. 'argumentation': 'Reasoning; the act of reasoning'.
6. See Herodotus, IV.1–4.
7. Horace, *Art of Poetry* (tr. T. S. Dorsch), 192: 'And there should not be more than three speaking characters on the stage at the same time', and Aristotle's *Poetics*, IV.
8. *Réfléxions*, IX.
9. 'uncouth': 'Odd; strange; unusual'.
10. The words are actually spoken by Lady Macbeth. In the *Dictionary* Johnson quotes from this passage under 'dun': 2 'Dark; gloomy'; 'knife': 'An instrument edged and pointed, wherewith meat is cut and animals killed'; 'to peep': 2 'To look

Notes to Pages 92–98

slyly, closely or curiously; to look through any crevice'; 'blanket' (where it is misattributed to *King Lear*): 1 'A woollen cover, soft and loosely woven, spread commonly upon a bed over the linen sheet, for the procurement of warmth'; 'pall' (v.a.): 'To cloak; to invest'; 'keen': 1 'Sharp; well-edged; not blunt'; and 'dark': 1 'Darkness; obscurity; want of light'. For this passage in the edition of Shakespeare Johnson refers the reader to this essay.

11. *Iliad*, VIII.111.
12. The translation from Lucan is Johnson's.
13. 'academic': 'A student of a university'.
14. *Aeneid*, I.586–93.

Dedication to Mrs Charlotte Lennox's Shakespeare Illustrated *(1753)*

For Johnson's hand in Mrs Lennox's *Shakespeare Illustrated* see above, pp. 6–7. The text follows that of the first edition, published in three volumes in 1753–4. There is important new material about the relations between Mrs Lennox and Johnson in Duncan Isles, 'The Lennox Collection', *Harvard Library Bulletin* 18 (1970), 317–44; 19 (1971), 36–60, 165–86, 416–35.

1. John Boyle, fifth Earl of Orrery (1707–62), was a friend of Swift and Pope, and also of Johnson who had a poor opinion of his literary abilities. His *Remarks on the Life and Writings of Swift* appeared in 1752, and in 1759 he contributed the Preface to Mrs Lennox's translation *The Greek Theatre of Father Brumoy*. See Paul J. Korshin, 'Johnson and the Earl of Orrery', in *Eighteenth-Century Studies in Honor of Donald F. Hyde*, ed. W. H. Bond, New York 1970, pp. 29–43.
2. 'invention': 3 'Excogitation; act of producing something new'.
3. 'catastrophe': 1 'The change or revolution, which produces the conclusion or final event of a dramatic piece'.
4. Pliny the Elder dedicated his *Natural History* to the Emperor Titus, praising him as a critic and judge.
5. 'pathetic': 'Affecting the passions; passionate; moving'.

Selection from the Dictionary *(1755)*

For the fourth edition of 1773 Johnson revised many of the definitions in the *Dictionary* in the light of his new work on Shakespeare (see

Notes to Pages 98–106

above, p. 11); to save space in the new edition he tended to shorten and omit the illustrative quotations. On account of this the text of the definitions is usually taken from the fourth edition of 1773; the text of the quotations is taken (except where noted otherwise) from the first edition of 1755. A sixth edition published in 1785 drew on some further revisions which Johnson made; one of these has been noted below. Most of the etymologies have been omitted; some of Johnson's more interesting revisions are noted below. Quotations from authors other than Shakespeare have been identified more fully than they are in the *Dictionary*.

1. CANARY In 1755 this read 'seems to signify to frolic'.
2. CASE 'leanness . . . "fat"': in 1755 this read 'leanness, or health'.
3. CESS 'though . . . "reckoning"' added in 1773.
4. CONTEMPTIBLE 'contemptuous' added in 1773.
5. CROWKEEPER 'The . . . controverted' deleted in 1773.
6. DARKLING 'or perhaps . . . "youngling"' added in 1773.
7. DIVERT 'unless . . . sense' added in 1773; Johnson defines the first sense as 'To turn off from any direction or course'.
8. HAVING 'It . . . here' added in 1773.
9. HEND 'or . . . possession' added in 1773.
10. INHERIT 'Not used' added in 1773.
11. INJOIN 'Not used' added in 1773.
12. INSTANCE Johnson quotes from the second half of this passage in his *Life* of Dorset (*Lives*, i.307).
13. KIDNEY 'Sort' replaced 'Race' in 1773.
14. MINNOCK The two quartos read 'Minnick' and 'Minnock'; most editors follow the folio's 'Mimmick' by printing 'mimic'.
15. MINUTELY 'Happening . . . minute' added in 1773.
16. MODEL (n.) 5 'Something representative' added in 1773 to replace 'Something formed or produced'.
17. MODEL (n.) 6 'for . . . measure' added in 1773. Johnson illustrated the third sense, 'A mould; anything which shows or gives the shape of that which it encloses', by quoting *Richard II*, III.2.152.
18. NONSENSE Pope's note refers to the folio's reading, 'a table of green fields' (*Henry V*, II.3.16), which Pope did not print in his text. Theobald's emendation, ''a babbled of green fields', appeared in his edition of 1733. Johnson quotes the same passage under 'Editor'.
19. PEAK 'from "pique"' added in 1773.

20. PILGRIMAGE In 1755 the definition ended 'improperly' and there was no quotation.
21. PLAYHOUSE In 1755 the quotation from this most famous of Pope's comments on Shakespeare's life ended after 'Style the divine'.
22. PLUCK 'It . . . "into"' added in 1773.
23. QUILLET 'petty cant' added in 1773.
24. SOOTH This definition was added in 1773; 1755 quotes the same passage under the definition 'Truth; reality. Obsolete'.
25. SQUARE 'Though . . . "capacity"' added in 1773.
26. TERMAGANT 'It was . . . shows' added in 1773.
27. THENCE 'yet . . . authorities' added in 1773.
28. TIDY 'or irony' added in 1785.
29. TRISTFUL Johnson is quoting the folio reading; Q2 has 'heated'.
30. TUCKET SONANCE In 1755 Johnson defined this as 'A word apparently derived from the French, but which I do not certainly understand; "tucquet" is a hat and "toquer" is to strike.' Both 1755 and 1773 print the two words as one.
31. UTIS '"Utis" . . . festivity' added in 1773.
32. VIRTUE 'opposed to vice' added in 1773.
33. WHIP 'always . . . use' added in 1773.
34. WOE 'which . . . ungrammatical' added in 1773.

Proposals for Printing by Subscription Shakespeare's Plays (1756)

For the history of these *Proposals* see above, p. 20. The text follows that of the first edition.

1. 'unfortunate': 'Not successful; unprosperous; wanting luck; unhappy'.
2. 'depravation': 1 'The act of making anything bad; the act of corrupting; corruption'.
3. 'revisal': 'Review; re-examination'.
4. 'sublime': 3 'High in style or sentiment; lofty; grand'.
5. 'embarrassed': 'To perplex; to distress; to entangle'.
6. 'uncouth': 'Odd; strange; unusual'.
7. 'sentiment': 1 'Thought; notion; opinion'.
8. See *Spectator* 285. Richard Bentley's edition of *Paradise Lost* appeared in 1732.
9. Sir Thomas Hanmer's edition of 1743–4 was printed and published at Oxford.

10. 'obtruded': 'To thrust into any place or state by force or imposture; to offer with unreasonable importunity'.
11. Johnson lists the earlier eighteenth-century editions of Shakespeare: Rowe, 1709; Pope, 1725; Theobald, 1733; and Warburton, 1747, whose 'more important studies', which had delayed his edition by about twenty years, were theological as well as literary.
12. Pope and Warburton marked their favourite passages and scenes with these symbols.

Preface to the Edition of Shakespeare's Plays (1765)

The text is taken from the first edition of 1765. Johnson's revisions made in 1768, 1773 and 1778 have been incorporated in the text: some of these revisions are noted below. Johnson's revisions in proof are described by Arthur Sherbo in 'The Proof-Sheets of Dr Johnson's Preface to Shakespeare', *Bulletin of the John Rylands Library* 35 (1952–3), 206–10.

1. 'opacity': 'Cloudiness; want of transparency'.
2. 'Pythagorean scale of numbers': Aristotle, *Metaphysics*, I.5.
3. 'revision': 'Review', but Johnson means 'revision' in the sense of 'editing'.
4. 'his century': Horace, *Epistles*, II.1.39, '*Est vetus atque probus, centum qui perficit annos*': 'Who lasts a century can have no flaw, / I hold that wit a classic, good in law' (tr. Pope).
5. 'devolved': 2 'To move from one hand to another'.
6. 'a precept': Cicero, *Familiar Letters*, XVI.8.
7. Hierocles of Alexandria, a neo-platonist of the fifth century AD, wrote a commentary on Pythagoras' *Aurea Carmina* in which this anecdote appears. Peter Needham published an edition at London in 1709; Johnson projected undertaking 'Hierocles upon Pythagoras, translated into English, perhaps with notes', but observed that 'This is done by [John] Norris' (*Life*, iv.381). Johnson owned an edition of Hierocles' commentary (*Sale Catalogue*, lot 147).
8. Petronius, *Satyricon*, I.1.
9. Preface (1725); in *Eighteenth Century Essays on Shakespeare*, ed. D. Nichol Smith, 2nd edn, Oxford 1963, p. 45.
10. 'agency': 1 'The quality of acting; the state of being in action; action'.
11. 'approximates': not in the *Dictionary*, but defined in the OED

Notes to Pages 124–128

12. 'mazed': 'To bewilder; to confuse'.
13. John Dennis, 'On the Genius and Writings of Shakespeare', 1712, in Nichol Smith, op. cit., p. 31; Thomas Rymer, 'A Short View of Tragedy', 1693, in *Critical Works*, ed. Curt A. Zimansky, New Haven 1956, pp. 164–9. Johnson refers generally to Voltaire's Shakespeare criticism contained in *L'Appel à toutes les nations de l'Europe*, 1761, and seems specifically to be thinking of the condemnation of Claudius's drunkenness in his *Dissertation sur la tragédie ancienne et moderne*, 1748. Voltaire's Shakespeare criticism has been collected in *Voltaire on Shakespeare*, ed. Theodore Besterman, Studies on Voltaire and the Eighteenth Century 54, 1967: see especially p. 57.
14. 'superinduced': 1 'To bring in as an addition to something else'.
15. 'adventitious': 'That which advenes; accidental; supervenient; extrinsically added, not essentially inherent'.
16. Cf. Horace, *Art of Poetry*, 343–4: 'The man who has managed to blend profit with delight wins everyone's approbation, for he gives his reader pleasure at the same time as he instructs him' (tr. T. S. Dorsch).
17. All the editions from 1765 to 1778 read 'alteration'; in Malone's *Supplement to the Edition of Shakespeare's Plays*, 1780, the text was altered to 'alternations'. The proofs read 'vicissitudes'.
18. 'pleasing melancholy': cf. Milton's *Comus*, 546: 'Wrapped in a pleasing fit of melancholy'.
19. 'unwelcome': 'Not pleasing; not grateful; not well received'.
20. 'The interchanges ... likewise': in the proofs this passage originally read, 'It is not common to be so much moved by fictitious calamities, but that the attention may be immediately transferred to different objects; and though it must be allowed that the mind may be sometimes interrupted in a state of pleasing melancholy, yet it must likewise be considered.'
21. John Heming and Henry Condell, Shakespeare's friends and fellow actors, issued the first folio in 1623.
22. Sir John Suckling and Sir Robert Howard both supplied different endings to their plays *Aglaura*, 1637, revised 1638, and *The Vestal Virgin*, 1665.
23. 'nicely': 1 'Accurately; minutely; scrupulously'.
24. 'seasonable': 'Opportune; happening or done at a proper time; proper as to time'.

25. Johnson is answering criticisms of *Hamlet* and *Othello* made by Rymer (*A Short View of Tragedy*, ed. Zimansky, pp. 131–64), and Voltaire (*L'Appel à toutes les nations de l'Europe*, in *Voltaire on Shakespeare*, ed. Besterman, pp. 63–80).
26. *A Short View of Tragedy*, ed. Zimansky, p. 169.
27. 'The stream of time, which is continually washing the dissoluble fabrics of other poets' originally read in the proofs, 'The stream of time, which is continually shattering the frail cement of other poets'; in correcting the proofs Johnson may have written 'wasting' rather than 'washing'.
28. 'adamant': 1 'A stone, imagined by writers, of impenetrable hardness'.
29. 'candour': 'Sweetness of temper; purity of mind; openness; ingenuity; kindness'.
30. 'catastrophe': 1 'The change or revolution which produces the conclusion or final event of a dramatic piece'.
31. Pope's Preface, ed. Nichol Smith, op. cit., p. 53.
32. 'tumour': 2 'Affected pomp; false magnificence; puffy grandeur; swelling mien; unsubstantial greatness'.
33. 'amplification': 2 'It is usually taken in a rhetorical sense and implies exaggerated representation, or diffuse narrative; an image heightened beyond reality; a narrative enlarged with many circumstances'.
34. 'evolved': 'To unfold; to disentangle'.
35. The editions before 1778 read: 'But the admirers of this great poet have never less reason to indulge their hopes of supreme excellence, than when he seems fully resolved . . .'.
36. This sentence was added in 1778.
37. 'frigidity': 2 'Dullness; want of intellectual fire'.
38. 'quibble': 'A low conceit depending on the sound of words; a pun'.
39. Johnson alludes to the story of Atalanta who was won by Hippomenes when she stooped to pick up three of the golden apples of the Hesperides which he had dropped, and so lost her race against him.
40. Corneille discussed the (supposedly Aristotelian) unities in the third of his *Discours dramatiques*, 1660.
41. 'the dragons of Medea': after Medea had killed Glauce and two of her own children she fled from Athens to Corinth with Jason in a chariot drawn by dragons.
42. 'calenture': 'A distemper peculiar to sailors in hot climates,

wherein they imagine the sea to be green fields, and will throw themselves into it if not restrained' (Quincy).
43. 'recreated': 2 'To delight; to gratify'.
44. Addison's *Cato*, 1713, V.1.
45. Cf. Johnson's general observation on *Othello*.
46. 'positive': 4 'Settled by arbitrary appointment'.
47. Lucan, *Pharsalia*, III.138–40 (tr. Nicholas Rowe, 1718):

> Nor time nor chance breed such confusions yet,
> Nor are the mean so raised, nor sunk the great,
> But laws themselves would rather choose to be
> Suppressed by Caesar than preserved by thee.
> (III.216–19)

48. 'deliberatively': not in the *Dictionary*, but all the editions after 1765 read 'deliberately' (of which 'deliberatively' is the obsolete form): 'Circumspectly; advisedly; warily'.
49. *Aeneid*, II.610–14.
50. 'philology': 'Criticism; grammatical learning'.
51. Tudor humanists and scholars: William Lily (c. 1468–1522), first High Master of St Paul's School, compiled the standard Latin grammar which Shakespeare used and of which Johnson owned a copy (*Books Associated with Johnson* no. 203); Thomas Linacre (?1460–1524) taught at Oxford and Sir Thomas More (?1477–1535) was Henry VIII's Chancellor. Reginald Pole (1500–1558) was Archbishop of Canterbury during Queen Mary's reign; Sir John Cheke (1514–57) taught Greek at Cambridge; Stephen Gardiner (c. 1490–1555) was Bishop of Winchester and, like Pole, a Chancellor of Cambridge University. Sir Thomas Smith (1513–77) and Walter Haddon (1516–72) were statesmen and diplomats, professors of civil law at Cambridge; 'Clerke' is probably Bartholomew Clerke (?1537–90), who also taught civil law at Cambridge and translated Castiglione's *The Book of the Courtier* into Latin; Roger Ascham (1515–68), whose English works Johnson helped to edit in 1761, was Latin Secretary to Queen Mary and Queen Elizabeth.
52. 'literature': 'Learning; skill in letters'.
53. Sir Thomas Malory's *Le Morte d'Arthur* was first printed by Caxton in 1485; Ascham refers to the popular taste for Malory in *The Schoolmaster*.
54. *Palmerin* and *Guy of Warwick* were chivalric romances of the sixteenth and fourteenth centuries. The Palmerin cycle was

translated into English by Anthony Munday between 1588 and 1602; *Guy of Warwick* was printed by about 1497. Samuel Rowlands's *History of Guy of Warwick* was reprinted throughout the seventeenth century.

55. *The Tale of Gamelyn* was included in editions of Chaucer until Tyrwhitt's edition of 1775; Lodge took the story of his *Rosalynde*, 1590, the source for *As You Like It*, from the tale.
56. Colley Cibber (1671–1757), actor and playwright; this anecdote does not appear in his *Apology* for his life (1740). There is a 1608 edition of *The History of Hamlet* translated from Belleforest. Mrs Lennox printed a translation of the story of Hamlet from Saxo Grammaticus' *Historia Danica* in her *Shakespeare Illustrated*.
57. Sir Thomas North's translation of Plutarch's *The Lives of the Noble Grecians and Romans* was first published in 1579.
58. In *L'Appel à toutes les nations de l'Europe*, op. cit.
59. See Jonson's verses on Shakespeare prefixed to the first folio: the correct reading 'less Greek' instead of 'no Greek' was introduced in 1773.
60. Zachary Grey in his *Critical, Historical and Explanatory Notes on Shakespeare* (1754), ii.53, compared *Richard III*, I.1.144, with Terence's *Andria*, 171.
61. In *The Tempest*, III.2.144, Caliban says, 'I cried to dream again'.
62. 'confessedly': 'Avowedly; indisputably'.
63. William Warner's translation of 1595 appeared too late for Shakespeare to have used it in *The Comedy of Errors*.
64. Mrs Lennox (i.90) notes that Shakespeare took details from William Painter's translation of Bandello which were not in the original.
65. 'construction': 3 '(In grammar.) The putting of words, duly chosen, together in such a manner as is proper to convey a complete sense' (Clarke's *Latin Grammar*).
66. Pope's Preface, ed. Nichol Smith, op. cit., p. 49.
67. 'indigent': 2 'In want; wanting'.
68. From Rowe's 'Some Account of the Life [of Shakespeare]', prefixed to his edition of 1709.
69. See Thomas Birch, *The Life of Robert Boyle*, 1744, pp. 18–19.
70. Paraphrased from *Troilus and Cressida*, III.3.224.
71. 'effused': 'To pour out; to spill; to shed'.
72. 'On the Genius and Writings of Shakespeare', ed. Nichol Smith, op. cit., p. 24.

Notes to Pages 146–155

73. *Gorboduc* by Thomas Norton and Thomas Sackville was acted in 1561 and reprinted in Dodsley's *Select Collection of Old Plays* in 1744.
74. Thomas Kyd's *The Spanish Tragedy* was first printed in 1592; it was reprinted by Dodsley.
75. John Upton's *Critical Observations on Shakespeare* appeared in 1746 and again with new material on Warburton's edition in 1748.
76. 'ideal': 'Mental; intellectual; not perceived by the senses'.
77. *The Old Bachelor* (1693) and *Love for Love* (1695).
78. All the editions until Malone's *Supplement* of 1780 read 'their'.
79. Warburton's Preface, ed. Nichol Smith, op. cit., p. 89.
80. 'As of . . . Rowe': until 1773 this read: 'Of Rowe, as of all the editors, I have preserved the Preface, and have likewise retained the author's life'.
81. 'compendious': 'Short; summary; abridged . . .'.
82. The Shakespeare apocrypha, including *Pericles*, was first published in the third folio.
83. Pope's Preface, ed. Nichol Smith, op. cit., p. 57.
84. Johnson is probably thinking of the *Dunciad*, of which Theobald is the 'hero' in the first version.
85. Warburton's Preface, ed. Nichol Smith, op. cit., p. 93.
86. William Warburton was installed as Bishop of Gloucester in 1759; his edition of Shakespeare had appeared in 1747.
87. 'Achilles' was replaced in 1773 by 'Homer's hero'; the words are taken from *Iliad*, XXI.106–14.
88. Thomas Edwards and Benjamin Heath; Johnson did not get the title of the latter's work correct until 1778, calling it the *Review of Shakespeare's Text* until then.
89. Paraphrased from *Coriolanus*, IV.4.5 (quoted in the *Dictionary* under 'puny' 2 and 'spit' 1), and *Macbeth*, II.4.12: the lines incorrectly began 'An eagle' until 1773. In the *Dictionary* he quotes them under 'To mouse' 1 (with the reading 'An eagle' again – corrected in 1773), 'pride' 5 and 'To hawk' 2.
90. Upton: see above, note 75.
91. 'empiric': 'A trier or experimenter; such persons as have no true education in, or knowledge of, physical practice, but venture upon hearsay and observation only' (Quincy).
92. Grey: see above, note 60.
93. 'scholiast': 'A writer of explanatory notes'.
94. *2 Henry VI*, IV.1.106: 'Small things make base men proud'.

95. 'controvertist': 'Disputant; a man versed or engaged in literary wars or disputations'.
96. 'laborious': 1 'Diligent in work; assiduous'.
97. 'table book': 'A book on which anything is graved or written without ink'.
98. 'stricture': 3 'A slight touch upon a subject; not a set discourse'.
99. 'animadversion': 1 'Reproof; severe censure; blame'.
100. It is usually thought this remark was directed at Garrick. See above, pp. 12–13.
101. 'perspicuity': 1 'Clearness to the mind; easiness to be understood; freedom from obscurity or ambiguity'.
102. 'interstice': 1 'Space between one thing and another'.
103. Pierre Huet (1630–1721), *De interpretatione*, 1661 (*Sale Catalogue*, lot 140).
104. 'points': 11 'Note of distinction in writing; a stop'.
105. 'evanescent': 'Vanishing; imperceptible; lessening beyond the perception of the senses'.
106. 'When in doubt, don't': Pliny, *Letters*, I.xviii.
107. *Temple of Fame*, 37–40: Johnson incorrectly printed 'efface' for 'deface'.
108. 'invention': 3 'Excogitation; act of producing something new'.
109. Joannes Andreas (1417–c. 1480), librarian to Pope Sixtus VI; Richard Bentley (1662–1742), one of the greatest of English Latin scholars.
110. 'regimen': systematic rule (this sense is not in the *Dictionary*).
111. 'Our conjectures make us look foolish, put us to shame, when we later come across better manuscripts': Joseph Scaliger, *Epistolae*, Leyden 1627, letter 248 to Claude de Saumaise, 14 July 1608.
112. The quotation (paraphrased by Johnson in the preceding words) comes from the commentary on Tacitus by Justus Lipsius (1547–1606).
113. *An Essay of Dramatic Poesy*, 1668; the Latin quotation from Virgil's *Eclogues*, I.25, means 'as the cypress soars above the drooping undergrowth' (tr. E. V. Rieu).

Selections from the Notes to the Edition of Shakespeare's Plays (1765)

The text of these notes is taken from the edition of 1765; some of Johnson's subsequent revisions are noted below. Many of Johnson's

Notes to Pages 166–181

lengthy quotations from the plays have been shortened, except where this would otherwise obscure the point of what he is saying.

1. In Book I of *The Laws of Ecclesiastical Polity*, 1593.
2. Casaubon: Méric Casaubon (1599–1671) in the Preface to *A True and Faithful Relation of Dr John Dee*, 1659.
3. In 1710 Charles Gildon (1665–1724) contributed a tenth volume to Rowe's Shakespeare containing the *Poems* and critical remarks on the plays.
4. The substance of the first sentence appeared originally in the Appendix to 1765; the rest of the note in 1773. Benjamin Heath (1704–66) was the author of the anonymous *Revisal of Shakespeare's Text*, 1765.
5. 'engrossing': 4 'To seize in the gross; to seize the whole of anything'.
6. *Roscius Anglicanus, or An Historical Review of the Stage*, 1708, by John Downes (*c.* 1640–*c.* 1710).
7. Michael Drayton (1563–1631) was Shakespeare's close contemporary; his *Nimphidia* was first published in 1627.
8. This paragraph first appeared in the Appendix to 1765. Books I to III of *The Faerie Queene* appeared in 1590; they were reprinted with IV to VI in 1596.
9. 'inextricable': 'Not to be disentangled; not to be cleared; not to be set free from obscurity or perplexity'.
10. The second paragraph was added in 1773.
11. 'shambles': 1 'The place where butchers kill or sell their meat; a butchery'.
12. 'vulgar': 2 'Mean; low; being of the common rate'.
13. 'exquisitely': 'Perfectly; completely: in either a good or ill sense'.
14. Lasco visited England briefly in 1583 and took the magician John Dee into his service.
15. 'Duke of Bavaria': John Casimir, Elector of the Palatinate and Duke of Bavaria, was installed as a Knight of the Garter in 1583.
16. 'fable': 4 'The series or contexture of events which constitute a poem, epic or dramatic'.
17. 'wild': 10 'Done or made without any consistent order or plan'.
18. From Virgil, *Georgics*, IV.238: 'lays down his life in a wound'.
19. *The Lady of May*, probably written in 1578 and first printed in 1598. Henry Peacham's *The Compleat Gentleman*, 1622; Johnson drew on this book for the *Dictionary*.

20. Castiglione's *The Book of the Courtier* was translated into English in 1561.
21. The title-page of the first quarto of 1598 says the play 'was presented before her Highness this last Christmas'.
22. These comments were first printed in 1773.
23. 'close with': 3 'To come to an agreement with; to comply with; to unite with'.
24. The last paragraph was omitted in 1773.
25. 'sensibility': 1 'Quickness of sensation'. 2 'Quickness of perception'.
26. 'from the very depths of the mind'.
27. *The Troublesome Reign of John, King of England*, an anonymous play in two parts first published in 1591; the nature of its relationship to Shakespeare's play is disputed.
28. The second paragraph was omitted in 1773.
29. 'revised': the fourth quarto of 1608 has 'new additions of the parliament scene and the deposing of King Richard'.
30. 'indetermined': 'Unsettled; unfixed'.
31. 'scenery': 3 'The disposition and consecution of the scenes of a play'.
32. This note was omitted in 1773.
33. The fault is corrected and this paragraph omitted in 1778.
34. The quarto of '1608' (actually published in 1619) preserves a reported text of the play; Johnson seems to believe that the folio text was revised by Shakespeare.
35. The final sentence was added in 1773.
36. 'So much does the open and artless confession of an error become a man, conscious that he has enough remaining to support his character.' Johnson's paraphrase of the quotation from A. Cornelius Celsus is taken from *Rambler* 31.
37. The 1727 Drury Lane production with Booth as the King was put on in honour of the coronation of George II.
38. 'perspicuous': 2 'Clear to the understanding; not obscure; not ambiguous'.
39. The Elizabethan chronicler John Stowe records that in 1409 'the parish clerks . . . played a play at the Skinners' Well, which lasted eight days, and was of matter from the creation of the world'.
40. 'factor': 1 'An agent for another; one who transacts business for another. Commonly a substitute in mercantile affairs'.
41. In *Tatler* 117 (1710).

42. 'involutions': 2 'The state of being entangled; complication'.
43. Joseph Warton contributed five articles on Shakespeare (three on *King Lear*) to the *Adventurer* in 1753–4. In 1770 Johnson wrote to Warton: 'I formerly misrepresented your opinion of *Lear*' (*Letters*, no. 239).
44. By Addison in *Spectator* 40. Nahum Tate's version, *The History of King Lear*, was first performed in 1681 and enjoyed great success until the first part of the nineteenth century.
45. Addison's tragedy *Cato*, first performed in 1713, prompted John Dennis to publish his hostile *Remarks upon Cato* in the same year.
46. Arthur Murphy (1727–1805) published two pieces on *King Lear* in his *Gray's Inn Journal* 65 (12 January 1754) and 87 (15 April 1754).
47. In *A Discourse Concerning the Original and Progress of Satire* (1693) Dryden quotes from Virgil's *Eclogues*, III.26: 'All you were good for was to stand at the crossroads and scrape a miserable tune out of one squeaking straw' (tr. E. V. Rieu).
48. This paragraph was added in 1773.
49. Johnson is thinking of the reference to *Titus Andronicus* in the Induction to Ben Jonson's *Bartholomew Fair* (1614).
50. This paragraph, which alludes to Francis Meres's mention of *Titus* as one of Shakespeare's plays in *Palladis Tamia* (1598), was added in 1773.
51. The story that Shakespeare had to leave Stratford for London because he had stolen deer from Sir Thomas Lucy at Charlecote was first printed by Rowe in his life of Shakespeare (1709).
52. Edward Ravenscroft's *Titus Andronicus, or The Rape of Lavinia* was performed in 1678 and first published in 1687.
53. 'surcease': 'Cessation; stop'.
54. This note was added in 1773.
55. This note was added in 1773.
56. In the *Dictionary* one of the meanings Johnson gives to 'May' is 'the early or gay part of life', and quotes from *Henry V*, I.2.119, and *Much Ado About Nothing*, V.1.74.
57. 'nice': 5 'Formed with minute exactness'.
58. 'illusive': 'Deceiving by false show'.
59. 'speculative': 1 'Given to speculation; contemplative'.
60. James Harrington (1611–77), *Aphorisms Political* (1659), no. 5.
61. 'amusing': 1 'To entertain with tranquillity; to fill with

62. 'unaffecting': 'Not pathetic; not moving the passions'.
63. 'tumid': 3 'Pompous; boastful; puffy; falsely sublime'.
64. '*Cape . . . pastor*': 'Snatch up stones in your hand, shepherd, snatch up staves', Virgil, *Georgics*, III.420.
65. 'inartificial': 'Contrary to art'.
66. 'equivocal': 1 'Of doubtful signification; meaning different things; standing for different notions'.
67. For Caxton's book, see note 19 to the *Miscellaneous Observations* above; Chapman's *Seven Books of the Iliads* and *Achilles' Shield* first appeared in 1598.
68. 'conduces': 'To promote an end; to contribute; to serve to some purpose'.
69. 'detorted': 'To wrest from the original import, meaning or design'.
70. Paraphrased from *An Essay on the Dramatic Poetry of the Last Age* (1672).
71. 'ductile': 3 'Tractable; obsequious; complying; yielding'.
72. From Dryden's Preface to *Fables, Ancient and Modern* (1700).
73. 'sentences': 3 'A maxim; an axiom, generally moral'.
74. In May 1776 Johnson admitted to Boswell that this note was 'disputable' (*Life*, iii.55).
75. 'Stuff': 5 'Essence; elemental part', quoting this passage.
76. 'occasionally': 'According to incidental exigence; incidentally'.

Miscellaneous Remarks, Conversations and Anecdotes

1. The essay continues by arguing that 'Good humour is indeed generally degraded by the characters in which it is found'.
2. The essay *Of Dramatic Poesy* was first published in 1668.
3. Longinus, *On the Sublime*, XVI.
4. Johnson visited Versailles ('a mean town') with the Thrales on 22 October 1775 (*Life*, ii.395). *The Englishman at Paris* is by Samuel Foote.
5. George Steevens is the source for this anecdote. Johnson worked on his tragedy *Irene* from as early as 1736 or 1737; it was first produced and published at the beginning of 1749. The manuscript draft of the play shows that Johnson abandoned the passage which he felt was too close to Cassio's speech and replaced it with what appeared in the published version as

V.6.5–6: the cancelled passage is printed in *The Poems of Samuel Johnson*, ed. David Nichol Smith and Edward L. McAdam, 2nd edn, Oxford 1974, p. 393. See J. C. Maxwell, 'Othello and Irene', *Notes and Queries* 202 (1957), 148.

6. The veracity of Murphy's anecdote is open to question.

7. Almeria's speech in Congreve's tragedy of 1697 comes in II.1:

> No, all is hushed and still as death – 'Tis dreadful!
> How reverend is the face of this tall pile,
> Whose ancient pillars rear their marble heads,
> To bear aloft its arched and ponderous roof
> By its own weight, made steadfast and immovable,
> Looking tranquillity. It strikes an awe
> And terror on my aching sight; the tombs
> And monumental caves of death look cold,
> And shoot a chillness to my trembling heart.
> Give me thy hand and speak to me, nay, speak
> And let me hear thy voice;
> My own affrights me with its echoes.

Johnson praised this passage again in his *Life of Congreve*, calling it 'the most poetical paragraph' in 'the whole mass of English poetry' (*Lives*, ii.229). For Johnson's opinion of the Dover Cliff speech, see above, p. 220 Mrs Piozzi further records Johnson's telling her

how he used to tease Garrick by commendation of the tomb scene in Congreve's *Mourning Bride*, protesting that Shakespeare had in the same line of excellence nothing as good: 'All which is strictly *true*' said he, 'but that is no reason for supposing Congreve is to stand in competition with Shakespeare: these fellows know not how to blame, nor how to commend.' (*JM*, i.186)

8. John Philip Kemble (1757–1823) succeeded Garrick as the leading Drury Lane actor and producer of Shakespeare's plays.

FOR THE BEST IN PAPERBACKS, LOOK FOR THE 🐧

In every corner of the world, on every subject under the sun, Penguin represents quality and variety – the very best in publishing today.

For complete information about books available from Penguin – including Pelicans, Puffins, Peregrines and Penguin Classics – and how to order them, write to us at the appropriate address below. Please note that for copyright reasons the selection of books varies from country to country.

In the United Kingdom: Please write to *Dept E.P., Penguin Books Ltd, Harmondsworth, Middlesex, UB7 0DA*

If you have any difficulty in obtaining a title, please send your order with the correct money, plus ten per cent for postage and packaging, to *PO Box No 11, West Drayton, Middlesex*

In the United States: Please write to *Dept BA, Penguin, 299 Murray Hill Parkway, East Rutherford, New Jersey 07073*

In Canada: Please write to *Penguin Books Canada Ltd, 2801 John Street, Markham, Ontario L3R 1B4*

In Australia: Please write to the *Marketing Department, Penguin Books Australia Ltd, P.O. Box 257, Ringwood, Victoria 3134*

In New Zealand: Please write to the *Marketing Department, Penguin Books (NZ) Ltd, Private Bag, Takapuna, Auckland 9*

In India: Please write to *Penguin Overseas Ltd, 706 Eros Apartments, 56 Nehru Place, New Delhi, 110019*

In Holland: Please write to *Penguin Books Nederland B.V., Postbus 195, NL–1380AD Weesp, Netherlands*

In Germany: Please write to *Penguin Books Ltd, Friedrichstrasse 10–12, D–6000 Frankfurt Main 1, Federal Republic of Germany*

In Spain: Please write to *Longman Penguin España, Calle San Nicolas 15, E–28013 Madrid, Spain*

In France: Please write to *Penguin Books Ltd, 39 Rue de Montmorency, F–75003, Paris, France*

In Japan: Please write to *Longman Penguin Japan Co Ltd, Yamaguchi Building, 2–12–9 Kanda Jimbocho, Chiyoda-Ku, Tokyo 101, Japan*

FOR THE BEST IN PAPERBACKS, LOOK FOR THE 🐧

A CHOICE OF PENGUINS

Adieux Simone de Beauvoir

This 'farewell to Sartre' by his life-long companion is a 'true labour of love' (the *Listener*) and 'an extraordinary achievement' (*New Statesman*).

British Society 1914–45 John Stevenson

A major contribution to the Pelican Social History of Britain, which 'will undoubtedly be the standard work for students of modern Britain for many years to come' – *The Times Educational Supplement*

The Pelican History of Greek Literature Peter Levi

A remarkable survey covering all the major writers from Homer to Plutarch, with brilliant translations by the author, one of the leading poets of today.

Art and Literature Sigmund Freud

Volume 14 of the Pelican Freud Library contains Freud's major essays on Leonardo, Michelangelo and Dostoyevsky, plus shorter pieces on Shakespeare, the nature of creativity and much more.

A History of the Crusades Sir Steven Runciman

This three-volume history of the events which transferred world power to Western Europe – and founded Modern History – has been universally acclaimed as a masterpiece.

A Night to Remember Walter Lord

The classic account of the sinking of the *Titanic*. 'A stunning book, incomparably the best on its subject and one of the most exciting books of this or any year' – *The New York Times*

FOR THE BEST IN PAPERBACKS, LOOK FOR THE 🐧

A CHOICE OF PENGUINS

The Informed Heart   Bruno Bettelheim

Bettelheim draws on his experience in concentration camps to illuminate the dangers inherent in all mass societies in this profound and moving masterpiece.

God and the New Physics   Paul Davies

Can science, now come of age, offer a surer path to God than religion? This 'very interesting' (*New Scientist*) book suggests it can.

Modernism   Malcolm Bradbury and James McFarlane (eds.)

A brilliant collection of essays dealing with all aspects of literature and culture for the period 1890–1930 – from Apollinaire and Brecht to Yeats and Zola.

Rise to Globalism   Stephen E. Ambrose

A clear, up-to-date and well-researched history of American foreign policy since 1938, Volume 8 of the Pelican History of the United States.

The Waning of the Middle Ages   Johan Huizinga

A magnificent study of life, thought and art in 14th and 15th century France and the Netherlands, long established as a classic.

The Penguin Dictionary of Psychology   Arthur S. Reber

Over 17,000 terms from psychology, psychiatry and related fields are given clear, concise and modern definitions.

FOR THE BEST IN PAPERBACKS, LOOK FOR THE 🐧

A CHOICE OF PENGUINS

The Literature of the United States   Marcus Cunliffe

The fourth edition of a masterly one-volume survey, described by D. W. Brogan in the *Guardian* as 'a very good book indeed'.

The Sceptical Feminist   Janet Radcliffe Richards

A rigorously argued but sympathetic consideration of feminist claims. 'A triumph' – *Sunday Times*

The Enlightenment   Norman Hampson

A classic survey of the age of Diderot and Voltaire, Goethe and Hume, which forms part of the Pelican History of European Thought.

Defoe to the Victorians   David Skilton

'Learned and stimulating' (*The Times Educational Supplement*). A fascinating survey of two centuries of the English novel.

Reformation to Industrial Revolution   Christopher Hill

This 'formidable little book' (Peter Laslett in the *Guardian*) by one of our leading historians is Volume 2 of the Pelican Economic History of Britain.

The New Pelican Guide to English Literature   Boris Ford (ed.)
Volume 8: The Present

This book brings a major series up to date with important essays on Ted Hughes and Nadine Gordimer, Philip Larkin and V. S. Naipaul, and all the other leading writers of today.

FOR THE BEST IN PAPERBACKS, LOOK FOR THE 🐧

PENGUIN CLASSICS

John Aubrey	**Brief Lives**
Francis Bacon	**The Essays**
James Boswell	**The Life of Johnson**
Sir Thomas Browne	**The Major Works**
John Bunyan	**The Pilgrim's Progress**
Edmund Burke	**Reflections on the Revolution in France**
Thomas de Quincey	**Confessions of an English Opium Eater**
	Recollections of the Lakes and the Lake Poets
Daniel Defoe	**A Journal of the Plague Year**
	Moll Flanders
	Robinson Crusoe
	Roxana
	A Tour Through the Whole Island of Great Britain
Henry Fielding	**Jonathan Wild**
	Joseph Andrews
	The History of Tom Jones
Oliver Goldsmith	**The Vicar of Wakefield**
William Hazlitt	**Selected Writings**
Thomas Hobbes	**Leviathan**
Samuel Johnson/ James Boswell	**A Journey to the Western Islands of Scotland/The Journal of a Tour to the Hebrides**
Charles Lamb	**Selected Prose**
Samuel Richardson	**Clarissa**
	Pamela
Adam Smith	**The Wealth of Nations**
Tobias Smollet	**Humphry Clinker**
Richard Steele and Joseph Addison	Selections from the **Tatler** and the **Spectator**
Laurence Sterne	**The Life and Opinions of Tristram Shandy, Gentleman**
	A Sentimental Journey Through France and Italy
Jonathan Swift	**Gulliver's Travels**
Dorothy and William Wordsworth	**Home at Grasmere**